PAINTING ∘ COLOR ∘ HISTORY

COLLECTION PLANNED AND DIRECTED BY

ALBERT SKIRA

MODERN PAINTING

contemporary trends

TEXT BY NELLO PONENTE

Translated from the Italian by James Emmons

o

Distributed in the United States by
THE WORLD PUBLISHING COMPANY
2231 West 110th Street - Cleveiand 2, Ohio

o

The latest trends in the history of modern painting are studied and illustrated in this new volume of the series "Painting ○ Color ○ History". A sequel to our previous volume by Maurice Raynal devoted to the genesis of modern painting and its evolution in the first half of the 20th century, this book traces the developments that have taken place since the Second World War. In its wealth and variety the achievement of the last fifteen or twenty years forms a panorama as undulating and diverse as could be desired. Even so, to illustrate all its facets and aspects with significant works called for a rigorous selection made strictly in accordance with our guiding aim: to single out and focus attention on the ideas and necessities that have made present-day painting what it is. Our work has been facilitated by the opportunities for study and comparison offered by the great international exhibitions of contemporary art, such as Documenta at Kassel and the biennial exhibitions at Venice, Sao Paulo and Paris; to the organizers we tender our grateful thanks. We also take pleasure in thanking the directors and curators of museums and the many private collectors who, with unfailing kindness, have given us access to the works of art in their keeping. Without their generous cooperation this book could never have been made.

Introduction

What most of us have in mind when we speak of post-war painting is the work of those painters whose aim is not to reproduce the outward appearances of things but to investigate the underlying significance of reality. It must not be forgotten, however, that this kind of painting already has a tradition of its own; it originated in the movements of the early 20th century which, stimulated by Cézanne, transformed the relationship between the artist and visual reality. What before had been an attitude of passive acquiescence on the part of the painter, became now a dialectical relationship; the painter asserted himself and penetrated, as he never had before, the inner life of things and images. "Expression, as I see it, does not lie in the passion lighting up a face or breaking out in a violent movement. It lies in the whole arrangement of my picture: the position of the figures, the empty spaces around them, the proportions, all this has its part to play." Matisse expounded these principles in a magazine article in the **Grande Revue** of December 1908. Over fifty years later they still hold good, they have lost nothing of their importance. And painting, all the while, has never ceased to evolve; the revolutions and counter-revolutions of art have added their lessons and precedents to these principles, and painters have constantly sought to suit their language to the conditions of the time, fully realizing that no return is possible to the outmoded standards of the past. But for all the changes that have come about in recent years, however sweeping, there is a connecting link, traceable stage by stage, between all the successive experiments of painters from the beginning of the century to the present day.

It seemed at one time that the limits had been reached: between the violent outbursts of Fauve color, heralding the first art revolution of the 20th century, and **Broadway Boogie Woogie** of 1942, which virtually brought the curve of Mondrian's career to a close, all possible meanings, both artistic and moral, seemed to have been wrung from reality and expressed in paints. Beyond this point it seemed impossible to go. But painting is not an escape mechanism. It has always reflected man's estate or predicament at a given time, it is bound up with human history, and is at the same time the history of the artist. If it is to remain alive, a tradition of artistic endeavor and research must necessarily evolve and renew itself; new ideas and aims supersede the old, and are themselves superseded in time. Painting can never really serve as the pretext for an academic evasion from reality, from society, from the climate of the times, even when it repudiates representation and narration. Today less than ever, with the example before us of the masters, like Matisse and Mondrian, who, in working out new solutions of their own, have shaped the taste of our century. In the great paper cut-outs made at the end of his life Matisse embodied the flowing arabesques of his paintings in a heavier, more immediately effective medium. Mondrian's **Broadway Boogie Woogie** broke through the two-dimensional patterns of Neo-Plasticism and initiated that rhythmic repetition of image-forms which, since the war, has led to a more drastic dissolution of the old limits of form and design.

But what link remains between the achievements of the early 20th century masters and the solutions proposed by those painters who have come of age (artistically speaking) and produced their maturest work since 1945? What is the relationship, for example, between Cubism and Action Painting? Or between Fauvism and French Abstract Impressionism? The words of Matisse quoted above point to the nature of this relationship, while the common denominator of all the investigations and experiments of 20th century art may be defined in the words of Mondrian.

"All modern art is distinguished by a relatively greater freedom from the oppression of the subject. Impressionism emphasized the impression of reality more than its representation. After the impressionists, all art shows a relative negation of nature's aspects; the cubists delivered a further blow; the surrealists transformed it; the abstract artists excluded it." [1] Freedom of expression, then, with respect to the subject, this is the common denominator of art in our time, in our century. But this does not mean that the artist has ceased to express the shifting yet permanent sum of features and factors that go to make up the human situation in all its complexity. The fallacy of superficial detractors of non-figurative art is to suppose that it signifies a more or less complete abandonment of reality; on the contrary, it probes into reality more deeply than ever before. This is as it should be. The artist cannot divorce himself from a state of society which, on the one hand, is profoundly disturbed by doubts and anxieties, but which, on the other, has achieved a great deal in the way of technical advances and social betterment. Why should painting reject new conceptions of time, space, matter and energy (and the new sensibility perforce bound up with those conceptions) when the other forms of artistic expression accept them? Already in Proust we read of the painter Elstir, that his "effort to exhibit things, not as he knew them to be, but in accordance with those optical illusions of which our first glimpse of a thing is compounded, had led him to emphasize certain laws of perspective, thus rendered peculiarly striking, for his art was the first to disclose them." And what is **le temps retrouvé** of the final volume of Proust's masterwork, but a new dimension of the mind, a new sensibility, transcending the measurable, chronological lapse of years, days and hours? It is not for nothing that we find Proust writing in 1919 of "the great, the admirable Picasso." [2]

Here, then, is the subtly modified approach to reality with which all the painting of our century has swung into line, for, as Apollinaire said, "the plastic virtues, purity, unity and truth, hold nature vanquished underfoot." And the work produced by the younger generation of moderns even before the end of the Second World War justified the historical importance of the avant-garde movements which, before the First War or immediately after, had charted the way and raised the problems of the future. Fauvism and Cubism, Futurism and Expressionism, Neo-Plasticism and Constructivism, Dada and Surrealism, and all the rest, were the successive aspects of a change taking place, but a change which, far from being clinched and accomplished, required to be made again after the explosion of rage and pain with which Picasso, in **Guernica,** reacted to one tragedy and gave instant warning of another. After **Guernica** there could be no question of reverting to the old familiar language, there was no turning back to a bygone classicism; the old "call of Italy" now goes unheard, for it is cut off forever from the realities of life. "One never paints what one sees or thinks one sees; one paints, under stress of a thousand vibrations, the shock received." Such is the affirmation, thoroughly pessimistic at bottom, of a painter like Nicolas de Staël, who never quite succeeded in overcoming the implicit contradiction between his human condition and his desire to single out a point of stable equilibrium in a flux of appearances which he felt to be too remote from reality, or too contingent on it, for him to identify the hidden thread of growth and purpose running through it.

The Nazi campaign against "degenerate art" and the return to imperial classicism preached by the Italian Fascists failed to disrupt the logical development of European art along the lines indicated above. Most important of all, the new concept of painting which, from the time of the first cubist experiments, had superseded the credo of Impressionism, remained intact. Painting, for the Impressionists, had amounted to an exploration of the sensations. Now it had become an exploration of the human consciousness, a creation of something, participation in a world which the artist himself shaped and molded. From the time Cézanne began projecting a multiplicity of perspectives on the canvas, in order to accentuate the emotional dimension of space at the expense of representational accuracy, he automatically stated the basic problem of all contemporary painting. From then on, sensation was superseded by consciousness, and representation by reality. Cubism proceeded to make the most of the lesson: it identified space and time, thus delivering the pictorial image from the relativity of space understood as a chronological sequence, as a succession of events, and projecting it into the present. And Cubism being the movement that contributed more than any other to the shaping of the new artistic language, it served to justify the impossibility thereafter of any return to the representation of visual appearances.

The breakdown of the subject was followed by the breakdown of the object, at a time when painters were losing faith in apparent reality. The Cubists resolved the crisis by creating another dimension in which the objects represented lost their usual meaning and acquired a new significance, often disconcertingly new, but one that resulted in those forms which, as Malraux has said, "had always fascinated men in the grip of enemy gods, those forms with clean-cut planes which look like men without imitating them."[3] The Cubists, however, were not introverts lured in search of some transcendental truth—as the metaphysical painters later proved to be. They were Cartesians, and in this they stand apart, for example, from a parallel movement equally abstract in tendency like Italian Futurism, or from abstractionizing Expressionism which, with the German Blaue Reiter group, achieved complete abstraction about 1909-1910. Italian Futurism, with its avowed aim of glorifying a mechanical civilization, soon exhausted the novelty of its subject matter—which, however, did not prevent it from producing some highly suggestive works of lasting value and significance. Kandinsky, on the other hand, together with his Blaue Reiter friends, including Klee (though Klee's artistic personality was in every respect dissimilar, a law unto itself), arrived at abstraction by setting out from Secessionist premises and then by resorting to the formal and chromatic coercions of Expressionism, which had not a little in common with the experiments of the French Fauves. Kandinsky, much like Delaunay in France, who followed up an original path of his own that kept him apart from the Cubists, repudiated naturalistic light and by doing so cut himself off from any further commerce with the apparent forms of nature—nature for him representing the material world in irreconcilable opposition to the spiritual. For Klee, on the other hand, expression was not so much an outpouring (inevitably romantic) of passionate emotion as a statement of the psychic associations which led him to create a form, "quite a small formal motif," as he wrote in his Diary (June 22, 1902), and to add to it other forms, by an almost automatic chain of ideas. The work of art thus came to convey, with telling immediacy, images stored up in the consciousness, with which the images of the visual world might well coincide, but not necessarily. It is clear that for both Klee and Kandinsky the spontaneous workings of the irrational mind had more value than the familiar patterns of normal vision. Reality, these artists seem to be saying, is something else: it lies within the human being, not in the world outside and around him.

As for the De Stijl group in Holland, these painters sought an absolute rationale. "Gradually I became aware," wrote Mondrian, "that Cubism did not accept the logical consequence of its own discoveries; it was not developing abstraction toward its ultimate goal, the expression of pure reality. I felt that this reality can only be established through **pure plastic.** In its essential expression, pure plastic is unconditioned by subjective feeling and conception."[4] In 1866 Zola had declared that the work of art results from the combination of a fixed element (nature) and a variable element (man). After all the transformations which had left this idea more or less intact, Mondrian, by way of Cubism, finally rejected the concept of nature as a fixed element, and then, entirely on his own, rejected the variable element as well. His aim was the creation of a **constant reality:** "While our perceptions and feelings may change our impressions, forms conserve their own expression. This fact emphasizes that, in order to establish a true image of form and space, an objective vision is necessary... The expression of life in the surrounding reality makes us feel alive and from this feeling art arises. But a work of art is only 'art' in so far as it establishes life in its unchangeable aspects as pure vitality."[5]

It is a grave mistake to regard Mondrian, as some have done, as an isolated phenomenon, devoid of consequences, in the general development of artistic taste. He represents, on the contrary, a precise historical stage of modern art, with which several collateral movements in sculpture and architecture are closely connected. And even in the case of painters intent on other solutions, Mondrian's example proved to be serviceable and even important to them in their efforts to penetrate the new meaning of reality. In Russia, for instance, Constructivism and Suprematism approached closely to Dutch Neo-Plasticism, just as the great artistic and literary flowering that grew out of Cubism and Futurism reaped the benefit of the advances made by all the avant-garde movements. Malevitch, who aspired to a **supreme reality** in many ways similar to Mondrian's **constant reality,** has left a definition, in a book published in Moscow in 1915, of what he meant by Suprematism: "the supremacy of pure sensibility in art." In 1913, with this idea in mind, he painted a picture of a black square on a white ground, in order to "relieve art of the dead weight of the object."

These rationalist tendencies, however, by no means exhausted the field of inspiration and experiment confronting the new painters who set to work after the Second World War. Dada and Surrealism have both left their mark on the artists of the younger generation, some of whom have even chosen to call themselves Neo-Dadaists. Dada was a clamorous, deliberately irrational protest against reason and the thinking mind, which, it claimed, were responsible for the outbreak of war in 1914. It was not only an art (or anti-art) movement but a political movement. It pinned its faith on the laws of chance and left it to them to recreate a spontaneous, unprejudiced order, which set art free and gave to man, as Hans Arp said, the image of a world waking up in a hand of crystal. Surrealism too sought to go beyond appearances, to capture and express the sensations of the unconscious, to create a new beauty by associations of incongruous objects—such beauty as might result, in the words of Lautréamont, "from the chance meeting of a sewing machine and an umbrella on an operating table." The really lasting successes of Surrealism were scored in those cases where it contrived to create original forms (not entirely dependent on appearances) vividly expressive of a dramatic picture content and to restore its poetic significance to the painter's medium, at the same time redeeming the literary nature of its inspiration by the purity of the pictorial means employed. Accordingly, for the familiar "logic" of the old way of seeing, the artist had to substitute his powers of intuition in order to render, in pictorial terms, a full account of the human condition in all its complexity, and not just a one-sided vision of the physical man—because, as Ionesco puts its, "here's no such thing as pure logic, it's all a hoax."

These were the values, rational and irrational, that post-war painting was led to reconsider and, very soon, to assimilate and reassert, offering fresh solutions both in Europe and America, in countries with a long-standing artistic tradition and in those which the modern tradition has placed on the map of the art world for the first time. The dividing line between the rational and irrational has not been so clearly marked as perhaps it was before the war. The facility of communications and the steady broadening of cultural horizons have resulted in a ceaseless exchange of ideas. Some of the basic characteristics of the various trends of pre-war painting have, however, been consistently maintained: on the one hand, fidelity to a tradition of logical discipline, which seems on the whole to be typical, for example, of the French achievement; on the other, well exemplified by Wols, a kind of phenomenological suspension of the flow of life, as if the artist had succeeded in sidetracking the world altogether. Or again, self-identification with action and movement, as in the work of Jackson Pollock and in so much American painting. But common to painters of all trends has been the effort to forge a link with a new reality, along the lines laid down by the modern masters, and to foster the growth of the artistic taste of our century, until it has finally and fully counteracted what has been called "post-impressionist staidness," jolted art out of its immobility and emotional deadness, and instituted a new order of active participation, even at the risk of overemphasizing the dramatic aspects of this new situation. We shall see in the following pages how our contemporary painters have so far acquitted themselves of their task.

AUGUSTE HERBIN - ALBERTO MAGNELLI - MAX BILL
JOSEF ALBERS - VICTOR VASARELY - GEER VAN
VELDE - RICHARD MORTENSEN - BEN NICHOLSON

elapsed in vain, and successive experiments had all left their mark behind them. Dada and Surrealism seemed forgotten, and yet before long they were to regain their value as pointers to the future. But to most members of the surviving generation of artists who had not betrayed their ideals, who had made no concession to any revival of the figurative which would have broken the logical evolution of 20th century painting—to them the tradition of geometric abstractionism seemed the purest and indeed the only possible tradition susceptible of further development. Today we see that this development did not take place, and that art turned toward other solutions. But nevertheless it must be acknowledged that this order, this moral clarity of an almost puritanical flavor—which of course could not last in a world where participation (and not detachment) was increasingly required of the artist—has left a lesson behind, and one that may yet be expected to bear fruit. Not, however, until there comes a re-examination of present aims, today so eagerly and, at bottom, uncritically pursued. When that happens there may be a change leading not to geometric abstractionism, but to a deeper faith in human reason.

But even now, at the present time, there can be no denying the contributions to pictorial idiom which these painters have made, even apart from the quality of their works. It cannot be forgotten that geometric painting was the direct heir of Cubism, at least in the years between the wars, and was the only painting capable of indicating the quality of a space which, projected on to canvas, served not only to envelop form and reveal it fully in a given perspective, but also, as Argan has said of Mondrian, "to attain to perceptive space, that is to say to space which does not precede form but comes into being with it." [6] This space is obviously a derivative of Cubism, but in Cubism it was still a place where dramatic encounters and situations could arise. In geometric painting, the policy of "non-intervention" laid down in the manifesto of 1920 led to a complete repudiation of this dramatic element; it led, that is to say, in the last analysis, to a refusal to solve the problem of language and expression in a historical dimension, and, in consequence, to a virtual repudiation of history itself. This was a patent contradiction, inasmuch as the geometric method had aimed at establishing a constant dimension of reality and life, which could only be achieved in a precise historical and social condition of the individual, as shown by the rationalistic experiment of the Bauhaus founded by Gropius. And Mondrian realized this when his sense of the historical responsibility devolving on him became so acute as to induce him to break up the space determined by squares and interrelated vertical and horizontal lines, and to seek a variant of this space which, with its increased animation, was more in keeping with his will to intervention and participation.

All this forms, as it were, the prelude to the period which concerns us here: the period following the Second World War. To the theories of the post-war years, however, we cannot apply any generalization that would not be superficial and false. Let it not be forgotten, for example, that the policy of non-intervention did not prevent Otto Freundlich, an artist who in reality had never been an adherent of Neo-Plasticism, from dying in a Nazi extermination camp. "It is by constructive action that man breaks the fatality of nature, the fatality of his birth and death. For it is constructive action alone which creates the continuity of his evolution." [7] Thus Freundlich defined another aspect of the search: reason, the thinking mind, through its constructive efforts, gives meaning to life and an absolute comprehension of things. And yet in the end there stands in opposition to it a cooler, more unfeeling faculty of reason, against which the moral sense inherent in man, and in the perfect form created by him, is powerless. The perfect form as created by Freundlich appeared on the cover of the catalogue of the exhibition of "degenerate art" held by the Nazis in 1937.

Of course, once an absolute pictorial language had been worked out, once the external appearances of visual reality had been definitively set aside, it may seem strange to find artists again identifying the forms represented with those of visual reality. Afterwards, however, at least for a time, the path followed by most painters of the younger generation was a very different one. But as regards the painters who already between the wars had been enthusiastic exponents of abstract art of an exclusively geometric order, they carried on after the war with a constancy and indeed a moral fervor that have never admitted of any compromise. So that a rational order

Alberto Magnelli (1888). Two-way Conversation, 1956. (51¼×63¾") Galleria Nazionale d'Arte Moderna, Rome.

of geometry, the identification of space and form reduced to their simplest terms, was held to afford the picture's only chance not of representing but of **being** reality, in the very sense indicated by the early masters of geometric abstractionism, who had declined to describe their work as "abstract art" and chose to call it "concrete art," by which they meant art at its realest and purest, existing in the absolute truth of its forms.

"The means at the painter's command are such that pictorial expression, in detail and in the aggregate, is always particular and concrete and is never capable of conveying the generalization of an idea." [8] Thus wrote the late Léon Degand, one of the most observant and intelligent champions of post-war geometric painting. This painting, then, is not to be dismissed as merely the fruit of a yearning for absolute beauty, identified with the purity of geometric forms, a notion already clearly outlined in Plato. It cannot be so dismissed precisely because it makes no claim to represent the generalization of an idea; its abstract—or, if you like, concrete—representations can never embody absolute and general concepts, but are always the product of individual activity. So we see how erroneous is the classicistic interpretation sometimes given of this painting. In spite of the rationalistic spirit pervading it, its means of expression and the language of its regular forms have something in common with the irrationalism of Dada. How many of the Dada artists used geometric space and regular forms? Even before 1914 Arp had executed works thoroughly geometric in design, which he later modified not so much by varying the regularity of forms as by breaking up their mechanical arrangement with **papiers déchirés** or

papiers froissés. Moreover, if we place ourselves at the opposite pole from rationalism, with Klee or Schwitters, we realize the extent to which both of these artists used geometric elements; they are plain to see in Klee, probably owing to the influence exerted on him by the Bauhaus; less apparent in Schwitters, though discernible in the regular, rhythmical cadence of some of his wood carvings whose forms are pure enough to differentiate them from the logical break-up of design peculiar to Dadaism. Mention perhaps should also be made of the geometric forms in movement in the **rouleaux** and films of Hans Richter; and in the works of Enrico Prampolini too, who numbered among the first Futurists and later moved on the periphery of the Dada movement, before finally working out a precise and regular formal order of his own, enriched by the use of sand and bitumen.

Alberto Magnelli (1888). Miscellaneous Forms, 1958. (57½×45″) Owned by the Artist.

To these a few more names should be added, for the moral lesson imparted by the geometric idiom has been momentous and long-lasting. In America geometric painting was the first to achieve a real originality, in the works—which proved to be influential—of painters like Josef Albers and Fritz Glarner, both Europeans transplanted to the United States, and also in the sublime example of Mondrian, who finished his career in New York. Geometric painting still seems today, at the time of writing, the only valid painting in South America, in Argentina in particular. In Italy the work of such abstractionists as Reggiani, Soldati, Radice and the early Licini formed one of the few vital trends that in the years after 1930 was able to pit its strength against the conformism of Fascist art and to express itself in a broadly European idiom. In Germany, Belgium and Holland, not to speak of France which was of course the focal point of all tendencies, geometric painting was a stimulating admixture to the experience of all

Max Bill (1908). Six Centers of Energy, 1949-1950. (Diagonal, 46¾") Private Collection.

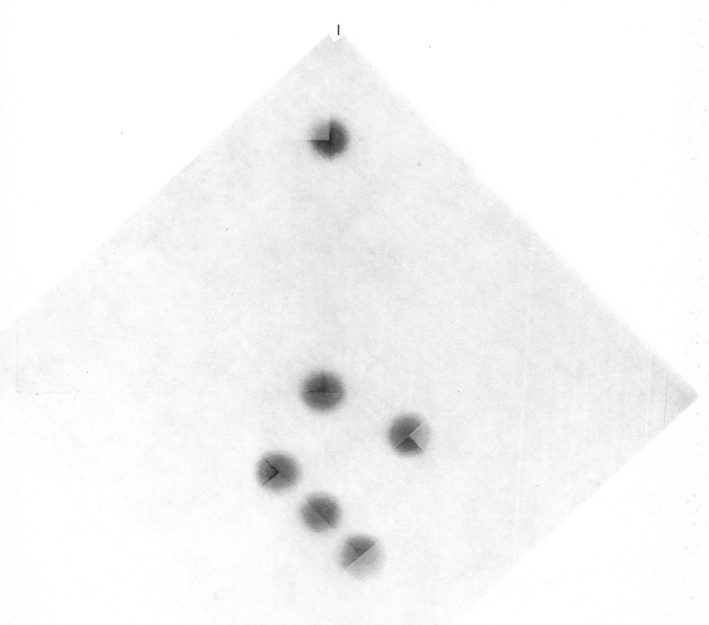

Josef Albers (1888). Homage to the Square: Ritardando, 1958. (30×30″) Courtesy Sidney Janis Gallery, New York.

artists, even of those who later turned to other solutions. Its lesson exerted a notable influence, notwithstanding the post-war controversy between the geometric painters and the younger men intent on a different type of abstraction. Geometric painting, as Léon Degand pointed out, had dispelled once and for all the "figurative obsession." All artists, of whatever convictions or tendency, thus found themselves enjoying a freedom which had not existed before, and which they could use as they saw fit, uninhibited by that obsession.

So once again, in spite of any semblance to the contrary and the inevitable polemics, there was a very real continuity, not exactly of language (this would have been impossible after the rupture of the war years), but a continuity of artistic effort in a direction and tradition that were genuinely European. And several geometric artists not only continued to produce works of outstanding quality, but arrived in the post-war years at some of their finest achievements, for now geometric painting had left all doubts and misgivings far behind and, perhaps in reaction against them, regained full confidence in itself at the very time when its esthetic was about to be eclipsed. It now gave proof of its best qualities, exhilarated by the sense of being the direct heir of the movement that had broken completely with every established canon of representational art:

Victor Vasarely (1908). Eridan II, 1957. (63¾×51¼″) Dotremont Collection, Uccle-Brussels.

the Neo-Plasticism of Mondrian. And in its ranks were not only accomplished, experienced painters, but younger recruits too; this fact alone vouches for the vitality of their work and gives the lie to those obtuse enough to maintain that geometric abstraction always led to the same results in all its practitioners.

A few examples, chosen among the most significant, will show plainly how wrong-headed it is to suppose that all these artists arrived at identical solutions. For while it is true, as Mondrian said, that the reality represented by geometric painting had to be a **constant reality,** unaffected by the fluctuations of individual sensations, the fact remains that the relations between forms and the creation of a space and a surface are necessarily affected by the artist's individuality and its embodiment in a personal style. Compare the works of, say, Herbin, Magnelli, Soldati and Albers, to take painters belonging to an older generation than that of men like Vasarely and Mortensen; comparison shows at once the profound differences separating works which, nevertheless, are all founded on a community of taste and culture. And the personality of each of these artists stands out sharp and clear, markedly original, without any trace of repetition from the work of one to that of another.

The work of art, according to Auguste Herbin, is "a world in itself, the expression of the man with a discipline peculiar to himself and means peculiar to himself, founded on the exclusive relationship of the man to the work."[9] This idea underlies all his constructions, even though it has never crystallized into a formula or a cut-and-dried system. Herbin, with his abiding concern for reality combined with his love of experimentation, has given food for thought to the younger generations. A painter of cubist origins, and later one of the founders of the Abstraction-Creation movement, Herbin has always been preoccupied with geometric order, ever since he set out to insert simplified forms of great purity in a space essentially cubist in its characterization, in order to infuse every possible sensation into those forms, while deliberately disregarding any relation they might have to any extrapictorial suggestions whatsoever. And yet his painting has never been a mere mathematical alchemy devoid of human implications, thanks to his unflagging insistence on this fundamental relationship, so important to him, between the man and the work. The pulse of life accordingly makes itself felt in the work, it alternately swells and subsides in a dialectic of forms and colors, in a way far removed from any romantic emotionalism—which of course is not to say that those forms and colors are lacking in human content, on the contrary.

If there is one thing Herbin sets great store by, one thing that cannot be subjected to preconceived schemata, it is color. He has studied, long and deeply, the relations between colors, and above all between various colored forms and colored space reduced to the two basic dimensions of the picture surface. The theories he puts into practice are summed up in a book he published in 1949, entitled **L'Art non figuratif non objectif.** And in an article in the review **Art d'aujourd'hui** of December 1953, Herbin gave an interesting account of his working methods: "I carry on with my constructive work, now and then modifying the proportional relationship between colors and, above all, adding to the precision of those relationships. The problem of space I regard as a false problem. After all, a painting cannot exist without space; color creates a space of its own. How do I go about my work? In the most ordinary way: with an easel and a palette arranged in due order from the brightest to the darkest. I make a point of using a very wide range of colors, and I like my colors as pure as possible, which I find the best way of ensuring their solidity and permanence. Mixing them with synthetic and natural resins has always given me good results. Lastly, I have banished gray from my palette."

When we look at a picture by Herbin, what particularly strikes us is the continually **invented** character of his forms. Triangles and squares, circles and other geometric patterns, have all lost their established associations; they have turned into something else unconnected with the geometric figures consecrated by tradition. And this is why his works cannot be described as reproductions or schematizations of forms: they are real inventions, they coincide with **constant realities** each time worked out afresh, and each time recreated in a space or spatial characterization deriving in each picture from color alone, in a scale ranging from the brightest to the darkest.

That the expressive capacity of color is one of the major preoccupations of geometric painting subsequent to Neo-Plasticism, is further confirmed by the work of two Italian painters: Alberto Magnelli and Atanasio Soldati, who certainly rank among the best representatives of Italian art in the years before and just after the Second World War. Soldati's experience was almost entirely Italian, though needless to say his connections with European painting as a whole are readily traceable. Magnelli, on the other hand, is an artist with an international background, and one of international stature as well. He went to Paris for the first time in 1913, made many long stays there in the next two decades, and since 1933 has lived in France almost uninterruptedly. His first abstract works date from his early stays in Paris. Yet Magnelli has remained a Florentine at heart, enamored of beautiful forms. He is a thoroughgoing modern, in the forefront of the avant-garde, who has lost none of the opportunities afforded in the first half of the 20th century by the new developments of painting. But he has always been fascinated by a regularity of form giving full scope to the blandishments of color, to undertones of a dreamworld. Of all the exponents of geometric art, this great artist is the one furthest removed from any hidebound rationalistic system, and the one who more than any other, by tradition and culture, by the very blood that flows in his veins, is drawn toward an ideal order of figuration. Arp has touched on this facet of his friend Magnelli's personality: "In the dark, unreal years of 1941 and 1942 the reality of beauty was the only consolation of our little circle at Grasse, made up of Sonia Delaunay, Sophie Täuber, Susi Magnelli, Alberto Magnelli, and myself." [10]

The "reality of beauty" is certainly the only reality that counts for this cosmopolitan Florentine. Fantastic apparitions of forms as if emerging at times from an atmosphere, carefully poised relationships and juxtapositions of colors, precise correlation of form with form, all go to build up a composition which aspires to a pictorial absolute, a clean-cut definition, calculated to embody in form, and to convey through form, a maximum of expression. But without any primness or undue austerity, for color plays its part with peerless elegance in creating an indivisible unity of formal purity and chromatic richness. Magnelli himself has explained the motives that guide him. "For me," he writes, "art is form, with the colors added which are necessary to its efficacy. To work out the form necessary to its expression, that is the one undisputed fact of the matter. Color without form is like a poem made up of disconnected words. But color applied to carefully worked out forms goes to complete the whole; both are necessary if the work of art is to have a lasting value. They are the two poles which jointly govern the image and create that mystery which prolongs vision in depth."

So for Magnelli the perfect fusion of regular form with the color that exalts it serves to break up the two-dimensional surface and to create a picture space of limitless dimensions, transcending visual appearances and partaking of a new time dimension and a new vision of the world— a picture space which, while no longer that of Piero della Francesca, yet preserves something of the gentle rhythmic cadence of Renaissance art. Magnelli belongs to that race of artists for whom chromatic richness signifies not a riotous display of colors, but concentrated harmonies instinct with power and intensity. Hence the fact that, even at its soberest, Magnelli's color has a peculiar fascination; even when reduced to the juxtaposition of flat tints, it always retains an intensity and subtlety which seem to kindle reminiscences of some irretrievable tonal harmony. Color is, however, one of the elements that the painter calls his plastic means, and with Magnelli it is one of the most characteristic and powerful of those elements. Thanks to his ability to enrich form through color, to sustain and strengthen it with an atmosphere born of color, Magnelli's art stands apart from the accepted cultural patterns and has no place in any of the present-day movements; it achieves a higher reality of its own, a higher embodiment of the pictorial image, beyond accidentals, in a timeless metaphysical sphere.

The painting of Atanasio Soldati answers perfectly to his aspiration toward a formal architecture. He took his degree in architecture, as a matter of fact, and this aspiration is already present in the landscapes and still lifes he painted before 1930, works distinctly Cézannesque, though at that time he had not yet seen an original painting by Cézanne. The years between the wars were a difficult period for painters in Italy, but Soldati held a steady course all the while, pursuing an ideal of purity without any concessions to official taste. A Mediterranean painter, as he liked to describe himself, he flooded his forms with color and light, always giving unstintingly of his best, always faithful to the statement of aims he made in 1935, in the prehistoric days, as it were, of Italian abstract art: "For dramatic expression, no knives or corpses, no cannons or flags are required, but only lines, colors and surfaces, all the means peculiar to painting, with no

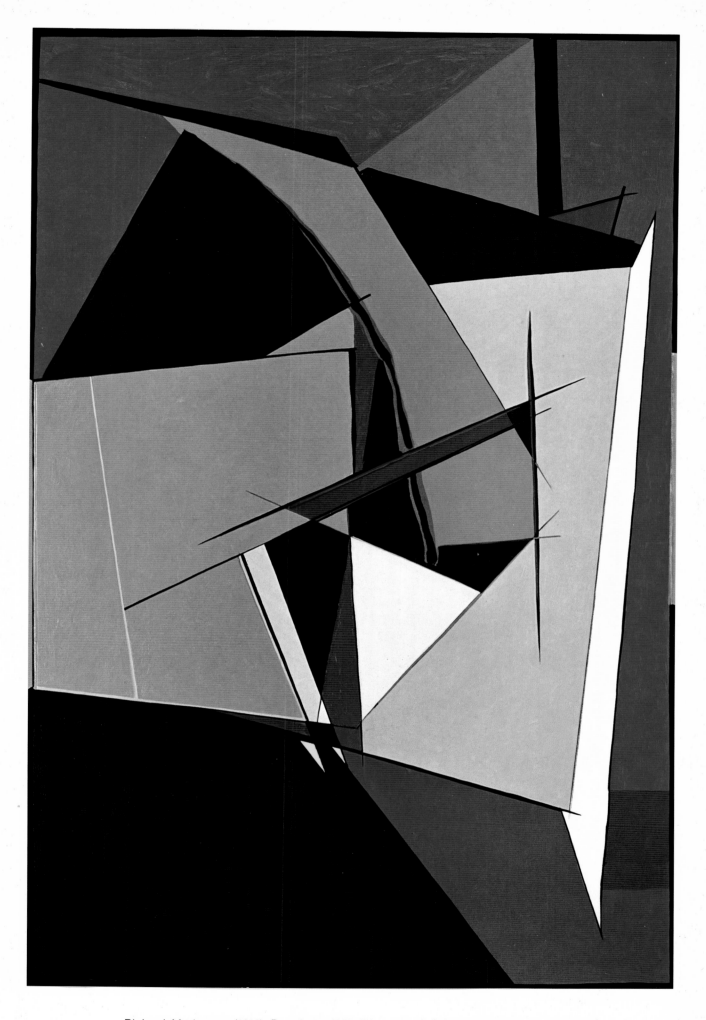

Richard Mortensen (1910). Propriano, 1960. (76¾×51¼″) Galerie Denise René, Paris.

Geer van Velde (1898). Painting, 1960. (57½×52¾″) Owned by the Artist.

preconceptions of any kind, and with no literary allusions." Nor was this a mere reiteration of the famous definition of modern painting made some years before by Maurice Denis; it was a plain statement of fact, acknowledging the new reality, that of form, with which painters were now concerned.

Soldati's, as it so happened, was not a dramatic temperament. He was at his best in a lyrical key, when freely exulting in the song of color. And his color is such as to excel even the absolute perfection of form. His colors are born of the mind, of a mind that had the knack of interpreting the chaotic impulses of the spirit and presenting them coherently, ordered and purified. Color with him, then, is not an intellectual plaything, but a vibration of his whole being, an emotional projection of his own humanity, reticent and perhaps even shy of itself, yet somehow no less passionate and expansive in its way. Soldati's painting gives form to his own humanity.

Its mysterious, ancestral geometry often has a metaphysical flavor, but a flavor always free of literary overtones, though often akin, strangely enough, to the metaphysical quality of Morandi's art. And in that eye-flattering geometry of his the keen observer can always detect a keynote of clarity and purity, an almost moral rigor embodied in crystalline forms suspended in space and time. Soldati was the poet of solitude: his form creations stand above contingencies, above any possible conflict, in silent yet vibrant isolation, suffused with warmth, not in a bleak or disquieting realm but in a haven of peace and composure, where there may be melancholy, but not despair.

Belonging to the older generation of painters born before 1900, Josef Albers is one of those who have contributed most to the great post-war flowering of American art. A German by birth, first a student, then a professor at the Bauhaus, he left Germany when the Nazis came to power and emigrated to the United States, where he still lives. For Albers geometry and rational order are not ends in themselves, are not limited to the structure of the painting. Indeed this structure can always be broken up by innovations in design; these are determined sometimes by simplified linework, sometimes (as in some of his more recent works) by the organization of light as expressed in the plenitude of its observable gradations. Younger than Albers, but with a very similar background, the sculptor, painter and theorist Max Bill apparently seeks to reveal the poetic reality of mathematical abstractions and to harness the expressive power of forms which seem to proceed from man-made theorems. It should be remembered that Max Bill has been the moving spirit behind the Hochschule für Gestaltung at Ulm, which may well claim to be the direct heir of the Bauhaus, and which has raised the basic problems of a new rationalism, utterly different from the rationalism of art between the wars.

Two other aspects of geometric painting, which tends to draw apart more and more distinctly from the art of the older geometric masters, are personified by Richard Mortensen and Victor Vasarely, the first a Dane, the second a Hungarian, though both have lived in Paris for many years. What seems to distinguish their painting is the intense will to participation which it evinces. "A sense of the great, refined and elementary rhythms characterizes the painting of Mortensen... Vasarely's geometrism takes on the most varied aspects of line and form, both static and dynamic, beautifully textured and with a fine breadth of composition." Thus Léon Degand described their work in the first issue of **Quadrum** in 1956; as usual, his judgment is sound, and his words show these artists in the right light. The main room in the Danish Pavilion at the 1960 Venice Biennale focused attention anew on Mortensen's work, at the very time when the esthetic of geometric abstractionism was thought to be moribund. Not that painting today is looking backward; there is nevertheless a very real need, felt in many quarters, to regain such an ideology as will justify the return to a pictorial order which is not geometric and which does not repudiate or do violence to the historical past.

That geometry need not be synonymous with rigid patterning has been amply demonstrated by Geer van Velde, who as a matter of fact had already demonstrated it at a time when it was still possible to detect a semblance of real images in his work. It was the space created by these interrelated images that became abstract—a space glowing with chromatic luminosity and extending not only along the surface but in depth as well. Geer van Velde has a lifetime's experience of painting behind him, and through the years he has continually enriched his means of expression, responding successively to all the tendencies that have gathered momentum around him, from Cubism to Post-Cubism. After finally discarding the last figurative traces lingering in his work, he continued to capitalize, more effectively than ever in fact, on his superlative faculty of creating suggestive space. The verve and fantasy of his colors, moreover, prevented forms from interlocking too sharply or rigidly. Van Velde's colors today have lost nothing of their vividness; well thought out and well controlled, they glow with an inner light that is not to be found in nature.

The work of painters like Victor Pasmore and Gaston Bertrand, among others, testifies to the continued pursuit of a non-schematic art unhampered by the limits of absolute geometry. The work of a painter like Maldonado, who succeeded Max Bill as director of the Ulm Hochschule,

Ben Nicholson (1894). Feb. 1959 (Half Moon). (63×58¾") Galerie Charles Lienhard, Zurich.

testifies to the same aspiration. It is surely no longer possible to revert to an art of geometric purity. The most fruitful line of research now seems to lie in the direction of forms released from the thralldom of physical space. Intensive experimentation is called for, guided by reason and the experience so far gained. From the pre-war masters to the younger men who have followed their lead, geometric painting has produced some very fine works, and has above all perhaps demonstrated the validity of principles which have by no means outlived their usefulness.

If no mention has yet been made of Ben Nicholson, the reason is that he stands apart; it will not do to classify him as a geometric painter and leave it at that. Ben Nicholson is the greatest painter England has produced in the past half century, and in spite of the modernity of his esthetic and the European spirit in which he works, he is also the most characteristically English artist of our time. It is no paradox to say that in him is perpetuated the great English tradition which has contributed so much in the way of ideas to European art—the tradition which, beginning with Constable and Turner, found its theorist and spokesman in Ruskin, who regarded painting, and artistic activity in general, chiefly in the light of its moral intentions and the qualitative values they reflect on the work of art. It is this attitude, with its high ideal of pictorial purity and simplicity, that has remained unshaken in England throughout the long evolution of art, and its attendant upheavals, since Ruskin's time. This does not in any way imply constraint or impoverishment, where sensations and their textural expression are concerned. But it means that the artist's attitude of humility before his forms assumes considerable importance and lends a peculiar character to the work. In this Nicholson is thoroughly English, and on this account alone stands apart from those European artists to whom he owes much, without however re-echoing the manner of any one of them. His work shows how well an exceptionally gifted artist can assimilate a stylistic trend—first Cubism, then Neo-Plasticism (under certain aspects), in Nicholson's case—without ever lapsing into the monotonous repetition of borrowed forms. Indeed, he has amply repaid his debt by opening up fresh possibilities of development in the use of geometric patterning.

About 1920 Nicholson began looking to Cubism for inspiration, but he took care at the same time to go back to the sources: the emotional density of the pictorial image, with its well articulated volumes, is an obvious reference to Cézanne, but in a different, more delicate tonality, which remained typical of his work even when he took the plunge and entered a wholehearted cubist phase, pursuing it in a spirit rather closer to Braque than to Picasso. Then spontaneously, as if moved by an inner necessity, he followed it up with a new phase, akin to Neo-Plasticism in the firm control Nicholson now felt impelled to exercise over form. He had met Mondrian, as a matter of fact, in Paris in 1934, and the two men were again in touch from 1938 to 1940, when the Dutch artist took refuge in England. But Nicholson remained very much himself.

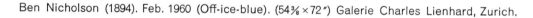

Ben Nicholson (1894). Feb. 1960 (Off-ice-blue). (54⅜×72″) Galerie Charles Lienhard, Zurich.

His color in particular, always confined to a scale of great simplicity, now acquired an almost metaphysical flavor. His colored reliefs were not only an attempt to renew the traditional language of painting and to break down the material barriers between the different forms of artistic expression; they also constituted a direct experiment with the chromatic values of new materials.

The geometric modulation of his paintings seems to owe relatively little to collateral tendencies; it did not lead him to the exclusive creation of forms unconnected with visual reality, for at times the artist assigned the same absolute formal value to various real objects. So a point had been reached where no distinction could any longer be made between a purely geometric form and, for example, the curve of a drinking glass, the latter having been stripped at once of its real, symbolic and illustrative associations. Nicholson never reverts insistently to an established pattern, never locks his architectonic rigor in a preconceived schema, nor subjects forms to an unimaginative automatism. The clarity of his expression, kept intact in his latest works, testifies to a coherent vision constantly fixed on an ideal of purity expressed in terms far removed from objective reality, terms imbued with courtly refinement and lofty poetry.

2

ROGER BISSIÈRE · JEAN BAZAINE · ALFRED MANESSIER
JEAN LE MOAL · RENATO BIROLLI · EDOUARD PIGNON
GUSTAVE SINGIER · MARIA-ELENA VIEIRA DA SILVA

Roger Bissière (1888). Gray, 1958. (45¾×35") Galerie Jeanne Bucher, Paris.

2

Bearing in mind what Kandinsky had to say about the "inner compulsion" actuating the artist at the moment of creation and lifting him above the contingencies of apparent reality, we realize the extent to which, ever since the opening years of the century, modern painting has sought to individuate a real event, of valid efficacy and scope, not only through the exchange between the artist and his source of inspiration, but above all through the relation in which he stands toward his work. Kandinsky went on to say that a patch of color can mean as much and have as high a potential of poetic expression as a figure or an object. The 20th century has endorsed a tradition whose guiding aim, from the Impressionists onward, has been to achieve an autonomous pictorial language; no matter whether that language proves to be the product, or better, the stylistic elaboration, of personal sensations. Nature could therefore continue to serve as a point of departure and could even be reproduced on the canvas; but the painter was free to interpret it as he saw fit, to vary its aspects and order of presentation, to adapt it to a rhythm, composition and space which, being peculiar to painting and no longer conditioned by appearances, embodied natural elements in a new context and changed their meaning.

Geometric painting, as we have seen, solved the problem of autonomous pictorial expression by reducing reality to purely architectural forms and cutting the artist off completely from any contact with the world of nature. But changing patterns of thought and culture after the Second World War, and changing social and political conditions too, called for different solutions. A need was felt to resume the dialectical exchange between man and nature, to respond again to sensations in so far as they could be controlled, crystallized and made to contribute to a conscious elaboration of visual data on the abstract level of style. So reality and abstraction came to coincide, thus on the one hand launching a reaction against the concrete painting of the geometric artists, while on the other avoiding any return to that more or less faithful reproduction of the subject characteristic of the period of lassitude which had set in after the avant-garde successes of the first twenty years of the century. This new move in the direction of pictorial autonomy bore fruit, both in France, where it had all the weight of the cubist tradition behind it, and in those countries which, after long years of political and cultural oppression, were emerging from the backwaters of an official art sponsored by dictatorial régimes, and were eager now to partake of the European spirit and taste a freedom so long denied them.

Confining our horizon for the moment to Europe and to a single aspect of painting subsequent to 1940, we see clearly enough that this new trend, while running counter to geometric painting, was by no means a venture into the irrational; so true is this that it coolly refrained from exploiting the conquests of surrealist automatism, not even admitting them as incidental means of enrichment. In short, the Second World War failed to produce an art movement of reaction and protest, such as Dada had been in the First War. This painting found its great source of inspiration in Cubism and, in addition to Cubism, in the personal achievement of Picasso, regarded in its entirety as an object lesson, from the cubist works to **Guernica** and **Night Fishing at Antibes,** and taken not as a pattern to cleave to, but as working capital and a stimulating indication of

Roger Bissière (1888). Painting, 1955. (21¼×31⅞") Hélie Lassaigne Collection, Paris.

the way toward further developments. And it was a lesson whose import was not confined to painting alone, but extended to moral and even political issues, which artists now, fully alive to their active role in society, were bound to take into consideration.

All the conquests of artistic idiom handed down by the traditions of the modern movement were challenged and tested anew. So it is not by chance that the group of painters in France who, in 1941, sought to rediscover a non-figurative dimension opposed to geometric concretism, called themselves "Peintres de Tradition Française." Best known among them were Bazaine, Gischia, Manessier, Pignon, Le Moal and Lapicque. They refused to brook any compromise with classicism and naturalism, just as they refused to countenance either the grim deformities of Expressionism or the psychological slant of surrealistic forms. One of their acknowledged masters, in addition to Picasso of course, was Jacques Villon, because he had never set a limit to the use of color, even when his style was strictly based on the principles of the Section d'Or group. Color, vibrant and even at times atmospheric, in this respect faintly reminiscent of Impressionism, was one of the distinctive features of this painting.

It is important to form a clear idea of the exigencies that shaped this new trend, for it not only made its mark immediately in France, but its influence soon spread through Europe. In 1952, introducing the work of several Italian painters which at the time approximated very closely to that of the French group, Lionello Venturi wrote: "They neither are nor want to be abstract painters. They neither are nor want to be realists. They are determined to elude this antinomy which, on one side, threatens to transform abstraction into a return to mannerism, and on the other plays into the hands of political forces intent on destroying the artist's creative freedom and spontaneity... They are by no means Puritans in art, like the abstractionists; they take their inspiration wherever and whenever they find it, and make no secret of the fact." [11] This sufficiently defines the character of the new movement and indicates how different it is from geometric painting, not only in its means of expression but in the interpretation it gives of the world. Its novelty lies in its broad acceptance of things, of whatever comes its way, and in its capacity for sharing in their life. The post-war years brought with them a re-examination of moral and political values, of social and economic relations; the hope of a better and fairer organization of world society kindled new faith in man and a new sense of human dignity. Even though that hope may now seem over-optimistic and that faith ill-founded, both were salutary at the time. The artist felt committed to a definite line of action; he felt it his duty neither to estrange himself from reality nor to accept it passively; he recognized the necessity of participating in the life of Europe. Upheavals soon took place, of course, as faith in the future faded and the reaction set in, bringing with it apocalyptic outbursts of protest and, at the same time, renewed appeals in favor of a **peinture engagée.** The flowering of American painting came as the aftermath of this reaction. But undoubtedly this group of painters who appealed to the spirit of the French tradition has greatly contributed to enrich the autonomous language of painting; they have successfully rescued it from the impasse in which it was about to land itself by blindly accepting abstraction and reality as mutually exclusive opposites.

The lesson of Picasso, for these artists, was not only a stylistic but a spiritual one. With **Guernica** in 1937 Picasso had committed himself fully and irrevocably, projecting the violence of his feelings into semi-abstract forms and drawing on all the stylistic resources at his command. He had also shown that, from a purely artistic point of view, there was no difference between concrete forms and abstract forms. The painter delineates forms of his own creating which for him are real, which body forth his own substance, and which nothing prevents us from regarding as figures; their representational value is obviously the same, whether they stand for a person, an object, or a circle. A painter's capacity for expressing the real, then, does not depend on his ability to reproduce external appearances. Working in this very spirit, Jean Bazaine, who in 1941 had organized the exhibition entitled "Vingt Peintres de Tradition Française," could write as follows a few years later: "When we look at a figurative painting, what seems undeniably to awaken our memories of reality, what we actually remember or what is evoked in our minds, is not brute reality, not a given pre-established world, but such a creation of our own as pure contemplation enables us to make. At the very instant when we look at the picture, we create a corresponding reality. Hence the fact that people react in such different ways to the transposition effected by a work of art. The truth is that we never judge a work of art by its closer or remoter resemblance to this crude myth of a dead Reality, fixed and inalterable; we judge it by our ability to invent a world of our own." [12]

Who indeed could any longer believe in a cut-and-dried reality, standardized once and for all? As far as painters were concerned, reality could no longer be held to coincide with the traditional proportions and vision of classical art; this was a mere abstraction based on fixed canons which had had their day. Nor could it be identified with the visible integument of the material things that meet the eye, now that physics had shown matter to be a real phenomenon far more complex than it appears. Nor could it be reduced to the stable sensations of pure geometry. Many and varied indeed were the perceptible aspects of reality, and painters in a body, even those who later diverged from this trend, set themselves to investigate its possibilities, to create a new realism which no longer consisted in a mere pictorial inventory of appearances, but manifested the painter's "ability to invent a world of his own."

All this logically implied a new interpretation of natural phenomena and their transmutation into forms, once they had been committed to canvas. Ever since Impressionism, the subject had been subordinated to the personality and interpretative powers of each individual artist. And his sensations, what Cézanne had called "**ma petite sensation,**" not only intervened as the determining factor in the choice of a particular subject, of the detail of a landscape or a still life; they also ruled out any concern with the picturesque and invested the subject with a halo of personal feelings, an emotive content no longer directly dependent on visual data. The result was that the subject, as students of Impressionism have duly noted, was changed into a motif. Now this was a change which the post-war non-figurative painters have borne in mind, though of course there has been no question of an outright return to impressionist sensations. These painters set out to create such motifs as condensed and summed up their own personal presence; this meant that they undertook to establish a dialectical contact with nature, or with its repercussions in the individual consciousness, for they regarded nature as only one of the elements of a world which the artist has a perfect right to reinterpret and modify in his own way. The problem was one of participation, in consequence of this deliberate intervention on the artist's part, through which—to use the terms of existentialist thought—man accedes to the consciousness of being **(Sein)** and existence **(Dasein).**

If, when all is said and done, art has always been a magnificent abstraction, then the new painting, in repudiating visual appearances, was more than abstract; it should by rights be called non-figurative, inasmuch as it no longer had any need to refer to anything recognizable or immutable. It was itself the expression of a reality in movement, in a state of perpetual flux, a reality in which the artist himself actively participated with a full awareness of his history and of the value the act of painting may assume in its own right with the rediscovery of the moral implications of the painter's craft. Nothing, then, could be more real and less abstract than painting considered in this light. Bazaine himself has stated the case explicitly, with some telling examples to back it up: "Cormon is less lifelike (less abstract) than Klee, but Klee is less lifelike (less abstract) than the Douanier Rousseau. And Kandinsky is much less abstract than Bruegel, Vermeer and Van Eyck. Van Eyck in fact may well be the furthest extreme of abstraction in the whole history of painting." [13] This because, after all, a painter's force of creative intuition, his sense of style, the compulsion he feels toward pictorial expression, cannot be assessed with reference to a greater or lesser approximation to visual reality, but only with reference to "an inner world which includes the outer and yields its secret life and even the **pure rhythmic motifs of being.**"

These notions, while expressing the outlook and theories of one of the outstanding artists of the post-war period, do not apply to Bazaine alone; they do not represent a point of view peculiar to him. On the contrary, they indicate the prevailing tendency of all the research work carried out by the younger generation in these and subsequent years, up to the emergence of the new informal esthetic or action painting. And this generation came to the fore not only in France but all over Europe. It is only fair to add, however, that the renewal of pictorial idiom, which took the name of Abstract Impressionism in France and was known in Italy as Abstract-Concrete (though none of these names adequately describes the movement under way), patterned itself on that type of painting which was the logical outcome of a whole artistic (and even political) attitude toward the problem of interpreting visual and sensory data. This was so to begin with, at least. As time went on, an increasing sense of commitment to active participation, especially outside France, again came to modify the artist's language and his relation to reality. But each of the men who fostered the development of this trend made a personal contribution to it. This was logical enough now that artists were free to interpret reality as they saw fit, and were expected to arrive not at a visual norm applicable to all, as in the past, but at a personal, individual idiom of pictorial expression. None of these artists, moreover, even in the broader context of an international art culture, could forget or mask the national character of his own background and temperament.

The exercise of Cartesian control over inspiration and the **esprit de finesse** that goes with it are qualities particularly susceptible of development in a French cultural milieu. To continue to capitalize on the tradition of modern painting (which had remained unbroken in France) was a necessity: it alone pointed the way to the future. But at the same time this new approach to the problem of painting, by committing painters to an uninhibited freedom of interpretation, and by releasing artistic expression from its subjection to the demands of mere hedonism and acknowledging its spiritual mission, led to an increasing variety of styles. This variety grew very marked indeed by the time these painters had become sufficiently sure of their means of expression and powers of interpretation, sufficiently detached from nature-directed sensations, to profit by new ideological contributions, not only from France but also and above all from the United

States (for the first time in history), from Northern Europe too, and even from the philosophies of the East. Yet this could only have happened in the initial phase of research, which, while producing works and artists of outstanding quality, had not forced painting to fit into any **a priori** schema, but left each man free to handle forms as his own personality suggested, regardless of established geometrical canons.

Jean Bazaine (1904). Child and the Night, 1949. (36¼×28¾") L.G. Clayeux Collection, Paris.

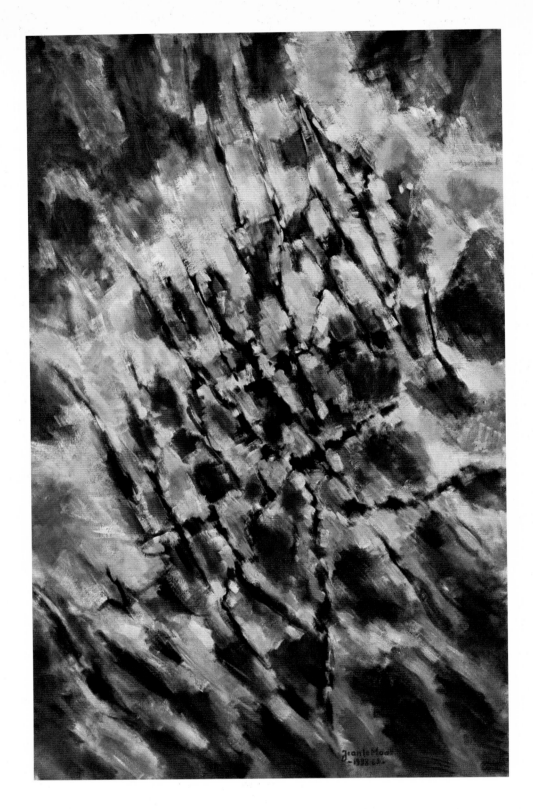

Jean Le Moal (1909). Autumn, 1958-1960. (51¼×31⅛″) Galerie Roque, Paris.

a purist esthetic. But the very fact that he has made a special study of artists like Seurat and Ingres, on the one hand, and Corot on the other, indicates the facets of his sensibility, which stands midway between the opposite poles of sensation and stylistic logic.

"Let us learn," Bissière has written, "to look around us less and to look more within ourselves. Therein lies the whole secret behind the strength of the French masters. They have never at any time repudiated the tradition of their race; they have accepted the abiding, unchanging laws handed down to them by their predecessors. But when it came to applying those laws, they have put on blinders and have sought no other exchanges but those which logically take place between the object and their own consciousness." The important thing for Bissière is that this conscious order should not cramp the artist's style, not impede his movements like a tight-fitting suit of clothes; but it should effectively exist, he feels, because this order, which cannot be geometrical (nor even partake of the geometry of Cubism, inasmuch as space is multidimensional), is capable of revealing the life of nature without representing it. Small signs and small colored forms are organized on the picture surface, others appear on a ground which has a different light intensity. The space we have here is no longer three-dimensional space, but is elaborated, extended, enriched by a time dimension in which the pattern of expression develops as a true, not an abstract, entity. With his intelligence—which is the form of his pride—and to the extent of his power of active intervention, Bissière proceeds to modify the apparent interplay of forms and colors, so as not to leave them at the mercy of any decorative caprice. These forms, in fact, are motifs which may legitimately fall into place in accordance with a rhythm born of intuition rather than thought. But the intelligence must intervene and displace them in order to fix the significance of their tonal qualities and their interrelationships. The human qualities of his work, though it has been completely non-figurative for years, stand out conspicuously and beautifully mirror the artist's mind and personality.

Perhaps the most acute theorist of post-war painting, as we have seen, has been Jean Bazaine, who expresses his ideas with a clarity that sheds light not only on his own work. His insights derive from a profound culture and thoroughly modern tastes (his partiality for Proust and Joyce is well known), and he also applies those insights to an analysis of his own painting. "I have always started out not from a preliminary drawing gradually filled out with color, but from color values intermingling in ever increasing complexity. These 'patches' are never gratuitous: from the outset they are values of space and atmosphere, they mean something, they are a reality, and the whole future development of the canvas depends on them. What evolves is this reality, or rather its power of evocation. Though the form comes through slowly, though memories and emotions give definition only gradually to this world of color, I always feel that the cycle has closed too soon. At any moment the canvas may come to a close, to a conclusion, but I always try to put off that moment." [14]

Here we touch on one of the peculiar qualities of Bazaine's painting: each work is a self-sufficient whole, circling back upon itself, beginning and ending its story. But this story continually stimulates the artist's consciousness, and from the natural world he elicits fresh rhythms. The reality it contrives to embrace is far more extensive than the reality summed up in an objective rendering of a given scene or incident. Some of Bazaine's paintings, especially those of several years ago, reveal that the artist is in direct communication with nature (even though he never paints from life), but his observation of phenomena is subordinated to a sense of style and interpretation which reshuffles their visual order, accentuates colors and intensifies the vibration of light. Dynamic lines and movements combine to convey a total impression of truth, fully mastered by the painter because formulated (at least in part) by himself. Certain chromatic passages in Bazaine's painting not only show an extreme finesse—so that it comes as no surprise to learn that Bonnard is one of his favorite painters—but also confirm his passionate participation in the life of things.

It would be an inaccurate simplification to say that Bazaine's is an art of evocation and contemplation. At its deepest level it is on the contrary a dramatic and restless art, criss-crossed by incisive rhythms alternately horizontal and vertical. Though the complementarity of colors is not always respected, their harmonies are used with consummate skill to break up the narrative continuity of the images, to point up a dramatic pause, to arrest a fleeting moment of silence and self-communion, before the thread of discourse is taken up again. But the approach so well defined by Bazaine in his theoretical writings and so ably realized in his painting has never amounted to a closed system imposing strict limits on the artist. His recent works suffice to demonstrate the contrary; they brilliantly evidence Bazaine's adventurous open-mindedness, his readiness to test out new elements and make new departures, always adding to his personal experience of nature and the world, while always developing the rich vein of continuity that links his later to his earlier work. Certain blues and whites which have recently crept into his palette, together with certain broken rhythms, tell of a vigorous capacity for continual renewal and extension of his poetic powers. It has always been his contention that the problem of reality cannot be reduced to the hard-and-fast equation of a single definitive solution, however carefully worked out, for the problem arises anew each time the artist comes to grips with reality, which each time calls for a fresh interpretation.

Very similar in many ways to Bazaine's approach is that of Jean Le Moal, who, like Bissière, cultivates an admirable sense of order and inward logic. Some of the landscapes he painted before 1950 are virtually encased in a geometric space, with their image-forms sustained by evenly pulsing rhythms. Then he gradually proceeded to free his surfaces from the too obvious patterning that underlay them, working out a more introspective order no longer subordinated to any deliberate geometry. This he was able to do by varying the quality of his colors, intensifying them and charging them with a stronger emotional appeal. In proportion as his colors were enriched, his forms opened out and expanded, gaining a new narrative felicity.

"Non-figurative art seems to me at the present time to offer the painter his best chance of working back to a reality of his own and retrieving a sense of what is essential in himself. It is only by regaining this vantage point that he can afterwards hit his stride and revitalize even the outward reality of the world. If man is a hierarchy of values, his outward appearance is no more than a transparent phantom if drained of its spiritual content."[15] Alfred Manessier, who wrote these words, is one of the few religious painters of our time, and undoubtedly the best of them, with the exception of Rouault.

Alfred Manessier (1911). Passion, 1955. (25⅝×31½″) Private Collection, Düsseldorf.

Alfred Manessier (1911). Painting, 1956. (38½×51¼") Klaus Gebhard Collection, Wuppertal.

Manessier is a Catholic painter. But his Catholicism is not confined to the immutable aspects of the liturgy, to dogmas that admit of no discussion. His is not a vague, mystical creed, but one of active commitment. He is a man who feels that the spiritual forces stirring within him, which his religious convictions foster, are creative forces. Religious art for Manessier can no longer be the old art of illustration, or the emotional art of popular imagery which the Church has too often sponsored in the past. For him, as for all great artists, art is an inner necessity enlisted in the service of human and spiritual values. Like all the artists of his generation, Manessier participates to the full in present-day life; only his aspirations, unlike those of his fellow artists, are primarily religious.

His art is pure. He makes no concession to official propaganda of any kind. Purity is the only word to characterize the pictorial elements that constitute his means of expression, his rich, resonant colors, and the tension and spareness of his forms. Like the other painters of whom we have spoken, Manessier maintains a dialectical relationship with reality, but this reality is not the outer world that meets the eye; for him it is spiritual truth that counts. It is true that man is made in the image of God, but this resemblance is an inner one; it lies in man's ability to distinguish good from evil, it lies in the exercise of free will, which can bring him closer to God or estrange him from God. The ostentatious painter, the vacuous academic artist, generally represents the divinity outright, because then he gleans some borrowed reflection of its glory which would otherwise never accrue to him, owing to his incapacity to participate in creation.

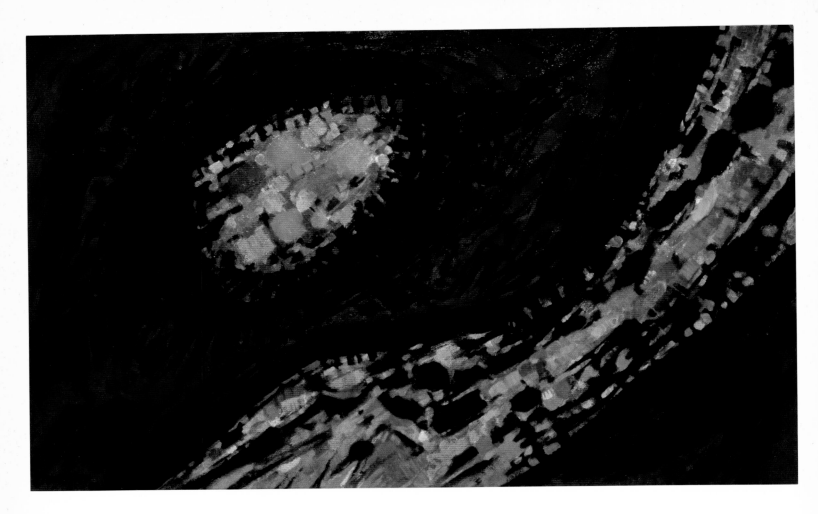

Alfred Manessier (1911). Christmas 1958. (31½×50¾˝) H. C. Bechtler Collection, Zurich.

Manessier rejects this type of representation, and is justified in doing so, for his spirit is present in his work and is something infinitely greater than any "objective" figuration and more profoundly true than the "transparent phantom" of appearances.

Hypocrisy is ruled out. No allusion to a figure is necessary. The free counterpoint of forms and colors suffices. The two commanding facets of Manessier's personality seem to be, on the one hand, an attitude of Franciscan humility toward his own work, from which he resolutely banishes facile effects; and, on the other, an unmitigated delight in exploiting the exuberant wealth of his palette and his pictorial means, which are the outward manifestation of his intense religious convictions. Even when (as in some of his recent works) he achieves full chromatic expression with only two colors, such as black and red, the harmony thus obtained is so rich and full-bodied that the spectator remains quite unmindful of this drastic reduction of the palette. He has also shown his fine technical skill and craftsmanship in the field of engraving and in the designing of stained-glass windows for churches. Manessier's style lends itself particularly well to the peculiar exigencies of the stained-glass window, which seems to intensify his rhythms and exalt the spirituality of his forms.

Even the landscapes and natural scenery which often inspire Manessier's work are always interpreted with a religious deference for all created things and with that simplicity of means which, as we have said, is anything but indigence. Light pours freely over these real forms and the compositional arrangement determines their spiritual meaning, because this arrangement springs from an inner compulsion which with him is also an inner order of spiritual harmony. Hence the full-sounding note of choral grandeur struck by these paintings, as if they were the echo of many voices raised in song: the artist yearns to communicate with all things, to embrace them all with fraternal good will, and to appreciate their value in the light of the spiritual truth he carries within himself.

While Manessier is a Catholic, Birolli, like Pignon, was a Communist—though both of them soon repudiated the esthetics of party-sponsored social realism. Their works, however, unmistakably convey that sense of personal commitment which characterizes their generation, in both cases a keen sense of social commitment, a deep-seated need to communicate which has nothing religious about it, or rather belongs to another religion which recognizes in man himself, in his social reality, the be-all and end-all of human activity. Pignon also took part in the 1941 exhibition of "Peintres de Tradition Française," but his painting now stands very much apart from that of his former companions: it is the painting of a robust extrovert who takes greater care in his choice of motifs and seems to set more store by the component elements of reality, which he transforms in his pictures, with almost expressionistic violence, but which he never abolishes outright.

Pignon needs this contact with real things; his sense of style organizes them in a frame of space and web of movement which are certainly not descriptive, though forms, the pictorial embodiment of sensations, are made to coincide with appearances in so far as possible. In a word, he is still confident in the possibility of probing into the meaning of the things the eye sees. For him they represent a means of communication which he cannot do without; his painting is

Renato Birolli (1906-1959). Fires in the Cinque Terre, 1955. (44⅞×47⅝") Emilio Jesi Collection, Milan.

therefore never inner-directed, but always faces toward the outside world. The motif, however, is always interpreted; Pignon is not the man to submit to the tyranny of objective visual data. He feels free to intensify his rhythms and colors, with all the means at his command, with an eye to concise, concentrated expression answering as nearly as possible to the vivacity of his temperament and the unquestionable sincerity of his intentions.

Renato Birolli worked in Paris in the years immediately after the war, but before that, in his native Italy, he had taken part in one of the movements which had arisen in violent protest against the official art sponsored (and imposed) by the Fascist régime: the Corrente movement. This was one of those loosely organized groups of non-conformist artists, of widely divergent aspirations, who produced their best work after the war. Birolli's art developed out of figurative Expressionism and, by way of the bracing disciplines of Post-Cubism, reached fulfillment (for Birolli died in 1959) in a highly personal form of non-figurative painting. His acquired style, however, was never such as to stifle the artist's temperamental virulence. Birolli has a way of seizing on reality in its most violent aspects. "For three days fires have been raging on these scorched hills," he wrote from Liguria to a collector of his work. "So I have set aside all the pictures I had begun and am tackling a large canvas on the **Fires in the Cinque Terre**. Now at last a grand contrast of reds, greens and blacks; of blacks, browns and reds; of violet-black

Edouard Pignon (1905). Shipyard, 1953. (28¾×36¼″) Prof. Funck-Brentano Collection, Paris.

Gustave Singier (1909). Sea Window, 1957. (82¾×67″) Collection of His Excellency M. Hugo Gouthier, Rome.

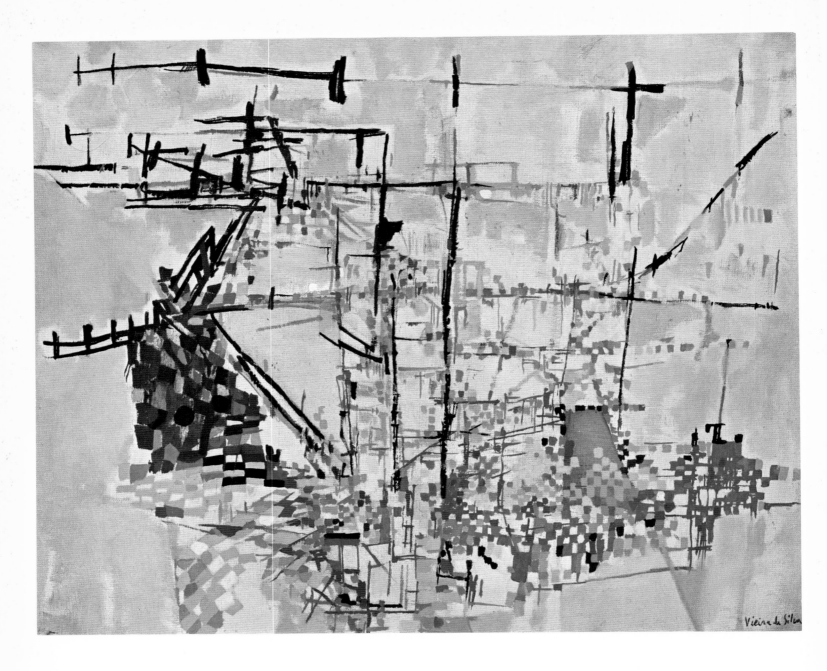

Maria-Elena Vieira da Silva (1908). Métro Station, 1953. (19¾×24″) Philippe Leclercq Collection, Hem (Nord), France.

and red or reds and violet." [16] In the course of his last trips to Flanders and his stays in the Cinque Terre region of Liguria, Birolli's color rose in a final swan-song of vibrant, broadly surging harmonies. Nature had leaped to life in his canvases, glowing, effervescent, infinitely suggestive, drawing power and energy from the sturdy compositional structure and from an intense vitality which, unfortunately, spent itself all too soon.

A well ordered composition gives Gustave Singier the foundation he needs for imaginative metamorphoses of form. "Any sight that catches my eye, landscape, still life or interior, spontaneously kindles within me a corresponding form or color emotionally bound up with it and inseparable from it. For many reasons, it would be impossible for me to tell why this or that particular form or color impinges on me. I make no attempt to analyze the matter, that's no business of mine. But as you can well imagine—such being the freedom the painter is privileged to enjoy—that particular form or color has only a remote connection with what people are pleased to call objective reality." [17] The outcome then is an autonomous image, and the degree of this autonomy is increased by the mysterious disposition of forms on the picture surface. So subtle are his color harmonies that Singier succeeds in giving an almost incantatory value to his pictures, beyond the contingencies of the moment.

Maria-Elena Vieira da Silva was born in Lisbon, but she came early to Paris where she studied both painting and sculpture. To the latter she probably owes that peculiar sensitivity to the plasticity of solid objects in space which she has so magnificently expressed in her painting. While her inspiration and her colors appear to be of a tremulous delicacy, actually her compositions are very carefully designed and constructed: real elements or symbols of reality (cities, houses, etc.) are inserted in a space peculiarly her own and acquire life and movement. Full of poetic intimations and a subtle lyricism best revealed in the flawless harmony of her color schemes, the works of Vieira da Silva evince an unerring mastery of style, whether frankly figurative or vibrant with colors and rhythms of signs and lines that shatter the figurative pattern. At every moment the artist's intelligence intervenes decisively in the pictorial elaboration of the data inspiring the work. Accordingly, the poetry and delicate grace with which she invests the picture elements are never merely the sentimental transcription of a mood or state of mind, because everything is concretized in the painting and becomes essential to the expression of her vision.

Vieira da Silva observes reality, records certain features of it in her pictures, and recognizes its value as a source of inspiration. But even before 1941 she had radically simplified it; selecting

Maria-Elena Vieira da Silva (1908). Studio, Boulevard Saint-Jacques, 1960. (31⅞×39¾″) Private Collection, Paris.

its dynamic elements, she isolated them and worked out the relationships of full and empty spaces, transforming the latter into emotive nuclei, vivified with subtle colors and geometrically ordered. Since that time she has always abided by these principles. She has made a point of ordering her emotions even when color texture itself, with its varying thicknesses and tenuities, acts as a vehicle of pure poetic expression. The resulting order is of course never imposed from outside; it is inherent in the painter's temperament, in her will to organize a concrete picture space capable of containing and intensifying all sensations. And this space, so necessary to the vibration of her colors, is not built up in terms of traditional perspective, it is not an ambience in which forms are simply suspended; it is an inward, a purely psychological space. "Though the world is present in Vieira da Silva's painting," writes René de Solier, "the elements of the work, the objects of her pictures, are considered as seen and felt from the inside."[18] This world, this presence of recognizable things, loses every descriptive or illustrational quality; everything comes to life as if by enchantment, in a projection controlled by the shaping imagination and the steady guidance of the intelligence. And the enchantment steals over the spectator, whose eye soon learns to make out the destinations of an imaginary journey and to thread its way through the clouded depths of glittering colors.

The dynamic rhythm of the work never flags. Small forms and filaments, hints of atmospheric values, vibrant colors skillfully attuned to whites, grays and tenuous blues, all these pure pictorial elements of which the painter stands in full possession combine to form fleeting images, to orchestrate movement, to create an emotional rather than illusionistic perspective giving scope for a new chronology of sensations, for a novel interpretation of truth, within a tightly constructed architecture which concedes nothing to the casual or equivocal. The painting of Vieira da Silva is there to show that the artist today, far from renouncing it altogether, has achieved a new mastery and a new awareness of reality.

3

NICOLAS DE STAËL · SERGE POLIAKOFF · MAURICE
ESTÈVE · BRAM VAN VELDE · ANDRÉ LANSKOY

Nicolas de Staël (1914-1955). Figure beside the Sea, 1952. (63¾×51¼″) E. Beyeler Collection, Basel.

3

"Awareness of the possible, unawareness of the impossible, and rhythm is free. Breathe... breathe... and never think of the definitive without the ephemeral. The tougher the thing is, the more one has to take it to heart." [19] Thus wrote Nicolas de Staël, less confident than the Painters of French Tradition in the possibilities of laying reality bare in the work of art. De Staël's artistic development seems to confirm the first crisis undergone by non-figurative art. His work amounts to a new elaboration of the painter's formal means, seconded by subtle color shading which modifies the interpretation of visual data. He not only scrutinizes those data in their apparent relations, before subordinating them (as many other painters did) to a deliberate process of stylistic transformation, but also explores the whole scale of variations to which they lend themselves. Much has been made of certain parallels between De Staël's investigations and those of others. Sometimes he is regarded as a painter who found it impossible to dispense with a figurative objectivization of the image, and his last pictures would seem to bear this out; again, particular stress is laid on his rational method; or else, taking the opposite view suggested perhaps by his tragic death, some critics couple him with Wols and Pollock, whose anxieties and loss of faith in the human condition and in the painter's traditional means of expression he is supposed to have shared.

De Staël, however, in spite of the fact that he committed suicide, does not seem to have been particularly concerned with dramatic expression, as Wols and Pollock were. He sought solutions of his own to the problems raised by the coexistence of objects and forms. The glowing texture of his colors and his manner of laying them on in broad, rich tracts, coat upon coat, were not meant to achieve that autonomy of expression in which color texture becomes the only possible reality (as in Pollock); nor, on the other hand, did his interpretation of the world resolve itself into a suspension of visual memories of the world (as in Wols). The three artists do admittedly have points in common: the novelty of their language; the symptomatic rupture, which each in his own way has contributed to bring about, of the time-honored relationship between the artist and nature; and their awareness of a possible extension of the painter's art which may constitute a reality in its own right, though logically very different from the apparent reality of visual experience.

But while Pollock gives us for the first time an art which represents a clean break with the modern tradition deriving from Impressionism, and while some of the informal painters have created a picture space altogether different from the space formulated by the Cubists, De Staël's painting, for all its manifest originality, appears more closely connected with the later developments of the modern tradition. His predilection for post-impressionist painting, for that of the Revue Blanche artists in particular, is a known fact. Important to remember too is his friendship with Braque, and also with Lanskoy, like himself a Russian-born artist whose full development—like his own—was only made possible by his transplantation into the French cultural milieu.

It is a fact, as we have already pointed out, that non-figurative art leaves each painter free to develop personal and national characteristics in what is perhaps their purest form. This is so true of Lanskoy that, in spite of the similar solutions he arrives at, we must take care not to couple him with Bazaine and Manessier. "A patch of color on a canvas," Lanskoy has been quoted as saying, "aspires to take form and contends with the other color patches on the same canvas. The outcome of this contest is the birth of the picture." [20] This statement reveals an abstract impulse fundamentally different from the motivation behind the art of the Painters of French Tradition. Lanskoy would seem to share that yearning for supreme reality implicit in the theories of Constructivism and expressed through a drastic simplification of the painter's means, so drastic as to reduce them to a few basic geometric patterns and to a few basic color combinations of black and white or even white and white. But for Lanskoy (and De Staël too) there is a moral responsibility in artistic creation which did not operate in the case of the Constructivists. It is no accident that the conflict between Lanskoy's happy instinct for freely handled colors and his strict sense of spatial organization results in a dynamism for which there is no exact equivalent in the work of any of his contemporaries.

De Staël, unlike Pollock and Wols, was not the prey of a rankling sense of despair. His was an introspective turn of mind, but one that liked to ponder on the whys and wherefores of existing things, on the connections between them, and on the value of their interrelations and interchanges. "Little by little I felt the futility of making an object lifelike, because even with a single solitary object before me I was always uneasily aware of the infinite multitude of other, coexisting objects." [21] With these words De Staël broached the possibility of resolving or reducing the aspects of reality, without there being any need for a violent break with the recent past and the useful lessons it had to offer. But at the same time he broached another possibility: that of following up the research work of his immediate predecessors along the lines laid down by post-cubist painting.

Did all this involve him in a contradiction? Did it break the cycle of his development and cause him to fall back on figurative elements amounting in effect to an evasion of pictorial reality?

Nicolas de Staël (1914-1955). Composition, 1951. (13×21⅝") Private Collection, New York.

Nicolas de Staël (1914-1955). Light-colored Composition, 1951. (23⅝×36¼″) Jacques Dubourg Collection, Paris.

Or have we here, after all, a reconquest of figurative representation achieved on the basis of an abstract idiom of expression? It is true that in the last few years of his life De Staël worked his way back to a figurative art which, since then, has been variously judged. Those who see in these last paintings the finest achievement of the artist's career thereby emphasize the continuity of meaning between this final body of work and his earlier paintings. Others, however, read into them the signs of a crisis affecting not only De Staël but a whole culture, a crisis from which he hoped to find a way out by turning back to the familiar landmarks of realistic art. This latter interpretation seems to the present writer absolutely at variance with the facts of the situation. The truth is that, with so rich and fruitful an experience of non-figurative art behind him, De Staël could never have reverted to outright figurative representation without deep-seated reasons; and these reasons must have been pre-existing, they must have been inherent in the earlier, non-figurative works. De Staël never denied that he wanted to paint objects; but he made it clear that he wanted to render them in their real relations of coexistence. This is not to say that he wanted to paint realistically. "Realist is an absurd misnomer if taken to mean what it actually implies"—these are De Staël's own words.

The alternative hypothesis mentioned above certainly seems to give a simpler, more plausible explanation of the facts. Even if we accept it only in part, De Staël's final paintings are seen, on this view, to have a logical continuity of meaning with his earlier work, though an important reservation must be made: considered as a whole, the later work does not quite come up to the standard of quality set by the earlier. Which may be taken to indicate, no doubt, that his final researches were broken off before they came to fruition, before he had time to work out the solutions which, as it is, we can scarcely presume to infer or imagine without distorting our judgment of his art as we have it. In our opinion, his finest work dates from the period when,

Serge Poliakoff (1906). Composition, before 1954. (45¾×34⅝″) F. C. Collection, Geneva.

Serge Poliakoff (1906). Composition, 1955. (51¼×38¼″) Serge Landeau Collection, Paris.

Maurice Estève (1904). Fleuriel, 1956. (23⅝×28¾″) Galerie D. Benador, Geneva.

without shrinking from the infinite complexity of visual relationships and the intricate coordination of space and form, he succeeded in avoiding the dangers of congestion by skillfully narrowing down the possible combinations of these relationships and setting them in good order. This period began about 1949 (even earlier in his beautiful drawings) and drew to a close by fits and starts after 1954, when these relationships, particularly that between surface texture and image, became too insistent and ostentatious; the artist, by this time, was trying so hard to reduce them to essentials, with so argumentative a sense of the issues involved, that the fine edge was taken off his creative spontaneity. The fact is—and this too is a clear indication of continuity—that the still lifes, the football players and the boats of De Staël's last phase are almost more abstract than the earlier paintings; they are certainly less real for anyone who does not judge of the truthfulness of a work of art by its fidelity to appearances.

So-called informal painting has at times enabled its exponents, as we shall see, to work back to a kind of figurative representation after starting out from wholly irrational premises. This was not the case with De Staël; in him, on the contrary, there occurred a progressive rationalization of the creative process, though this rational method "has nothing of the idealistically pre-established character peculiar both to Cubism and to Mondrian." [22] This is a thesis with which we entirely agree, while bearing in mind that this process of reasoning is **a posteriori** with respect to the compositional order, to the logical scansion of forms and rhythms (even of those apparently most palpable), to the structuring of space. But let it not be forgotten that this space, to begin with, is intuitively perceived in a dimension that is completely abstract, luminous, almost impalpable, but real. Equally real, moreover, is De Staël's instinctive participation in the life of nature and in the loveliness of its colors. In the last analysis, any categorical judgment of this artist and his achievement runs the risk of being too restrictive. The man is best summed up in the words of Braque: "Whatever the path he took or might have taken, we were certain of meeting a painter; this is the surest guarantee."

Like Lanskoy and De Staël, Serge Poliakoff is a Russian by birth and a Parisian by adoption. But the character of his painting seems to be altogether different from theirs, even though it reveals that scrutiny of pictorial relationships and that awareness of the possible which distinguish his pictures—as they distinguish Lanskoy's and De Staël's—so very sharply from those of Bazaine or Manessier. But Poliakoff has no need to go to nature for raw material. The possibilities he explores lie in colors and in a distribution of them whose constructive efficacy is intensified by the textural refinements of their superimposed coats. Poliakoff, whose technique represents the absolute antithesis of the **hautes pâtes** of the informal painters, is nevertheless well aware of the importance attaching to color texture and its expressive qualities. He has never hesitated to follow the example of the Constructivists (of Malevitch in particular), who were able to work out relationships between geometrical forms apparently identical and apparently of the same color—a white square on a white ground, for example—but who nevertheless always managed to arrive at differentiation, not at uniformity, and to build up a composition out of the variations of textural quality inherent in paints and canvas.

Grounded as it is on the differentiation engendered by successive layers of pigment, Poliakoff's painting develops out of a certain number of basic relationships. The constructive rigor which makes his work so very different from that of any other contemporary artist would seem to link it up with the geometric investigations of an earlier day. And, indeed, the end result of any given canvas by Poliakoff is an architectonic construction not established beforehand but worked out by successive dislocations and variations of color qualities and color quantities. "Put on by instinct," writes Dora Vallier of his working methods, "the initial tract of color extends from the edge to the interior and its expanse becomes a form. Other forms gradually surround it, all beginning from the edge of the canvas, after the painter has considered how they look with respect to the straight line delimiting the canvas and after he has duly weighed their values with respect to each other." [23] This, then, is a highly personal art of sensitized geometry, disrupted whenever the artist feels impelled to vary the rhythm and create a space which, by its very nature, cannot be postulated beforehand on **a priori** principles.

Apparently consisting solely of two-dimensional surface effects, this painting actually extends in depth along a very definite spatial dimension. In the first place, it is not meant to be a continual repetition of forms, even of forms straining the physical limits of the canvas; but everything takes concrete shape within the four sides of the picture frame, with a concentration of color power which, surging in from those outer limits, converges on the central nucleus and there discharges the full force of its expression—a climax which makes the inner movement and patterning of the colors all the more effective. The color texture, with its successive juxtapositions and stratifications, with its diversity of timbre, goes to define the chromatic ambience, in the end always unitary, which enables the artist to implement his will to act within the concrete limits of the actual painting, by making the most of the component elements of his medium and of the possible combinations of forms, without any naturalistic scaffolding or any allusion to the outside world.

Poliakoff's experience of abstraction now extends over many years. He executed his first non-figurative works in 1938, and since then he has steadily enriched and refined his style and affirmed its originality. No one before him had succeeded in making space arise so perceptibly not from the clash but from the mere juxtaposition of colored forms. Delaunay of course comes to mind and his name has been linked with Poliakoff's. But the difference between them is obvious and not only in their means, in their construction, in their organization of the picture elements; it is a fundamental difference of spirit and approach in their feeling for form and the significance attaching to it. Poliakoff's rhythms are calmer and broader; with him there is no question of the simultaneity of sensations. Rather than the dynamics of form, what seems to interest him is the positioning of tangible elements, consecutive in time, within a picture space which gives that time element a wholly abstract meaning. This process, controlled by the constant intervention of the mind (thus preventing an association of forms dictated by automatism), also opens up a possibility of logical reconstruction and stands as a lesson to be pondered on for the future development of non-figurative art.

The painting of Maurice Estève also shows a concern for the geometric organization of the composition—whose results and significance, however, are altogether different from anything to be found in Poliakoff. Estève too had a long and interesting figurative phase in the early part of his career, and there is undoubtedly an organic continuity between this and his later work. But, as Pierre Francastel has pointed out, Estève began about 1930 by "creating with tractable —if not realistic—figurative elements, a picture space through which the spectator moves; by introducing forms which, though not utilitarian objects, retain enough recognizable features to quicken the imagination." [24] This was a means of arriving at the full autonomy of pictorial expression, without sacrificing the evocative power of figurative elements. Accordingly, if space was not to remain a mere meeting place of natural elements, the relations between images had to be presented in such a way as to convey a sense of depth, and not simply form a backdrop. Estève solved the problem by emphasizing the chromatic quality of his images. The colors thus

Bram van Velde (1895). Painting, 1960. (51¼×76¾″) Galerie D. Benador, Geneva.

André Lanskoy (1902). Lack of Pity, 1958. (39⅜×28¾″) Galerie Louis Carré, Paris.

intensified were not handled naturalistically, but tended rather to condense into concrete forms. His greens, reds and yellows were not simple tracts of color, nor did they lend themselves to atmospheric effects. They were used far more tellingly: by filling up voids and so creating space, they became forms. The resulting rhythm, unfalteringly sustained, gave the painting a satisfying plenitude, expressive both of the artist's sense of a necessarily abstract style and of his deliberate intention to keep in touch with reality and appearances.

As he enriched his means and gained confidence in their expressive possibilities, Estève gradually simplified the figurative elements, intensified his colors and finally worked out a more organic conception of space where evolving images collide or go their way through interrelated zones of different colors. In these forms it is still possible to detect a connection with natural appearances, but only a very remote one, all but dissolved by the autonomous rhythm governing them. Colors seem to hint at lingering memories of real objects immersed in an atmosphere, but in the process of stylistic elaboration everything becomes autonomous. These faint suggestions of the outside world are redefined in exclusively pictorial terms. In the end they are no longer recognizable as transformations of natural elements; they are, if anything, a plastic equivalent of them, achieved by means of regular formal elements architecturally ordered within a chromatic space. A pure pictorial idiom thus expresses the artist's relation to natural phenomena and, by the same token, vouches for his determination to remain faithful to the basic realities of the human condition, without letting himself be overwhelmed by the violent and fascinating realities of nature, which he nevertheless feels bound to accept and take into consideration.

"The world is a mystery, the work of painting helps me to fathom it. What I want to express is too strange, too violent, for me to hold it in a word or a thought; it has to come out somehow and so I paint." So wrote Bram van Velde in a number of **Derrière le Miroir** in 1948, and his words go far to explain what painting means to him, and how necessary an outlet it is. From his very earliest works Van Velde has aspired to go beyond the limits of any particular type or trend of painting. He wants to be free to make the most of each sensation as it impinges on him, to give expression to it uninhibitedly in the most effective way, without forcing it into any prescribed schema. He is never at a loss for motifs, but invents them as he goes along, with unfailing readiness. They correspond to nothing the eye sees, but arise in response to an urgent need to communicate. Forms are combined in accordance with a rhythm unhampered by logical considerations, and expand whenever the rhythm calls for a continuous sequence on the picture plane. Space never abides by hard-and-fast rules, but is variously created by the varying relationships of one form with another. Anything can happen on the picture surface; what is unreal may at any moment become real, because painting is an inner necessity, giving shape and substance to the shadowiest visions of the artist's mind—shadowy and elusive, and therefore all the more fascinating.

4

HANS HARTUNG · PIERRE SOULAGES · GÉRARD
SCHNEIDER · WILLI BAUMEISTER · EMILIO VEDOVA
FRITZ WINTER · ROBERT MOTHERWELL · FRANZ KLINE

Hans Hartung (1904). T 1956-22, 1956. (63½×40¾˝) H. C. Bechtler Collection, Zurich.

4

Modern art is virtually founded on the principles of interchange and intercommunication. It is possible for a painter living in Paris to know in the same day what his fellow painters are doing in New York. The result is a give-and-take between artists all over the world that is more immediate and more effective than ever before. All this militates against a well-defined classification of present-day art trends. We hear a good deal about informal painting and action painting; the first is supposed to be a European creation, the second typically American. But the facility today with which ideas are exchanged and notes compared makes it absurd even to attempt to draw any clean-cut dividing line between them. Hans Hartung, for example, may seem distinctly closer to the American approach than to the irrational poetics that preside over informal painting. Yet Hartung is perhaps the most typically European of all modern painters and his first abstract works date from 1921-1922, whereas American action painting has only developed since the end of the Second World War. Some of the black-and-white works of Pierre Soulages have been compared with those of Franz Kline; the meaning they convey, however, is altogether different; the two painters have evolved their language without any reciprocal influences and indeed from widely different points of departure. The case of Emilio Vedova also comes to mind. His painting seems to combine the liberties of informal abstraction with a spontaneous configuration of black turbulent signs. But in reality Vedova is the only Italian painter who has proved capable of renewing the link with Futurism.

At the same time there is no denying a certain community of interests and aims in the investigations pursued by these painters. Not an identity of interests and aims, of course; but a common desire to cut painting adrift from its traditional ties, even from the recent tradition of abstract impressionism and so-called abstract-concrete art. So the last contact with nature has been broken, and the new men have fallen back on pure form, beyond the reach of naturalistic allusions and equally remote, probably remoter than ever before, from the architectonic eurhythmy of geometric painting. It is no easy task sorting out the various trends; their rise is too recent, in some cases too tentative as yet, for the contemporary observer to chronicle them without resorting to arbitrary subdivisions made merely for the sake of convenience. Michel Tapié, who coined the expression **art autre** which has gained currency as an indication of the exigencies governing the new art now in the making, has written as follows: "For the time being I have designated this venture by the name **signifiance de l'informel.** Those who have contributed to it in a masterly manner by the spirit of their investigations (but without any thought of team work, which is all to the good, in every way) are: Tobey, Hartung, Bryen, Hofmann, Sutherland, Riopelle, Guiette, Soulages, Serpan, Graves, Brauner, Ubac, De Kooning, Appel, Gillet, Rothko, Sam Francis, Ronet, Russell, Arnal, Philip Martin, Capogrossi, Dova, Kline..."[25] Even here we obviously have an attempt at a general classification of the artists who presumably represent the new avant-garde. But Tapié himself has admitted, for example, that "Hartung, Wols, Soulages and Bryen explore in their own way other actual zones of that untold, unfigurative no man's land: each one is carrying out an experiment so peculiarly his own, and in sectors how fortunately have no chance of encroaching on each other, that the only conclusion to be drawn is that the unknown is incommensurable and that each individual is free to take his chance and play for the highest stakes..."[25] Perhaps the reason why the term **art autre** has gained currency is that it denotes a necessity felt by all, but a necessity that did not require the same solution of everyone. The key to that solution, in its manifold forms, lay in a common desire to break up the form-patterns of the modern tradition founded by Impressionism; in the individuation of a new space beyond the four dimensions of Cubism; and above all in a new relationship which the artist sought to work out, not with nature or phenomena, but with history, in which he participates and to the evolution of which he contributes. It seemed possible for each artist to arrive at some such solution by falling back upon his innermost self.

The currents of modern thought, as a matter of fact, are in keeping with this aspiration, and so are political and economic trends. In his **Eloge de la Philosophie,** published in Paris in 1953, the French thinker Merleau-Ponty wrote: "The presence of the individual in the institution and of the institution in the individual is clear in the case of changes in a language. For it is often the triteness of a form of speech that suggests the idea of resorting, in accordance with a new principle, to the means of discrimination available at a given moment in the evolution of the language. The constant need for communicating leads us to coin words and justifies the use of words in a new way, not consciously thought out but systematic nonetheless. Such by-products, endorsed by the will to expression, take their place and have their significance in the history of the language in question."[26] Even before this, in **Sur la Phénoménologie du Langage,** Merleau-Ponty had dwelt on the fact that certain forms of speech decline when overtaxed and drained of their expressive capacity. An analogous process occurs in art, and we may accordingly observe not only the new significance but the new elaboration of forms in

Hans Hartung (1904). T 1951-12, 1951. (38×57½″) Kunstmuseum, Basel.

Hans Hartung (1904). T 1956-9, 1956. (70⅞×54″) Collection of Madame Anna Eva Bergman, Paris.

the most recent paintings of several artists whose works are reproduced in this chapter. Each exponent of the trends subsequent to Post-Cubism completely ignores the problem of man's relationship with nature, though at times he may arrive at a new formulation of his artistic means by starting out from premises which presuppose that relationship. Take for example the sign, the black sign which forms so integral a part of the language used by these painters. It wells up and takes shape, it dilates over the picture surface—but not in order to constitute a solid foundation on which to raise a subsequent construction. The sign expands, multiplies, and takes on the significance of form independently of any ulterior motives: it is, in a word, autonomous, it is a new element, or anyhow an element employed in a new manner, deliberately substituted for the old familiar forms used hitherto, now sapped and drained of meaning. In actual practice, the sign does duty on the one hand for geometric figures and, on the other, for color-form built up (more or less) from naturalistic data or from sensations.

There was a time when the artist gladly interpreted nature, though he often took it to imply a far greater breadth of meaning than is conveyed by appearances alone; a time too, thereafter, when he came to treat it as a storehouse of autonomous forms, elicited by the stylistic trans-formation of visual data. Then at last he felt compelled to go beyond nature, and indeed, as has happened recently, to ignore nature altogether. In order to arrive at this result, the sign has had to be stripped of the meanings usually attaching to it, has had to be detached from its calligraphic associations. Franz Kline, for example, has quite rightly protested against the parallels sometimes drawn between his painting and Japanese calligraphy. Rightly, because by drawing such parallels critics run the risk of inverting the process of stylistic interpretation. Today, it is safe to say, we Westerners take a greater interest in Japanese calligraphy, but not in its semantic value. In short, the channel of thought only runs one way, from West to East and not vice versa. The signwork of Japanese calligraphy interests us only in so far as it elicits an esthetic response and conveys a sense of space intelligible to us now that we have had some experience of Western signwork, which is not calligraphic. The chances are that at one time or another Kline actually took an interest in Japanese calligraphy; but if he did it was only in the above-mentioned sense. To take another example: the large and small sign-forms which Capogrossi reiterates in his pictures were unquestionably suggested by some ancient symbology, by ancestral symbols but they retain none of their ancient meaning; pictorially speaking, they are autonomous.

Herein lies the absolute novelty of the new painting, which seems to mark the sharpest cleavage yet made with the art of the first half of the 20th century. This chapter will be concerned with only one aspect of this new artistic language. But we shall see later on how it has proved possible to take a familiar image or figuration—as Dubuffet, among others, has done—and make it express an entirely new meaning in terms of the new syntax and vocabulary at the artist's command. If we want to look for antecedents to all this, and for traces (uncertain at best) of continuity with the researches of the recent past, then we must go not to Picasso or the Cubists, but rather to Kandinsky and Klee, to the latter above all. The full implications of Klee's achievement are now becoming apparent, thanks to his unrivaled ability to elicit, from familiar appearances, forms imbued with new meaning. Painters today of course go even beyond this point. With what end in view? According to a young Italian painter, Achille Perilli, "we stand at the outset of a quest, that much is certain, without even the clue of a possible solution... Since picture texture is not governed by any law, and since composition, tonality and color are not governed by any laws, no law-in-itself can be said to exist. And we have no intention of creating any. We mean to do away with all previous experience, to work back from the informal to form, from form to image, from image to sign, from sign to token, from token to memory, from memory to the unconscious, from the unconscious to the true, absurd, immediate poetry of something which is not only ourselves, as we are today or tomorrow or yesterday, but everybody, always and everywhere." [27] And meanwhile? Meanwhile the work goes on of stripping familiar things, symbols and stylistic elements of their familiar meaning, in order to reshuffle them and substitute them for others, to give expression to a new world and a new estate, to a new and poignant relationship, often (but not always) the product of despair. Yet in the last analysis, in spite of all odds, the artist remains confident in his power to express not only himself and his inner life, but the world and society as they come within his experience or his intuition.

The sign, in earlier painting and until very recently, was a limit or indicator of rhythm, or the projection of an immediate intuition; it served as a complementary element, not to be employed as an absolute value. Today the sign is autonomous, it has the same importance as the color patterns which it replaces. It is essential, because no delineation of feelings or states of mind is any longer possible. The artist today feels irresistibly impelled to express too many things that lie beyond visual perception and beyond its reflections in the mirror of consciousness. Ocular experience is not our experience of life; too much escapes the eye for the painter to repose his entire trust in it. "Our experience," as Hans Hartung has said, "is made up of everything we have lived through. I feel cold, I feel hot, I suffer, all the inward movements of my body, this is what gives me access to a knowledge of the world. When we come into the world as babies, we cry out because life is really a terrible thing. Thus we get to know the world. What we feel affects us much more strongly than the mere reds and blues we see around us. It is for us painters to express all this. I need not go into the matter here, but experience reduced to vision alone makes neither the object nor the world known to us. I do not belittle the fact of seeing, on the contrary. But sight is not our only means of knowledge. We have many other ways of knowing." [28]

The approach to this kind of knowledge could scarcely have been any different from what has so far been achieved. Painters stood sorely in need of a new method of investigation which they could never have hoped to find either in known forms or in known space, nor in a pictorial ideology founded on methods and norms of vision which, however fruitfully developed in recent times, are nevertheless rooted in a long tradition. The attitude toward the object, toward visual data which have to be seized on and recreated in an unnatural dimension (for such is the surface of the canvas), has been more or less identical for centuries. What has changed, at every period and for every artist, is the way of interpreting that object, the way of adapting it to a personal style. Geometric painting (and not only that of today) repudiated the object, it is true; but it constituted an equivalent of it in which, at bottom, it was always possible to detect an element dependent on the artist's visual experience. But today the artist dispenses with visual perception. Of course he does not work with his eyes shut; the organ of sight is still the filter through which the picture elements must pass. But what he now deals with is the sum total of his sensations, the sum total of his experience of life, emotional, social and political; and all this cannot be considered in accordance with visual or visible equivalents. It is no longer a question of placing the spectator in the center of the picture, as the Futurists sought to do. It is a question now of achieving a presence, not a vague symbology of life, but a presence amounting to life itself perceived steadily and whole, and not with the eyes alone.

All this is embraced as a unity and no longer split up into different spheres of activity. We have mentioned the importance of Kandinsky's example; but looking beyond the spiritual and non-spiritual postulated by Kandinsky, that is to say beyond any distinction between the materiality of the object and the immateriality of pictorial form, we find the solution worked out by Klee, who synthesized the concepts of good and evil, thus neutralizing their antagonism and reasserting a unity beyond ideological distinctions. The latest trends of present-day painting aspire to this unity, which in theory embodies the artist's life experience in its entirety. Significant gains have already been made, for these new investigations call for new technical means; thus unusual materials have come into use, not for the purpose of mere surface enrichment, as was the case with the Cubists, but as the tokens of an immediate presence, as the presence in fact of the entire picture. In judging the works produced in the last few years, we have to bear in mind the artist's deliberate refusal to interpret visual or even geometric data. Granted that Impressionism, Cubism and subsequent movements have exerted an enormous influence on all modern painting; that Surrealism still continues to exert its influence, though in the form of a revaluation of Dadaist elements rather than those of classic Surrealism. Granted too that the painters of today have drawn abundantly on this rich accumulation of experience in order to clarify their own aims. The fact remains that, once those aims are clarified to their satisfaction, they have turned their back on the past and built up a painting of their own which no longer has any connection with it, and cannot possibly have any, because they have abolished both its precepts and its theories which, while helpful at certain stages of a stylistic evolution, would only have stood in the way of the ideological revolution that was required.

The drawings and paintings executed by Hans Hartung as early as 1921 and 1922 were already completely abstract; they successfully eluded, moreover, the Scylla of geometric patterning on the one hand and the Charybdis of cubist space on the other. The sign as it then figured in his graphic work was disconcertingly elementary for the period; he refrained from using it, however, in his watercolors and tempera paintings where it might have contrasted too strongly with the luminosity of his tones. Later on, one of Hartung's most fruitful departures lay precisely in considering the sign, the black sign, as a color value and handling it accordingly, in all possible affiliations with light. Then the **tache,** the color patch, came into being, floating or dissolving on the picture surface with an imperturbable calmness that had little or nothing in common with expressionist violence, apart from the expressive potentiality inherent in color itself. Instead of well-defined tracts of color, we now find superpositions of overlapping color patches, gradations of tone effected not by skillfully contrived transitions from one color to another through its complementary, but by the distension of the color patch, producing irregular effects of density and transparency. The patch thus seemed to well up out of these pools of color, and with its more decided density assumed the semblance of form. Here already we find the painter resolutely stripping this form of its possible associations and meaning; and while the effect may seem atmospheric, while the color thus gradated may almost convey the impression of light vibrations, actually this value has no reference to daylight or sunlight.

Then these color patches fell into what seemed to be a more logical order, and on top of them appeared signs spaced out contrapuntally with respect to the ground, thus creating an interchange between the different levels suggested by the painting. There loomed up other signs and other forms, like ghostly apparitions, but these forms were not determined by psychological promptings, they did not well up indistinctly from the unconscious; nor, moreover, did they fit into a geometric pattern. Certainly Hartung profited by such examples as the painting of those years could offer him; but the significance and results of every other experiment even remotely comparable to his own were necessarily different. Hartung, for his part, was already practised enough for his intuition to tell him when to embark on the definition of a form and when to leave off, because its value lay in the act itself—a value later recognized as the peculiar property of the gesture, of action. Hartung, then, well before 1940, had already disengaged some of the elements which have been thrown into prominence in post-war painting.

"Would it not be fitting," Gindertael asks, "to write a eulogy of Hartung's thinking hand?" Indeed it would. The hand that in his art delineates the sign and converts it into form always acts with a full awareness both of itself and of the value of its action. It combines a stern control of the rational and irrational forces behind it with a consummate craftsmanship which amounts to more than mere technical proficiency, for it is the agency through which Hartung defines the significance of his poetic vision. Not only his painting, but his engravings, with their admirable graphic refinements, and his pastels, for Hartung is unquestionably the best pastel painter of our century—all alike are born of this intermarriage of mind and instinct, of the mind's power to bring out the dynamism of forms by means of an organic composition, with the vigilant instinct so quick to record the vital essence of all the experiences that throng the consciousness. This is one of the finest qualities of Hartung's art: his faculty of unpremeditatedly coordinating, in the very act by which his hand creates form, all the promptings set in motion by his vital impulse. Simultaneity of order and instinct: what this implies is the creation of a new spiritual dimension in painting, made possible by the resolute rejection of the familiar, all too familiar meanings attaching to images and space, which for Hartung had long since been drained of their expressive content in the very sense indicated above in the words of Merleau-Ponty.

Pierre Soulages (1919). Painting, 21.6.53. (76¾×51¼″) Owned by the Artist.

Pierre Soulages (1919). Painting, 8.12.59. (79½×65″) Galerie de France, Paris.

Pierre Soulages (1919). Painting, 6.3.60. (57½×44⅞″) Raoul Lévy Collection, Paris.

Gérard Schneider (1896). Untitled, 1958. (32⅝×25⅝") Galerie Der Spiegel, Cologne.

Hartung's example stands alone, but it has played a key part in the recent developments of pictorial language, and in other respects too; because it testifies to a new attitude not only toward reality interpreted in this or that manner, but toward the whole adventure of being and existing. Everything implied by both informal painting and action painting is present in this artist's sense of style and in his approach to his work; but it is present at a particular level unrelatable to any other, because his commitment to a new departure in painting, which amounted in effect to a moral commitment, was incompatible with the continued manipulation of the traditional elements of pictorial language. Those elements now had to be changed. As early as 1921 and 1922 he was capitalizing on the power of poetic expression that lies in the juxtaposition of simple signs and variously shaded color patches. Today, now that we can appreciate the full value of the color patch overflowing traditional closed forms, he cuts the figure of a precursor. His recent achievements bear this out: Hartung's style and influence have grown by leaps and bounds since the bleak silence of the war years. Against the sufferings and demoralization of that period he has reacted with an energy unparalleled in his earlier work. His post-war paintings show no trace of any complacency or dreaminess of color and form; under the stress of experience, the artist's whole being, his outlook on life and his artistic reactions to the world have been violently transformed, yet at the same time refined. The delicate counterpoint of his colors, in conjunction with the buoyancy of his signs, serves to indicate the chromatic quality of his painting. Instead of the seething colors of the expressionist tradition, instead of the haunting emotional tonalities of Surrealism, we have unwonted modulations and compact pools of color that tie in with the signwork indispensable to them. And these sign-forms are all the more essential because divested, as we have said, of any reference to writing or calligraphy; they are the fulfillment of a gesture and render its full meaning. The black stroke and the color patch, together with the interweaving lines of force, express the poetry of action and assert the new significance of painting, to which all vital impulses may contribute.

"I believe abstract art to be a state disengaged from any outside influence," writes Gérard Schneider. "In front of his canvas the painter liberates everything within him, though it has no name." [29] How indeed are we to analyze his sensations, when the artist refuses to submit to the dictates of his eye and record what it sees? There is, he feels, something more complex than visual, nature-kindled sensations, something even more complex than the unconscious sensations stratified in the subconscious mind. Surrealist methods of pictorial composition are no longer of any use to him; they revealed many things, but not the complexity of all that man contains within himself. Like Hartung, Schneider rejects the automatic approach to pictorial forms; he rejects, too, any pre-arrangement of those forms. His is also a thinking hand which achieves a sought-for significance at the very instant of delineating a colored form. "The act must contain everything," is his credo. The vivacity of his temperament, so clearly mirrored in the dynamism of Schneider's unpredictable compositional rhythms, transcends the limits of Expressionism and overrides any opposition between rational and irrational impulses: "I do not seek to determine the share of the subconscious or the conscious mind in the canvases I work out. Expression is an inner necessity, to which the conscious mind supplies its plastic structure." [30]

Chary too of any superabundance of expressive content are several German abstract painters. After the stringent disciplines of the Bauhaus, where he studied under Kandinsky and Klee; after his repudiation of nature imitation and representational art, which was the logical consequence of this training; and after Germany's dark years of dictatorship and war, Fritz Winter has created works which in some ways, and certainly in the spirit behind them, approximate to those of the painters dealt with above. Broad black, white and red signs, forms apparently regular but in reality responsive to every rhythmic suggestion, and surface texture in perceptible relief often patterned into stringy linework—these combine to perfection to express the artist's private world. This concern with surface texture was also characteristic of the work of one of the leading abstract painters in Germany prior to 1940: Willi Baumeister. From 1919 date his first **Mauerbilder** (wall pictures) in which he attempted a kind of interpenetration between the

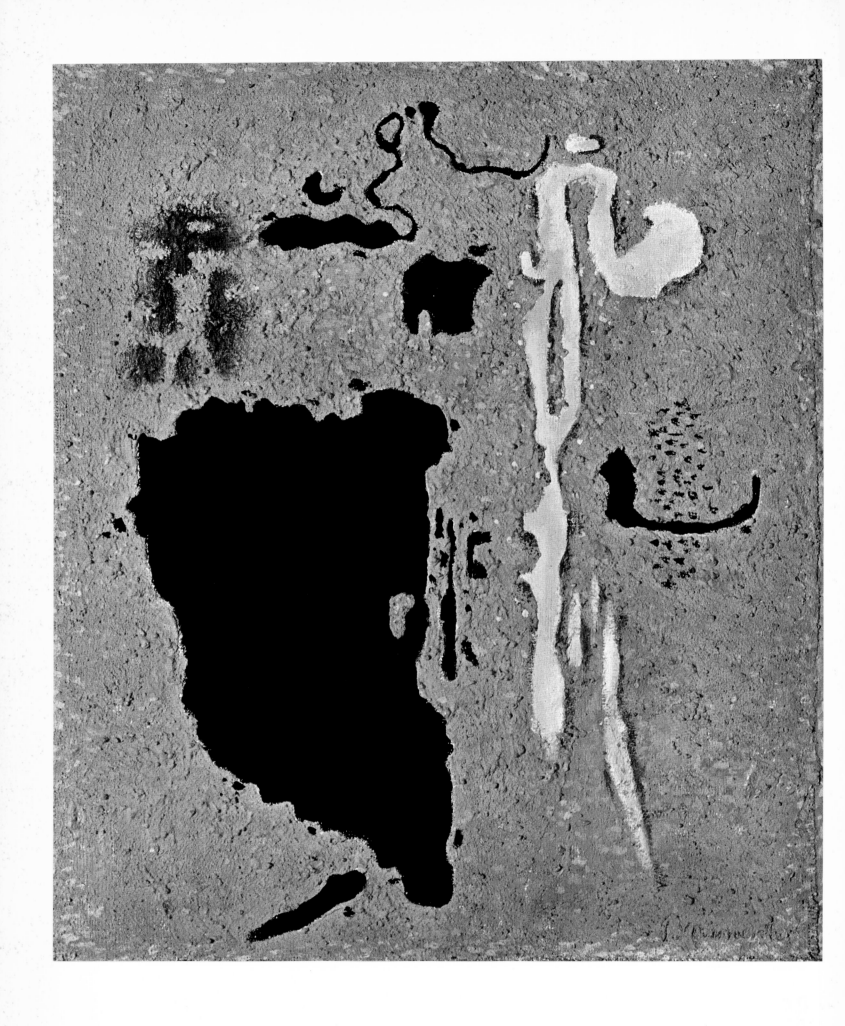

Willi Baumeister (1889-1955). Safer, 1953. (25⅝×21¼") Frau Margaret Baumeister Collection, Stuttgart.

wall and the painting. His formal researches thereafter cannot be said to have yielded results in any way similar to those of Hartung, or even to those of Winter, for they were based on the cubist formulation of space and on the geometric transposition of rhythms. But when, after 1945, in the ten years of life remaining to him, Baumeister—a "degenerate" artist outlawed by the Nazis—came to resume his earlier experiments, he did so with a detachment and purity of means in utter contrast to Expressionism. The forms he proceeded to create are like congealed outgrowths of texture, or like rents in the picture surface, while his signs are extended and amplified. The results thus achieved are disconcerting in their novelty and may confidently be expected to stand as a masterly example—together with that of Theodor Werner—to the German artists of succeeding generations; as an example, first and foremost, of stylistic clarity and due emphasis laid on all the means of expression at the artist's command.

Can any limit be set to the materials and techniques which the present-day painter adapts to his own ends? Probably not, we cannot help feeling, when we recall the **hautes pâtes** of Fautrier, the burlap bags and ironwork of Alberto Burri, the dripping technique and enamel paints of Jackson Pollock, not to mention the extraordinary variety of materials resorted to by American Neo-Dadaists like Robert Rauschenberg and Jasper Johns. If he is to give a new meaning to painting, then the artist is certainly justified in resorting to new and untried media

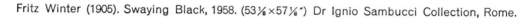

Fritz Winter (1905). Swaying Black, 1958. (53⅛×57⅛") Dr Ignio Sambucci Collection, Rome.

of expression (untried anyhow in painting), not only the new products thrown on the market by modern industry, such as the new synthetic glues, but also iron, wood and rags which, handled in a certain way, can be steeped in poetry to good effect. The old ideology, with its absolute scale of values and strictly limited means, no longer holds good. Even the classic media of oil painting and tempera painting have in our time been radically deformed and formed anew out of fresh materials.

As Jacques Lassaigne has said, speaking of Soulages and his thick black signs set off by colors which, though simplified, are no less resplendent, "a new kind of texture thus comes into being, midway between painting, stone and wood." [31] Yet painting it remains, whether oils or gouache, and in its breadth and sweep achieves an anti-rhetorical monumentality. The broad signs and black bars of Soulages, so deftly counterpoised against blues and tans, forming a color complex of great richness and potency, have something unshakably stable about them; they seem to convey a robust confidence in themselves as a self-sufficing means of expression. Soulages makes no secret of his predilection for Romanesque art, and his familiarity with it is reflected in his painting, in its stability and sturdy self-reliance.

We find no concessions to taste or fashion, no meretricious charms or prettiness in his color schemes, no diffused and vibrant light. The problem of lighting is solved in an entirely new way by the flashes and gleams that shoot out from beneath these great black signs. The composition hinges on the organic framework of these signs, whose effectiveness lies in their reciprocal interchanges. There is an order here, but not based on a geometrical hierarchy of form and space. What counts is the conscious gesture delineating the sign, dimensioning it in terms of vertical or horizontal cadences, particularly the latter in his more recent works. But the brushstroke never overflows the limits of form, never lapses into the informal color patch. "Painting," says Soulages, "always precedes thinking," and this is certainly the case when, as with him, the act of painting is a conscious moral act and not an arbitrary one. And this lucid awareness extends also to technique, to the handling of color, of the blacks which in Soulages are a color as vivid as any other, and which, for optimum expressive power, have to be applied in a certain way, with a certain fluidity, in a certain direction. "Soulages," writes Hubert Juin, "is a painter who likes to prepare his colors himself. He makes a point of selecting his own binding media, priming his canvas himself, and grinding his own colors." [32] What better earnest of self-commitment than this craftsmanlike concern with technique? The painting of Soulages is rude and rugged, both in its results and in the shock it produces on the spectator. It has the rudeness of absolute sincerity. Yet the means that fashion it are means of an extreme finesse, just as those of Romanesque sculpture are—an art he is passionately fond of. But this parallel must not be misconstrued: the painting of Soulages is primarily the expression of a modern state of mind, of an active concern with the problem of man's commitments to his fellow men here and now, and also of stable moral principles which cannot be challenged. His art is not of course a reflection of anguish or despair (and for this reason alone it is absurd to compare it with that of Kline). Nor is it even a reflection of balance and good sense. What it actually represents is the presence of a complex, well-defined reality and a confident faith in the ultimate destinies of painting and in the ethical principles implied by human workmanship.

Of all American painters, Robert Motherwell has the closest cultural ties with Europe. Though steeped in European culture and influenced by the great modern movements of French art, Motherwell has successfully surmounted these influences, like every other significant painter of his generation in America. There is one feature of the European tradition, however, which he has always retained: the painter-craftsman's diligent cultivation of technical perfection and his delight in surface effects. What he seems to owe to Surrealism is a knack of creating new forms emanating from irrational impulses—forms equally remote from anthropomorphism and from academic stylization. Critics have not failed to note that his sympathies lie rather with Schwitters and Arp than with Max Ernst, with Dali least of all. The paintings and **collages** he produced after 1940 testify indeed to a range of sympathies extending not only to Arp and Schwitters, but to Picasso and Matisse as well.

But he did not stop at this point. His personal theories and aspirations soon led him to a simplification of his means, in an effort to penetrate more deeply into reality. Frequently, as in the **Spanish Elegies,** the black sign becomes the vehicle of this approach. "The **Spanish Elegies,**" we read in the catalogue of one of his exhibitions, "are an effort to symbolize a subjective image of Modern Spain. They are all in black and white: they are funeral pictures, laments, dirges, elegies—barbaric and austere." It is difficult to say what the confines of reality are for Motherwell, and to what extent he excludes any reference to sensations and memories. From Surrealism he seems to have learned how to push back and blur those confines so effectively as to make them include every vital impulse. But any show of violence is foreign to his temperament, and none is to be found in the **Elegies** or the **Wall Paintings,** nor in any works he has produced in recent years, since the **collages.** Forms and dilating signs, whether black or colored, acquire a peculiar significance, not restricted to the reality of form but suggesting to the spectator's eye and mind further realities both personal and impersonal. Motherwell exercises an unrelaxing control over all this, obviating any risk of arbitrariness by virtue of his consummate technical mastery and his refusal to cater for the mere gratification of the eye, always abiding by the principle that "without ethical consciousness a painter is only a decorator." [33]

Robert Motherwell (1915). Elegy for the Spanish Republic XXXIV, 1954. (80×100″)
Albright Art Gallery, Buffalo, N.Y. Gift of Seymour H. Knox.

Franz Kline (1910). Initial, 1959. (100½×77½") Collection of Mr and Mrs Robert C. Scull, Great Neck, N.Y.

Franz Kline (1910). 1960 New Year Wall: Night. (119×183″) Courtesy Sidney Janis Gallery, New York.

It is a widespread misconception to suppose that contemporary American art finds its characteristic satisfactions in a boisterous violence of expression. The term "abstract expressionism" commonly used to define it is too sweeping to give a true picture of the situation. The case of Motherwell alone shows how inexact it is; his **Elegies,** though they strike at times a note of protest, have a prevailing calm of spirit and composition. But congenital violence, the immediate projection of emotions and impulses, a superabundance of inspiration which seems to outrun the painter's hand—these indeed appear to be genuinely characteristic of the painting of Franz Kline. And in this he must seem to many to be typically American. Though comparable in some respects to that of other artists both European and American, Kline's painting has a virulent energy that sets it apart and makes it inimitable. When he sweeps his dark brush over the white surface of paper or canvas, the resulting signs are really guide-lines of motive force, symbols—or rather the expression pure and simple—of clashing or interweaving energies which go their ways heedless, as it were, of the space generated in their wake, in a mesh of black and white. When Kline resorts to color, as he has done in some of his recent works, its whole import seems to be focused on the tragic implications of reds and greens which jar on one another or, together with tenuous pinks, strike a contrast with the black surfaces of his signs. But what chromatic finesse in spite of everything, what vibrancy concentrated in a tract of gray which, though apparently a single color, is actually composed of a delicate blend of colors!

"In Kline's pictures," writes Thomas B. Hess, "white and black count as colors, as they have done since Velazquez, but Kline eliminates all other hues. He endows the absence or totality of refraction with the range of the spectrum. This is achieved (as Willem de Kooning did in his related abstractions of around 1945-1950) by an emotional intensity that seems to burn all color out of art." [34] Here we have a typical example of action painting. More evident perhaps in Kline than in any other American painter are the experience and validity of the hand's gesture and movement, and his ability to guide the self-revealing sign unerringly over the canvas. The sign is a continuous presence in the picture; it really is, as the theorist of action painting, Harold Rosenberg, has defined it, "the abstraction of the **moral** element in art; its mark is moral tension in detachment from moral or esthetic certainties." [35]

In his latest works Kline has amplified his tracts of paint; he has adopted, as mentioned above, colors of reckless violence, reds, blues, and greens, in preference now to blacks, though he assigns the same spatial value to them. Hitherto his black signs were the only elements in contrast with the white ground of paper or canvas, but they were not calligraphic. The sign is an instrument of research into new meanings expressive of new emotion, connoting the presence and validity of action; it is a means of overcoming the intractability of the painter's materials, of keeping him on his guard against the facile effects to which they lend themselves. It would be absurd to seek in this painting for the transposition of images indistinctly welling up in the consciousness; absurd to ask of it the equivalent of sensations inspired by nature, or any delineation of a mood or state of mind. "To paint as a bird sings"—Monet's self-declared ideal—is obviously no longer possible.

Image of Time, Contrast, Collision of Situations, are titles of pictures by Emilio Vedova which have a violence of expression comparable to that of Kline's, yet very different from it. There came a time in Vedova's evolution when—if the metaphor is not too ascetic—he mortified his forms in a hair-shirt of geometric patterns, in order to quell the unruly surge of his instincts.

Emilio Vedova (1919). (Tumult) Image of Time, No. 6 V, 1958. (51⅛×77˝) Giuseppe Panza di Biumo Collection, Milan.

Emilio Vedova (1919). Warsaw No. 1 V, 1959-1960. (108¼ ×80¾ ˝) Collection of Mr and Mrs Maxim Hermanos, New York.

But this penance did not last long. "Excuse me," he wrote to me in a letter, "but I don't believe in artists who self-confidently succeed in mastering their own means, in artists who have no more problems, once they've overcome the false problems imposed by others and by history. Ever and always, painting, like life itself, confronts us with new choices to make, new responsibilities to assume... Nothing is easy for me, my hand won't move without months of preliminary study, without a continual deepening of consciousness. At times I seem to have forgotten everything, I feel that painting is difficult, when it must not and cannot be anything but a unison with ourselves, when we feel that every sign on the canvas bears a responsibility, that it must not be allowed to lapse even for a moment into a cliché or commonplace which may even be a manner of our own and is thus all the more dangerous."

Vedova's starting point was expressionistic, that peculiarly Italian Expressionism which centered before the war in the Corrente group. Yet even before that, as a boy, he had executed drawings in which his conception of space seems to have been suggested by the great example of Tintoretto in the Scuola di San Rocco in Venice (where Vedova was born and still lives). So that when he joined the Corrente group his choice had already been largely made: the figures he drew and painted within a dense network of thick brush or pencil strokes, almost making them burst the bounds of the bleak space in which they stood, could not help being very different from the type of Expressionism, often rather undecided, practised by the other members of the group. The rhythms he resorted to in order to condense his emotions were quite untinged with romantic Expressionism; they overcame the lure of formal violence, just as it had been overcome years before by Franz Marc and August Macke when they both felt the need to take a lesson from Cubism. Cubism, then, also had a lesson for Vedova, and he profited by it after the war, when Italian artists in a body were re-immersing themselves in European culture.

Yet Italy's recent past also had something to teach Vedova, something which, at a time of need, he found thoroughly congenial to his form of Expressionism and to his aspiration toward abstraction. Vedova was perhaps unique among Italian painters in this, that he alone felt the full importance of Futurism and proceeded to restate its lessons. He succeeded in doing so, because the dynamic movement now being achieved by the intensification of the sign had been part and parcel of his work as early as the time when, as a boy, he had spent long days drawing and sketching in the churches of Venice. But for him Futurism meant above all the discovery of a momentous possibility: that of throwing an aura of romantic emotion over wholly modern formal problems, and thereby regaining effective contact with Europe's cultural past. Thus it was possible for him, after rejecting geometry, to resuscitate the full violence of Expressionism, which with him became a moral protest, a commitment to a definite choice between the antinomies of being. And so he arrived at a complete autonomy of sign and structure.

The construction of space in Vedova's paintings has remained consistent with the principles on which he founded it, with the space of Baroque intensity which, by way of Tintoretto, he discovered about 1935. It is a space sharply projecting from the picture surface outward, with a buoyant vigor that almost seems to burst the frame. And within this highly vitalized space, first his forms, then his sign-forms, have been patterned and organized, without setting any limits to their movements or inhibiting in any way the anguish they body forth; they are violence incarnate, the harbingers of disaster, whose rigors scarcely admit of the blandishments of color. Vedova is no believer in "fine painting." Notwithstanding his picture titles and the indictments implied by his style, his painting is not meant to be a symbol; it is simply the reality of man's estate at the present time. The artist is an eavesdropper; he listens in on the world and records its essence in a moment. Such an artist is Vedova. He has no qualms about plunging into the depths of bleakest despair—and is quick to return with joyful tidings. Full and empty spaces show through an overgrowth of blacks and whites, torn asunder by flashes of color and pitted by concrete lumps of pigment. His message, aspirations and protests are expressed without recourse to symbols; dramas are enacted in space, in the encounters of signs, in the clash of forms. This is not propaganda painting; it is, however, the art of a man who has committed himself, and who through his art realizes a mode of being.

5

GIUSEPPE SANTOMASO - PIERRE TAL COAT
AFRO - KENZO OKADA - JULIUS BISSIER

5

If the sign had to be dissociated from any possible calligraphic reference, light too had to be invested with a different meaning by the painters whose temperament and training led them to use it abstractly. It ceased to act as a means of evoking atmosphere or defining space; above all it ceased to be the local indication of a naturalistic reference. We have seen how in the earlier non-figurative works of Bazaine and Manessier, notably in their landscapes of about 1948, light nevertheless continued to indicate such a reference, even when inserted in the composition as an autonomous rhythm. Indeed, at a given moment, light was the great quality of this painting, because, though an impalpable element indefinable except through personal experience, it enabled the painter to keep in touch with one aspect of reality, of which it constituted as it were a touchstone or equivalent, easily perceived by the senses and easily localized in terms of natural sensations. Light in fact had the advantage of being an element conveniently abstract and concrete at the same time: abstract because elaborated in accordance with a particular sensibility, concrete because affording ready reference to nature.

Once the naturalistic esthetic of abstract-concrete art had been repudiated, painters had to choose: either to ignore light as a picture element (which of course was out of the question for painters brought up in the impressionist tradition), or else to use it as a compositional element cut off from any reference to nature or to sensory data. This meant that each painter had to work out for himself an individual conception of light postulated as a pictorial reality in its own right and perceived as so many autonomous vibrations irreducible to naturalistic terms. Bazaine's latest works, as we have said, seem to fulfill these conditions. Many other painters akin in taste and culture to the Painters of French Tradition have gradually made a complete break with nature. They have revealed a new luminous space, no longer local but autonomous, by divorcing the vibrations, the preciosity and indeed the very quality of color from the descriptive rhythms of the composition; they thereby predicate the chromatic values as an immediate presence and the artist's handling of them as an action, or anyhow a particular type of action (not to be confused of course with that of American action painting). Now this modulation of images and space is foreign to Expressionism in any shape or form; yet it has a dramatic potential of its own, lying in the power of surface texture to intensify color contrasts and to assimilate them to psychological conflicts.

Undoubtedly the evolution of artistic ideas in the last few years, both in painting and other forms of expression (musical "pointillism" comes to mind, for example, and its validity is indisputable), has resulted in a reassessment of the light element and, above all, made it impossible to isolate it. The fresh scrutiny of every theoretical principle, the impatience now felt with the ideologies and precepts of the avant-garde movements of an earlier day, have contributed not only to a new interpretation but, what matters more, to a new quality of light. For the important point is this: it is no longer possible to assign a merely hedonistic role to light in the picture composition, no longer possible for light to go on tamely conveying that dreamy suggestiveness which in the past it always conveyed to the spectator. Light now, on

Afro (1912). Fondo degli Ulivi, 1958. (35½×55⅛″) Emilio Jesi Collection, Milan.

the contrary, has become an abstract dimension where we recognize a life experience or share a memory which the artist, by an act of will, situates in the present, not in the past. So that while we may speak of light to define a quality of color, it is inadmissible to speak of luminism. Into the gemlike colors and atmospheric values which several artists now employ, there enter no contrasts, no preoccupation with rhythms of light and shadow, scarcely more than the faint modulations required to differentiate form from the open rhythm of informal textures and from the dynamism of black signs. Any clean-cut distinction that may result is purely arbitrary. We have seen in Soulages, for example, how the luminosity of color shows through beneath the dense network of black signs; in Wols too we shall see how important this chromatic underlighting is. Nor can the quality of Tal Coat's sign be ignored, which fits so well, so satisfyingly, into the rarefied color scheme of his canvases; or the grooves and salient relief of Corpora's richly orchestrated color texture. It is, in short, for every artist to handle this light element to the best of his ability, without however exaggerating its importance or allowing it to overshadow other elements. At all events, it is worth while noting that every significant artist of the present day has given a meaning to the luminosity of color which it never had before.

It is well, then, to emphasize that, notwithstanding its chromatic characterization and the ground covered since the time of Impressionism, Fauvism and Cubism, this new non-figurative painting stands apart from every other trend of the recent past; it is in fact a wholly new departure. From contact with the reality of nature artists have now arrived at the autonomy of light elements; the signs that loom up through the color pattern, and even Julius Bissier's allusive figurations of objects, restore those elements to the field of human experience, to psychology in some artists, to memory in others, to action in the present in the case of still others. "The throbbing of your arteries and the fever heat of your blood, such is the driving impulse of that basic communication which resolves itself on canvas in a series of primary gestures, actual ciphers of all beginnings, origin and end in itself,"[36] writes Pierre Restany in connection with Tal Coat, precisely because it is no longer possible to go on dealing with private emotions at a time when the artist is striving to express a universality of more or less distinct sensations.

In Afro we have a painter who has achieved an absolute autonomy of color texture after an extremely profitable experience of both the figurative, before the war, and the non-figurative (of a kind similar to that of the Painters of French Tradition) after the war. But he soon departed from this latter vein. Afro is a Venetian, and the great Venetian color tradition is ingrained in his very nature; even so, it would not have sufficed, without the experience just mentioned, to create the highly individual language in which he expresses himself at the present time. To that tradition, however, he owes a chromatic conception of design and a wonderful ability to grasp the structure of the painting in terms of light and color, not as a linear framework in which to fit the colors. Logically enough, in the course of working out this vision, he was led to minimize the role of the subject; as he pressed on, the same fate befell the object. In the process many things came to impinge on and alter the figurative aspects of his earlier painting. The lesson of Cubism, for example, was important to him, the more so as Afro's keen interest in the technical side of the painter's craft made him particularly receptive to the pointers to be learned from such a master as Braque.

After the war, when Italian painters could breathe more freely and begin to broaden their outlook, he was led to pay off the debts contracted in the past and to branch out more boldly on his own, though in doing so he maintained a firm control over form and a certain detachment from it. Afro resolved the relationship between man and object, between man and nature, into the elements of a non-figurative style which, in Italy, as we have seen in the case of Birolli, was very close to that of the Painters of French Tradition. But rather than the transformation of objective data into formal rhythms, what he aimed at was an equivalent of those data in terms of the tonal values of colors—a ghostly apparition of colored forms in an intimated time dimension unassimilable to the unity of time and space postulated by Cubism. It is a time dimension with a different kind of unity: that of memory, which is necessary to the purification of all the elements, graphic, symbolic and psychological, that enter into the composition. On color, in Afro's work, devolves the task of preventing any isolation of the motifs and integrating them into a unitary order. In doing so, he found the post-cubist schema inadequate to his intentions, which were to express the fullness of human dignity and to reaffirm the presence of man not so much in the object as in an emotional form and space. What he was really trying to do was to regain the temporality of the image, to break up the set formulas of Post-Cubism, to work back to the origins with the resources which he had acquired, and whose most useful elements stood to lose nothing of their efficacy, on the contrary, by the effort to retrace his steps.

In the development of Afro's painting since 1952 we see this new awareness of style being steadily deepened and clarified. In the catalogue of the New Decade exhibition of European painters held in 1955 at the Museum of Modern Art in New York, Afro wrote as follows: "I like to think that my paintings give forth a sense of hope, a presentiment of dawn. I want them to contain a clear reflection of the world overridden by human passions, but at the same time to unfold with increasing assurance a vast open territory ready for contests, the sufferings and the celebrations of mankind. I want the sensations of the things, the symbols of reality to regain the warmth of a forgotten sentiment within the certainty of pure form. I think painting is getting ready to break away from its exclusive and closely guarded function of instrumental music; it is reaching for new modulations and tones that presage the entrance of the human voice raised in song."[37] What better way of realizing this dream of harmony and song than through the music of color and light? In Afro's hands color and light have shattered the hard shell of pre-established space, both geometric and naturalistic. The spatial dimension, with him, is psychological and emotional. It is the configuration of his world and his hopes, which it enables him to mold and control at will. Hence the necessity of a formal modulation exploiting all the luminous qualities of color, not only of color at its brightest but throughout all its gradations down to the dimmest and darkest. Only then could his painting illuminate the secret crypts

Afro (1912). Viale delle Acacie, 1958. (31½ × 47¼ ") Owned by the Artist.

of the artist's mind and consciousness; only then could he express himself without resorting to any violence of design or form, but with a freedom of plastic creation which seems to amount to a relinquishment of mental disciplines in favor of a psychological revelation.

Afro's art is actually an art of memory, of associations of images tinged with psychic emotions. A form, a color, an effect of transparency, are never the symbol, even less the representation, of the external phenomena of nature. Nor is there any falling back on the merely decorative: reality lies in the very form which gives concrete expression to the idea, it is a vital datum of the imagination and not merely the transformation of a sensation. Afro charges his work with the full emotional intensity of memory. The design of a picture by him is determined by an association of forms which, at the outset, may well be automatic, because engendered by the unconscious mind; but in process of time, as he works them up and recasts them, those forms come to be a fully conscious, fully thought out expression of the picture's organic structure. One form is complementary to another, a color disguises or discloses a plane, or gives an indication of space; above all, his palette supplies him with a seemingly inexhaustible wealth of colors, which he handles with rare refinement. Here a memory, recent or remote, finds its poetic embodiment, and as it soars beyond the narrow confines of figurative representation, this painting unfolds a world which Afro brings to light from the depths of his own consciousness, a world, as he has said, "where images are still rooted in their obscure origins, in their unconscious sincerity."

In 1952 Afro exhibited at the Venice Biennale with the other members of the group known as Eight Italian Painters: Afro, Birolli, Corpora, Moreni, Morlotti, Turcato, Santomaso and Vedova, artists of the most varied personalities, who seemed at that time to represent the best that the younger school of Italian painting had to offer. But there were other artists at work in Italy too:

Capogrossi, for example, of whom mention has been made; Spazzapan and Fontana; and of course Alberto Burri, who had already begun his experiments with new materials. The artistic culture of the Eight Italian Painters was that of Post-Cubism. Taking up the struggle for a renewal of pictorial language immediately after the war, they had all arrived at a non-figurative conception comparable, by and large, to that of their coevals in France. But having reached that point together, they proceeded to part company: each struck out on his own and a series of private ventures followed which have yielded diverse results. Moreni and Morlotti found fulfillment in a kind of informal art, emphatically dynamic in the case of the first, redolent of a curious naturalistic sensibility in that of the second. Turcato, in his recent works, has introduced various materials into the body of the painting in a neo-dadaist spirit. So that the unity of the group has definitely been broken up. "The experience of others," writes Santomaso, "may serve to clarify the problem of contemporary vision, but only through his own experience will a painter arrive at a degree of freedom which is more than a mere vagary."

Born in Venice, Santomaso feels a warm and stimulating bond of sympathy with the great Venetian color tradition—the tradition that paved the way for modern art. But Santomaso's

Afro (1912). Via della Croce, 1959. (43¼×51¼") Catherine Viviano Gallery, New York.

painting does not draw on the stuff of memory, as Afro's does. It is, rather, an immediate acceptance of the prolong them in the **real duration** of the consciousness. Space and dimensions, in order to phenomenon, an immediate seizure of **real data** at the moment of visual perception however, in his painting, are emotional space and dimensions, though admirably controlled for all that. Intense and vivacious though his colors are, the painter keeps to rational standards in the choice of elements, if not in his inspirations. He prefers to take for his point of departure a distinct emotion or the actual visual presence of a thing rather than the idea of it in his mind. So that his pictures, as has often been pointed out, presuppose an explicit reference to reality, either some glimpse of a thing behind the luminous veil of appearances or some insight into its essence. Needless to say, the embodiment of it in the painting is anything but a literal transcription. In fact what Santomaso ultimately gives us is the image of light, of luminous space issuing not from the progression or recession of planes but from chromatic pauses, often underscored with white or a darker sign, according to the quantity and quality of the form in question and the physical bulk and chromatic quality of the form beside it. But light here is the effective agent of reality: it marshals and binds together the images suggested by observation and empirical experience, images not transformed into gesture but modulated in a conclusive rhythm which, instead of being prolonged in tonal sequences, is resolved into the physical properties of the paints.

As Umbro Apollonio has noted (and he has been one of the most alert and sensitive observers of the artist's evolution), "Santomaso's most concrete stylistic dimension first asserted itself in 1942, when light came to enhance the significance of his objects, seen no longer in the confined space of the studio, but within the natural atmosphere of which they are part." [38] And he has greatly enriched his style since 1942. While the motifs of his inspiration have in many cases remained unchanged, they have come to be seen, not analytically, but within the overall circuit of their interrelationships and interactions. Santomaso has never departed from his highly characteristic conception of luminosity. The successive textural enrichments that have been so marked a feature of his recent work have not, however, induced the artist to surrender entirely to the lures of automatism; the delicacy of the colors and their flawless harmonies, unruffled by any stridency or any lapses of taste, increase the effectiveness of his formal modulations. With every barrier broken, form floods over the picture surface apparently unrestrained; actually it is governed by an underlying structural pattern, invisible but no less real, which enables the artist to identify himself totally with the image. The titles of Santomaso's paintings allude to travel impressions, to things seen and enjoyed in the vivid light of southern lands; his reds recall the blues, yellows and browns of those sights and scenes. Santomaso is a healthy extrovert, he likes to exteriorize the faith he pins on light, and on the form which his stylistic meditations impart to light.

A similar urge to contact with reality, but a reality simplified to the extreme limit in delicate, luminous and subtle renderings of the signs conveying the structure of objects, is also evident in Tal Coat's painting. A highly accomplished artist, he has constantly made a practice of simplifying or accenting forms so as to convey sensations in their most concentrated state and with the most telling emotive impact. Even in his most recent works the continuity of his style is unmistakable, a reflection of the persistence of the moral criteria he has always brought to bear not only on reality but on his own works too. His approach to Truth, whether his own or that of reality, is unvarying, the outcome of long years of solitary meditation on his art and of faith in a personal discovery owing nothing to the fluctuations of artistic tastes, but deriving from an insight into the underlying elements of the visible aspects of things and a perceptive eye for the pulsating life infusing them. Tal Coat is not concerned with non-figurative painting as such or for its own sake; what he is aiming at is, rather, to overcome the antinomy between abstract and concrete. Distinctive of the language he now employs is its ability to transmute natural images into signs, dynamic rhythms and gossamer-light tissues of colors, without abandoning anything of the intensity of sensations and the intellectual penetration that characterized his earlier work. As Jacques Lassaigne says, "his work is tending toward ever greater abstraction, in the sense of spareness, selectivity and transposition, and nevertheless it is more and more guided by an intimate understanding of nature, of the world and its physical substances, and by a will to achieve a balanced play of moving lights and stable dominants."

A native of Brittany, Tal Coat went to Paris in 1924 and entered on a long expressionistic period not altogether free of reminiscences of Gauguin. But his figures were dramatically intensified, swept with contrasts of darker and lighter colors, punctuated with strongly marked volumes. This phase culminated about 1939 in his **Massacres,** whose subject matter and compositional organization both constituted a violent expression of strong personal feelings. The lessons of Cubism and Post-Cubism were of course important to him, less as an impetus toward greater compositional rigor than as affording a possibility of enhancing the particular significance of

Giuseppe Santomaso (1907). Andalusian Song, 1960. (31 ½ × 31 ½") Private Collection Amsterdam.

Pierre Tal Coat (1905). Pathway at the Bottom of the Valley, 1956. (74⅝×76¾″) Musée d'Art Moderne, Paris.

each object represented. Then, as he stepped up the dynamism of his rhythms, these images underwent a steadily increasing process of simplification, losing their sharply stressed scansions and melting into a profusion of colors: there, as primordial and elementary signs, they silently floated in the depths of a new dimension of reality. Objects were thus immersed in the luminosity of the color tracts, yet they remained intact and effectively present. At first these were liquid objects—aquariums, streams of water, schools of fish; then, perhaps with greater forcefulness, the same fluidity was applied to the pictorial rendering of solid objects, released from their materiality and seen in the flux of ceaseless change. Through these signs, this chromatic luminosity and fluid, vibrant texture, the artist communicates with the world.

Tal Coat has lived for many years in Provence, in the vicinity of the Château Noir and the Montagne Sainte-Victoire, both of which figure in so many masterpieces by Cézanne. This landscape is present in Tal Coat's paintings, though transfigured; what he seizes on and renders is not so much its outward appearances as its inner forces and underlying rhythms. He opens up perspectives, projecting spatial vistas into every part of the canvas, in accordance with an emotional rather than a physical order. Colors grow more intense in certain zones in order to stress the solidity of the composition, which remains organic, though there is no longer the slightest reminder of any feature of visual reality. In other zones light is more tenuous and diaphanous, as if to indicate a space of different emotive intensity. The signs, which are also steeped in light, are governed directly by the artist's will, which arrests or amplifies them whenever the need to do so makes itself felt. The very act of painting, with Tal Coat, is the regained awareness of an immediate reality; it is the communion of his being with the totality of life, embracing not only the aspects of nature but also their inner significance, together with the indestructible presence of man within the organism of creation.

Kenzo Okada (1905). Height, 1959. (50½ × 47¼″) Courtesy of Betty Parsons Gallery, New York.

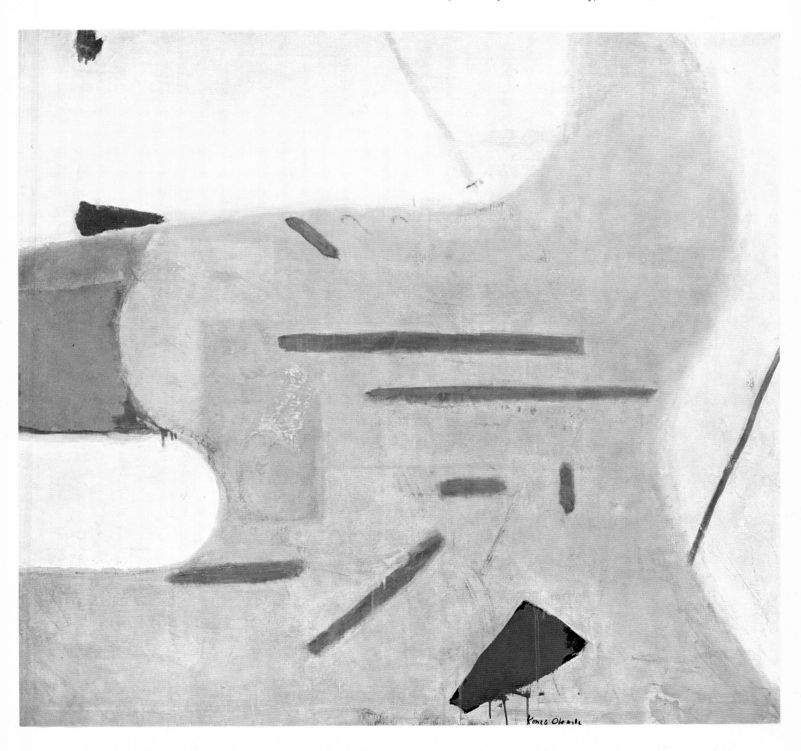

Born in Yokohama, Kenzo Okada studied in Tokyo and Paris. He went to the United States in 1950, where he now makes his home. After an early phase of realism, he has now oriented his painting toward abstraction. It should be said at the outset, however, that his work appears to owe nothing at all to the esthetic of action painting, which has characterized American art in recent years. The broad color tracts of his pictures, the juxtaposition of exquisitely delicate tints, his sound craftsmanship and skill with the brush, all seem to belong to a cultural background in which Europe plays the preponderant part. Yet, on the other hand, his detachment from form and the variegated images he mysteriously creates hark back to the moods and vision of Oriental art. But Okada's style is nonetheless firmly rooted in the modern tradition. Condensed in color textures, light is completely abstract; it refers to no figuration and makes no concession to appearances; it is reduced to an essence.

Julius Bissier feels thoroughly mistrustful of what he himself calls the world of natural patterns. This does not prevent him from conjuring up images of concrete objects against the gray, faintly illuminated ground of his "miniatures"—objects which he lifts to the plane of autonomous signs by stripping them of any reference to their practical utility or everyday function. Bissier himself calls them "psychograms." They appeared in his painting about 1930 and are like the calligraphic equivalent of a poetic sensation. They act as a simple, linear means of transcribing the artist's inner life, of concentrating it on the picture surface, attired in muted yet vivid colors and vagrant gleams of light. "From 1933 on," he writes, "I handled these signs so much like the counters of a game as to make them a wholly private sign language. But fortunately I could only elaborate them at the dictates of an inner prompting, until ultimately they became a genuinely legible script, a symbol universally valid." [39] A close friend of Willi Baumeister, Bissier has nevertheless worked out his style on his own and pursued wholly personal aspirations, with a puckish sense of humor and a mastery of his means which, though they may sometimes remind us of Klee, are the inalienable attributes of a highly original personality.

Julius Bissier (1893). 2 Sept. 59. (7⅝×10″) Owned by the Artist.

JOAN MIRÓ · ANDRÉ MASSON · MATTA ECHAURREN
ARSHILE GORKY · WILLIAM BAZIOTES · GRAHAM SUTHERLAND

Sidney Janis published a book in New York in 1944 entitled **Abstract and Surrealist Art in America.** In the fourth chapter, devoted to the American Surrealists, the following painters figure prominently: Morris Graves, Lee Gatch, Mark Tobey, William Baziotes, Arshile Gorky, Adolph Gottlieb, Mark Rothko. Alongside these names we even find that of Jackson Pollock, accompanied by a reproduction of one of his paintings, **The She-Wolf,** a work still half figurative. Seen from the vantage point of the present day, in the light of sixteen eventful years, particularly eventful in the United States, where so much has happened in the interim to change the face of painting, this classification may seem almost absurd. It would occur to no one today to describe Tobey, Pollock or Rothko as Surrealists; and even as regards the others, the term clearly fails to define the real trend and character of their work. Yet this classification, which today looks arbitrary, was not so then; there were sound reasons for it. What Janis had discerningly tried to do was, first of all, to group together artists whose style was oriented toward a larger freedom of compositional rhythms and forms; to segregate them from others whose handling of these elements was more strictly disciplined either by the dictates of geometry or by those of Cubism. Then he went on to define the quality of forms, distinguishing those that were frankly fantastic from those that retained even clandestine contacts with objective reality. For even at that time there were significant differences of pictorial language: what could be further from the textural refinements of Morris Graves, in the transformations of his **Birds** into autonomous color-forms, than the new space and unprecedented dramatic intensity already apparent in Jackson Pollock's **She-Wolf?**

Sidney Janis's book, then, helps us to find our bearings amid the disorderly ranks of American avant-garde art during the war years, when the shape of things to come was still very indistinct. Keen interest was then being shown not only in Cubism and in the far-ranging developments of Picasso himself, but more particularly in Surrealism, whose performances were well known in the United States, and were made even more influential thanks to the personal presence of André Breton, who took refuge in the United States during the war, and to that of artists like André Masson, Wolfgang Paalen (who was living in Mexico) and still others. No one can deny that the influence of Surrealism played an important part in shaping the taste of Pollock and Rothko. At the same time, of course, for artists of their calibre, it was only a kind of stepping stone; Surrealism for them represented a valuable assortment of means and procedures which had to be mastered before they could accede to more personal means and procedures answering to the needs of their own temperament.

Surrealism, judging anyhow by tangible results, seems to make little appeal to the contemporary sensibility, to awaken no vital echo in the consciousness of present-day painters, concerned as they are with clarifying the processes of the thinking mind, not with obscuring them. Certainly neither Tanguy nor Delvaux, neither Magritte nor Dali, can be shown to have exerted any notable influence on contemporary artists; their art is nowhere to be felt either as a lesson in style or as a force to be reckoned with in the renewal of pictorial language. Yet there is one exception

Joan Miró (1893). Figures and Dog before the Sun, 1949. (32⅛×21½″) Kunstmuseum, Basel.

that calls for special mention. We refer to the work of a young Spanish painter, Antonio Tápies, who, on the basis of some well assimilated influences, has in the post-war years achieved a truly original style of his own. Among those influences, perceptible in the paintings Tápies produced just before he entered his abstract phase, we find that of Max Ernst, of his surrealist landscapes in particular. Furthermore, while it is true that the latest researches of the informal painters cannot be considered to have any direct filiation with Surrealism, the fact remains that certain devices adopted as instrumental to a compositional order, and notably the reliance for that purpose on irrational impulses, correspond pretty closely with the procedures of Surrealism. In this connection Jackson Pollock comes to mind, as perhaps the most typical representative of a **peinture engagée**, who in his last works owes absolutely nothing to Surrealism (and this fact is worth emphasizing, in view of the misinterpretations of his last works that are still current). Yet Pollock himself, in a statement quoted again and again by critics, openly admitted that "when I am **in** my painting, I'm not aware of what I'm doing." [40] This is automatism pure and simple, and it may well be the result of an assimilation of surrealist procedures. Note, however, that Pollock speaks unequivocally of being **in** his painting; this alone would suffice to distinguish him from the Surrealists properly so called.

All this goes to show that Surrealism has indeed been a powerful leaven in the ferment of 20th century American art. It only really took effect, however, with the arrival of European artists in the United States, and with the arrival too of a young Chilean artist, Matta Echaurren, who in his painting developed the space that André Breton has defined as "the need for a suggestive representation of the four-dimensional universe." But for the artists who were to create a typically American form of Abstract Expressionism, it was the emphasis they laid on violence, that is to say the accentuation of one particular quality of Expressionism, that led them away from Surrealism, led them to participate more actively, with their whole being, in the gestation of the picture as it sprang to life in their hands—that led them, in short, to the concept of action as opposed to that of contemplation, whether unrealistic or surrealistic. But all the same, to achieve this participation, to put the concept of action into practice, a method had to be worked out and a whole artistic culture (to which Surrealism contributed much) had to be developed. With aspirations like these, Pollock had little to hope for from the reactionary teachings of Thomas Hart Benton, who had been his master, and even less from the routine craftsmanship into which the Mexican painters had lapsed, to whom, nevertheless, he owed some useful pointers. He began exhibiting at Peggy Guggenheim's Art of This Century Gallery in New York, where a whole group of abstractionists and surrealists forgathered, representing the two poles of an avant-garde which, though still European, was about to become American.

In addition to Picasso (as represented above all in the works produced after **Guernica**), Miró and Masson were probably the artists whose influence was brought to bear most decisively on the new American painting in its formative years. André Masson in particular played an important part here whose full scope has perhaps not yet been recognized; certain works by Pollock, like **Male and Female** of 1943 (which was reproduced in **Problems of Contemporary Art: Form and Sense,** by Wolfgang Paalen, Wittenborn 1945), certainly seem to show the distinct impact of Masson's art. Not so much the overt style of that art, of course, as the directive principles behind it. Pollock's personality was too strong to remain long confined within the narrow bounds of either a cubist or a surrealistic approach. But then the question arises: wherein exactly lies the influence that Masson has exerted on so large a sector of American painting? The clue to the answer is perhaps to be found in a statement by Masson himself in the catalogue of an exhibition at the Museum of Modern Art in 1945: "I was associated with Surrealism. With me Surrealism has been a cyclic affair. I was one of the first group of Surrealists. Then in a manner of speaking I became separated from them ... As a consequence I am solitary; I am too surrealist for those who do not like Surrealism, and not surrealist enough for those who do." His personal idiom of expression, increasingly independent of surrealist formulations, together with his love of Oriental calligraphy, of mysteriously evolving signs untrammeled by the strict limits of logic—this accounts for Masson's influence on an art in the making, which is just

André Masson (1896). Combat and Migration, 1956. (31¼×39″) Courtesy Saidenberg Gallery, New York.

what American painting was in the war years, an art in search of self-fulfillment and only too glad, in its eagerness for freedom and unrestrained experimentation, to welcome the irrational expedients of Surrealism but not its superannuated means of expression.

For in spite of the misleading and by no means disinterested claims of die-hard followers of Surrealism, it seems safe to say that any revival of the movement or its guiding principles, as laid down in the years between the wars, is now absolutely out of the question. The present-day esthetic of the irrational, of lyrical abstractionism, as exemplified in the work of European artists like Wols, Fautrier, Mathieu, Dubuffet, Bryen, and even Henri Michaux, not to mention the **langage parlé écrit** of a writer like Raymond Queneau—that esthetic has nothing to do with the "classic" Surrealism of thirty years ago. If the work of these men has its validity, its underlying necessity, its justification, these lie in the answers it gives to contemporary post-war problems; the problems of pre-war days are, for all practical purposes, ancient history. If we look for the "ancestry," the origins, in the recent past, of that impetus toward an irrational esthetic which remains so strong and effectively determinant even in the work of the younger generations of both European and American painters, we have to go back to Dada or to the ready-mades of Marcel Duchamp, not to Surrealism.

The work that perhaps corresponded more closely than any other in America to the intentions of Surrealism (though always with highly significant differences) was that of Arshile Gorky.

As he committed suicide in 1948, Gorky failed to play any part (assuming he would have cared to do so, which is doubtful) in the rise of action painting. He fashioned his style under the influence of several European masters: Picasso first of all, then Miró; after 1943 Matta Echaurren too seems to have contributed something to it. Gorky's painting cannot be described as abstract. The image is never carried to the point of self-determination, never quite attains to full autonomy of meaning; on the contrary, it is always justifiable in terms of another life, an inner, psychological plane of being. André Breton very aptly pointed out that in Gorky "nature for the first time is treated in the manner of a cryptogram on which the tangible imprint of the artist leaves its mark, as he lays bare the very rhythm of life." [41] But here a distinction must be drawn. In her remarkable monograph on Gorky, Ethel K. Schwabacher has elucidated the significance of the artist's debt not only to Miró but to Chirico; she further maintains, quite rightly, that nowhere in his painting are the technical procedures of Surrealism to be detected, neither those typical of Max Ernst nor those associated with any other Surrealist. There is no evidence in his work, moreover, of any researches akin to those of Duchamp, Arp or Picabia.

To sum up, then, Gorky may be said to have developed a pictorial language that was non-objective in the sense that it never involved a literal transcription of objects; and in this respect he departed from Surrealism. On the other hand, while objects are never literally transcribed in their familiar aspects, they are nonetheless present, inwardly present, bound up with the genesis of man and all created things; in this respect the artist does in fact keep to an interpretative procedure that is very definitely surrealistic. So we may infer that, while his manner of interpreting the actual presence of real objects is surrealistic, his manner of giving them concrete form is foreign to Surrealism.

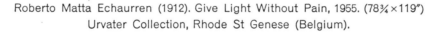

Roberto Matta Echaurren (1912). Give Light Without Pain, 1955. (78¾×119″)
Urvater Collection, Rhode St Genese (Belgium).

Arshile Gorky (1904-1948). Landscape Table, 1945. (36×48″) Collection of Mr and Mrs B.H. Friedman, New York.

An Armenian by birth, Gorky emigrated to the United States in 1920. The pattern of his development was essentially European and his sources of inspiration are clearly apparent. The works of 1923, for example, are modeled on Picasso, not on his cubist paintings but on those painted just before his cubist period—and modeled on them so closely, in certain works, that we find Gorky even taking over the same human types portrayed by the Spanish artist. At the same time, as might be expected, he made a profitable study of Cézanne, more particularly of Cézanne's novel conception of space and perspective, and did not fail to look to the Fauves for a lesson in color handling which stood him in good stead ever afterwards; here the closest link might seem to be with Matisse himself. Then came his discovery of the architecturally ordered planes of Cubism, of the geometrized forms of objects inserted in a space rigorously dimensioned by the artist himself—space which acts as form, no longer merely as atmosphere. In time these forms became less concrete, following no doubt the example of Picasso in his pictures subsequent to 1927.

Gorky, as it turned out, never evinced a capacity for affirming the symbol as an effective agent of reality; the ability to do this lay only within the province of Picasso's tremendous creative power. It was left for the American artist to make the most of a happy gift for self-communing and imaginative introspection rather than for any exteriorizing of the vital impulses of the conscious or the unconscious mind. This being so, a time soon came when the example of

Miró bulked larger for him than any other. His organization of space then became strictly psychological: the projection on to canvas of a mental plane peopled by forms which are like ancestral memories in restless metamorphosis. Gorky may have lacked the driving power of Picasso, he may have lacked Miró's irony and sleight of hand, but he had qualities of his own. Perhaps the finest was his sense of color—of color that seems to come from within and vividly transforms the ordinary into the extraordinary.

After 1943 the influence of Matta Echaurren may have helped Gorky to pursue his researches along more clearly defined lines. Matta handled space—and still handles it—in such a way as to afford new possibilities of stepping up the emotive power of the picture, of charging it with ghostly forms on the brink of collision, with fitful gleams of light impinging as if from an extra-dimensional world, with organic life sensed rather than seen, in a word with symbols born of the characteristic process of extracting symbols from forms which is typical of Surrealism. It was precisely at this point that, in conjunction with his native gifts, the knack of organizing space which he learned first from Cézanne, then from Picasso and Miró, proved to be so useful to Gorky. Unlike Matta Echaurren, he had the faculty of organizing form; of never surrendering it altogether to the rhythm of symbol sequences or to the irrationality of an immediate presence; of conjuring it up out of a chromatic luminosity which is certainly the most exquisitely refined ever created by any American painter.

Arshile Gorky (1904-1948). Dark Green Painting, c. 1947. (44×56″) Collection of Mrs H. Gates Lloyd, Haverford, Pa.

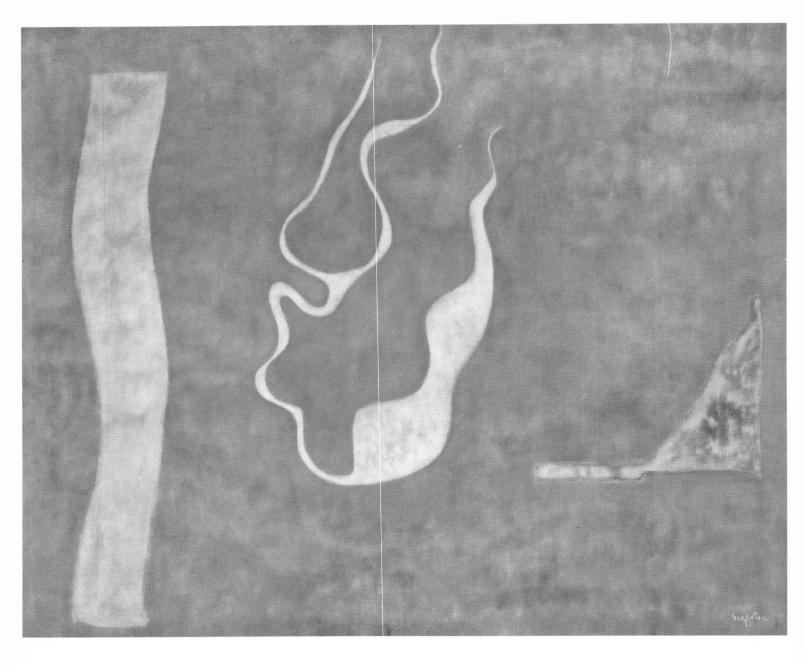

William Baziotes (1912). The Sea, 1959. (60×72″) Mr and Mrs Morris H. Grossman Collection, New York.

The evolution of Gorky's painting from 1943 to his death in 1948 consisted in an intensive purification of this form, stripping it of anthropomorphic symbols, while accentuating its psychological presence, not so much by a linear modulation or its characterization in images as by a highly personal distribution of colors—colors which seldom clash outright but form contrasts of mood by turns delicate and racy. Little by little the process of purification did its work: the definition of the image grew less and less figurative, forms less and less distinct, rhythms increasingly incisive because increasingly simple and linear. So in the end, instead of giving us the by-product of an esthetic—that of Surrealism—which had had its day, instead of merely repeating lessons learned from Picasso and Miró, Gorky's painting came to stand alone as a really admirable, wholly original formulation. His ability to dislocate forms arbitrarily (or apparently so) in a picture space which is always kept under effortless control, seems to have served as a useful indication for artists of all tendencies. It had its effect even on Pollock, whose work, though more complex and more definitely committed, also took shape in the formative period of mid-century American art which, before coming into its own, had been diligently assimilating the most advanced trends of modern art—assimilating them first, then bending them to its particular exigencies, before finally abandoning them altogether and striking out on its own.

"Each beginning suggests something. Once I sense the suggestion, I begin to paint intuitively. The suggestion then becomes a phantom that must be caught and made real. As I work, or when the painting is finished, the subject reveals itself." [42] Thus Baziotes describes his procedure, which consists in projecting an intuition on to canvas, in making it real and distinct. He shares to the full that will to action typical of present-day American art; on the other hand, he shows no propensity to expressive violence. His forms, which often look like the fantastic organisms of primordial life, emerge from the indistinct recesses of the subconscious in a way that is not without reminders of Surrealism. Even his color has an unreal intensity about it, like nothing

Graham Sutherland (1903). Hanging Form, 1959. (65¾×56″) Kunstmuseum, Basel (Emanuel Hoffmann Foundation).

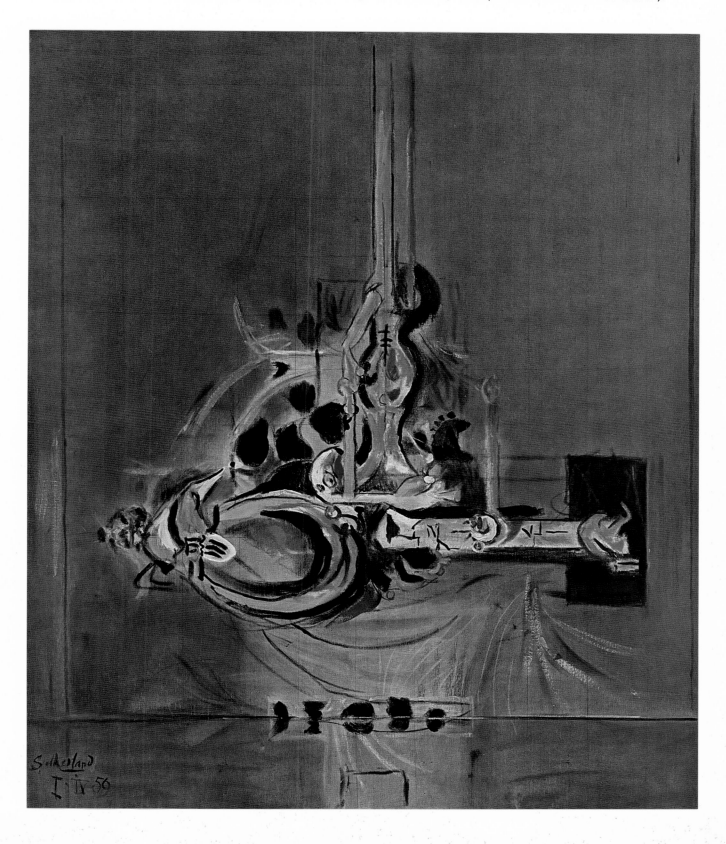

we may expect to find in nature, and it greatly enhances the psychological value of form. Unlike the Surrealists, however, once he has seized on the image and drawn it from the depths of consciousness or memory, he gives it life and meaning not by an automatic process of association but by working it out in the real action of pictorial creation.

In Europe the legacy of Surrealism was by no means exhausted, though operative only within the limits outlined above. Surrealistic elements, projections of anthropomorphic forms metamorphosed, as it were, by the incubi of consciousness—these are still to be found in the work of many different painters of the generation subsequent to that of the Surrealists. But leaving aside all the travesties and perversions committed in the name of Surrealism, we need only dwell here on the significant fact that in Europe the methods and spirit of the movement have by no means become a dead letter; in some notable instances their fecundating influence has given rise to works of great originality. André Masson came back to France after the war and Matta Echaurren too now lives in Europe; so does the Cuban painter Wifredo Lam. Masson has not contented himself with exploiting a manner of his own, but has proved a searching and imaginative innovator, not only in his handling of the sign, in the autonomous calligraphy of his pictures, but in his experiments with texture and new materials. He has gone to the length, on occasion, of inserting real objects in the painting, leaves for example, but even these objects are strictly subordinated to the mysterious and fantastic rhythms of the brushwork. The interest taken in a new definition of texture has led to significant modifications in the surrealistic imagery of painters like Victor Brauner. The painting of Alberto Giacometti—not to mention his sculpture—continues to exert a powerful influence on the development of the younger generation of artists, thanks primarily to his stark, elemental colors, to the contrasting signs which build up his images, and to the infinite depths of space in which those images have their being.

In England the direct influence of Surrealism is particularly noticeable in the case of such painters as Francis Bacon and Graham Sutherland, in spite of the fact, rightly emphasized by Sir Herbert Read, that they both owe more to the English romantic tradition than to any continental influence. Indeed we shall look here in vain for any exact correspondence with classic Surrealism and its reliance on automatism. The really surrealistic element in the work of the two English artists lies rather in the tantalizing aura of the fantastic and mysterious that clings to their images. William Blake and his disciple Samuel Palmer have undoubtedly had a considerable influence on Sutherland's work, though he has never relied on the literary content which is of course part and parcel of Blake's illustrations. Alive to their dramatic possibilities, he explores and follows up the transformations to which certain groupings of objects and real figurations lend themselves. Bacon, on the other hand, seems to draw openly on sources of literary inspiration, though it is difficult to put one's finger on any definite references; he skillfully uses their power of suggestion as a complementary element designed to enhance the purely pictorial features of the work. It is precisely this transformation of the meaning of one object through the impact of another, this suggestive literary enhancement of the painted image and the superadded touches of surrealistic humor which so often go with it, that the irrational tendencies of contemporary painting are reacting against in their militant advocacy of an art of unreserved commitment, which makes no secret of the anxieties and vexation of spirit underlying it.

WOLS - CAMILLE BRYEN - HENRI MICHAUX
JEAN   FAUTRIER   -   LUIGI   SPAZZAPAN
ANTONIO CORPORA - GEORGES MATHIEU
SIMON HANTAÏ - JEAN-PAUL RIOPELLE

7

There seems to be an absolute contradiction between the concept of the "informal," as now used to describe a particular trend of contemporary painting, and the concept of reality, in the traditional sense of the term, which the cultural background of many centuries has accustomed us to regard as being based on visual experience. But we stand today on the threshold of a new cultural era and indeed are participating in it already, unconsciously perhaps but no less actively for that. We are laying its foundations and building for the future at such a rate that in the past fifty years art seems to have made the strides of many centuries. Thanks to these substantial contributions to the new culture in the making, to the identification of being and becoming, of existence and activity, it is now possible to lay down a new, experimental concept of reality adequate to new conditions of life. For, after all, the concepts bequeathed us by a long-standing tradition of empiricism answered in the first instance to specific human needs: as those needs change, the concepts determined by them cease to operate, and new ones accordingly emerge. Such is the case today. The great intellectual adventure of modern culture, not only in our own time but ever since the Age of Enlightenment, lies in its rebellious defiance of prejudices, its impatience with the established order, and its aspiration, at every stage of its growth, toward a new conception of reality, whether social and political, like the French Revolution of 1789, or broadly cultural, like the romantic reaction against the conventions of neo-classical art.

So when we come to inquire into the relationship between the domain of the real and an art which, by definition, ignores visual experience, an art undulating and diverse which has only come into existence since the end of the Second World War, we must first of all cast off the yoke of prejudice—as the artists themselves have done—and try to determine not the external reality to which the picture corresponds, but the internal reality capable of modifying the variable reality outside. Hence the necessity of narrowing down the problem and seeking not a general solution but a fresh one for each case as it arises. And we find, in analyzing their experiments, that the exponents of informal painting, unlike other abstractionists, seem to have willfully discarded certain data of the thinking mind in favor of a more frankly fantastic, psychically motivated idiom of expression, in which the reins of control are left not so much to the unconscious mind, as in the case of the Surrealists, as simply to impulse. The cultural forces that have shaped society in the last fifteen years are profoundly different from those that came into play after the First World War. So that the reliance on dreams and the unconscious mind, and the exploitation of psychic automatism, which were the characteristic devices of Surrealism, have no place at all in the esthetic of informal painting, whose most authentic representatives dispense with symbolism altogether, thus avoiding—and this is one of their finest qualities—the optical and psychic illusionism which counts for so much in surrealist painting.

The problem, for these artists, is not just a matter of setting themselves up in opposition to previous trends or to those of their contemporaries. It lies in the recognition of certain facts and necessities which call for art of another kind, for the **art autre** postulated by Michel Tapié. "A pure act of existence," writes G. C. Argan, "free of any ulterior motives and any empirical

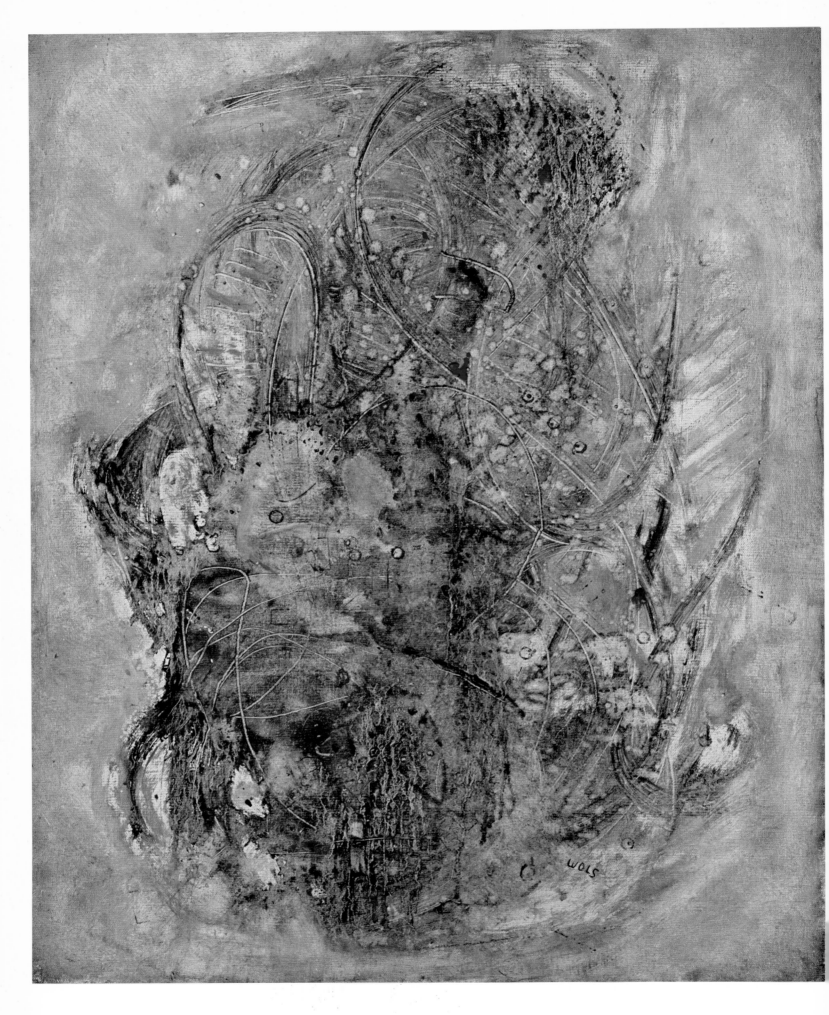

Wols (1913-1951). "La Turquoise," 1947. (25⅝ × 21¼") J. Janssen Collection, Lierre (Belgium).

reasoning, the informal work of art is an absolute alienation. It aims, that is to say, at reproducing in its entirety, in terms of 'otherness,' the experience undergone by the artist in producing the picture; and at thereby eliminating every difference of quality or degree between the determination to act and the completion of the creative act." [43] This is a condition which attaches in fact not only to painting, but also to certain aspects of contemporary literature and music. The **Colloque abhumaniste** written by a painter, Camille Bryen, might well be cited as a pertinent example in the domain of literature, and the title in this case amounts to a definition. As far as music is concerned, an abundance of recent experiments comes to mind, ranging from compositions based on the twelve-tone scale to electronic music. All such works mark a departure from the traditional conception of space, sequence and frequency.

The term "informal," however, embraces too wide a field for it to answer fully to the realities of the new situation. It has been applied indiscriminately to the work of Wols, Fautrier, Mathieu and even Jackson Pollock. The diversity of these men is too great for them to be lumped together, nor can matters be mended simply by classifying them all as lyrical abstractionists. Notwithstanding that diversity, there are of course discernible affinities between them. Informal art does not pretend to be a revolt against reason or against society; and though it may owe something to Dada, it is not and was never meant to be a kind of anti-painting, such as Dada claimed to be. It represents, on the contrary, a concerted inquiry into the real meaning of the human situation at present—an inquiry conducted outside the limits of any over-schematic, rational formulation. We have already dwelt on the fact that the elements of the artist's language must change or be changed when their expressive content is exhausted. But here it was not so much a question of changing the elements of expression as of overcoming opposing categories of

Wols (1913-1951). Composition, c. 1948. (6¾×9½″) Hélie Lassaigne Collection, Paris.

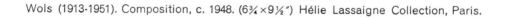

thought, of mental and psychic activity. None of these painters drew his forms from the unconscious depths of his being, nor moreover did any of them fit their forms into a logical order of space and composition. With all of them the color patch, the **tache**—hence the name **tachisme** by which informal painting is often designated—evolves with uninhibited freedom on the picture surface and in its depths; its only limits are those of color itself and of the evocative power of its manifold presence.

"Psychic non figuration" was the name given in 1947 to a **tachiste** movement launched by Mathieu and Bryen. Their aim, as the name indicates, was the immediate projection of psychic values on to canvas—not a symbolic transformation and metamorphosis of objects and anthropomorphic images, which had been the aim of Surrealism. If the dictates of the conscious mind were not to intervene in the picture in any positive sense, there was no reason for their opposite number, the promptings of the unconscious mind, to intervene either. For in this art there is no cleavage or time interval between the conception and the realization of form: the two coincide in a single simultaneous action. Nevertheless, as Kandinsky had pointed out in a different context, this inner compulsion has to be brought into play in a real, a tangible medium; for informal painting, which posits the work of art as a real entity sufficient unto itself, this medium necessarily becomes that of technique and surface texture, i.e. the painter's actual manipulation of his pigments and their materialization in the finished work. This process of materialization presupposes a traceable continuity and virtually a new time dimension. Hence the importance of the informal achievement for artists of widely different tendencies: it has enabled them completely to renew the function and significance of the materials they embody in their paintings. Burri is a case in point.

One of the major exponents of informal painting was Wols. Born in Berlin, he came in contact with the artists of the Dessau Bauhaus and later with Surrealism. He then settled in France, where he knew H. P. Roché, Sartre and Simone de Beauvoir, became a close personal friend of Camille Bryen, and exhibited at the Drouin Gallery where the painters of the new movement forgathered. But it would be absurd to judge his work from the limited viewpoint of a single movement. Wols must be recognized for what he is: one of the great representative figures of European culture in our time, not only because he reflects the conflicts and ideas of modern society and modern thought, but also and above all because he inherited, renewed and enriched the traditions sponsored by the masters of modern European art. Expression, in his work, is elaborated on the strength of a stylistic patrimony deliberately acquired and assimilated. His finest achievement lay in going beyond Surrealism, after assimilating and even improving on its methods, from automatism to the association of forms. The influence of Dada too can be detected, not so much in the quality of his expressive means as in his essentially negative conception of the world. The pictorial image, however, as Wols handled it, lies outside the known world, on a metaphysical plane which is not idealistic but existential, or better, phenomenological. So the artist no longer felt any need to create forms intended as psychological equivalents, or to probe into the mysteries of the unconscious. His, on the contrary, is preeminently an art of the conscious mind, whose immanent phenomena—and not those of nature—he called upon to build up a new pictorial dimension.

"The first thing I rule out of my life is memory." This note, in Wols's hand, figures on a sheet of his drawings, and it helps to clarify the problems raised by his artistic language. Psychic automatism as practised by Wols—and critics have pointed out how different this is from pictorial automatism—signifies an immediate, wholehearted participation in the building up of form. In the first place, nothing of memory or reminiscence enters into his inspiration; secondly, he makes play neither with naturalistic suggestions nor with the repercussions of visual phenomena in the subconscious mind, which had been so important a factor in surrealist painting. The pulse of life that we sense in his pictures, the organic vitality, the continuous germination of his images, all this is native to the painting itself and has no possibility of existence outside the painting. For Wols, things exist only in terms of form, life itself is form—form in the throes of ceaseless change, expansion, entanglement—form enamored of its attendant color-signs

Wols (1913-1951). The Vowels, 1950. (31 ⅞ × 23 ⅝″) Collection of Madame Grety Wols, Noisy-le-Roi (Seine-et-Oise), France.

Camille Bryen (1907). Drawing, February 1960. Galerie Raymonde Cazenave, Paris.

and subtly glowing or violently contrasting color-textures. Always, even in the most delicate or rhapsodical passages, texture is brought out and made to convey an exalted, forthright sense of life in flux, which the artist compels us to accept as the only possible reality.

For Wols the great lesson was that of Klee. He recognized its importance early in his career and assimilated its external features. What in Klee had been an abstract calligraphy of sign-forms and color-signs corresponding episodically to the appearance of a real image (though always subordinated to the exigencies of expression) remained in Wols's work up to 1945 a system of descriptive signs serving to indicate the chromatic dislocation of an object, and to reduce reality not so much to a purely pictorial dimension as to a decorative pattern. In time, however, as he experimented with Klee's subtle signwork, and thanks in part no doubt to the practice of engraving, Wols opened up a new realm of expression lying entirely within the mind and unconnected with the outside world. Klee had always held that there was no longer any point in representing the things we see or take pleasure in seeing, since visual reality is only a phenomenon isolated from the more complex reality of the cosmos. Wols reacted against appearances in much the same way. But the spirit in which he proceeded—and which, as we have said, is not without vague analogies with Dadaism—prompted him to advance from Klee's position and reject any possibility of correspondence between form and image, in order to achieve a simultaneity of expression on the only plane whose validity he recognized: the vital plane of his own emotions, their flow undeflected by any necessity to describe or explain them. The means he used to this end were exclusively pictorial: a new intuition of the world and the sense of a new relationship with it became real presences because expressed in a construction of forms and colors belonging exclusively to painting. In Wols the coalescence of image and brushwork occurs immediately, without any intermediary, because without any literary intentions or any romantic undertones. His object, as he himself said, was "to ignore the importance of man," though this by no means implies a rejection of human values, which are always an integral part of his work. What he set out to do, and succeeded in doing, was to suspend or ignore the outside world (in accordance with the phenomenological proposition of Husserl), the world of nature which, needless to say, continued to exist as a reality for the conscious mind, but which was effectually excluded from the picture. Hence the indivisible time unity of Wols's painting, which thereby, at one blow, rules out both chronological sequence and spatial sequence. The singular state of suspension thus achieved also represents a safeguard against the lure of romantic impulses. So in keeping with the spirit of his age, he rejected visual appearances out of hand as incapable of conveying the full force of his emotions and the lyrical sublimation of an essentially pictorial style. More important still, Wols's painting finds a new justification and opens new horizons by at last reconciling the cross-purposes so long implicit in the various trends of abstract art in the past half-century.

Henri Michaux (1899). India Ink, 1959. (29½×41⅜″) Private Collection, Paris.

Jean Fautrier (1898). White Construction, 1958. (28¾×36¼˝) Serge Landeau Collection, Paris.

A friend of Wols, Camille Bryen initiated almost at once that line of research which has steadily led up to his mature, highly personal style of informal painting, so remarkable for its precision and directness. Bryen is a writer and poet as well as a painter, and this gives his painting a quality which cannot be called literary, for his means are exclusively pictorial, but which infuses a lyrical vitality into form and space. For Bryen all psychic impulses can and must be exteriorized, for it is these that constitute the structural framework of the picture and take the place of visual data. The resulting space therefore fails to constitute a physical dimension; it becomes a labile element, waxing and waning with the ebb and flow of emotion; it is like an unexplored wonderland in which the mind ranges freely and comes at every turn upon the most surprising discoveries. There is a kind of wizardry here in the ease with which Bryen disrupts the logical order of sensations and their projection into the picture. He finds infinite possibilities in the adventure of artistic creation. There is neither time nor space nor anything stable in Bryen's world. Action and sensation are identified in the continuous elaboration of an unlimited flow of irrational and spellbinding impulses.

For Jean Fautrier informal painting does not represent a recently felt need. As early as 1928 he anticipated its developments, and it may be said that even before that date he had mastered the elements on which they were based. Fautrier proved original and far-sighted enough to create an art that owed nothing to Cubism—certainly a **tour de force** for any painter in the twenties. From the outset his work was characterized by the investigation of a picture space where texture and image were one, and whose modulations were neither those of cubist space nor, even less, those of impressionist space. This picture space of Fautrier's devising conferred a dramatic significance on texture and image, for a sense of impending drama arises out of the suppression of any reference to familiar space. Much has been said of the magic element in Fautrier's art. It is only fair to add that if this is magic, it never seeks evasion in metaphysical abstractions: it is materialized in human form and is never alien to the artist's experience of reality. In an interview with Pierre Volboudt in 1957, Fautrier was recorded as saying: "Not only does reality exist, but in no case should it be rejected outright. The act of painting is not merely a need to spread paints on canvas. It must be admitted that the desire to express ourselves springs originally from something we have seen. That this reality should be transformed, molded in the image of the artist's temperament, and that the resulting image should end up by becoming realer than reality itself—well and good. But appearances always underlie it, to a greater or lesser degree." [44]

Fautrier himself is skeptical of the term "informal" when it is taken to mean "no more than mere variations of texture, from veined paper to stucco." [44] This is natural enough, for of all the lyrical abstractionists he is the one who more than any other keeps to logical processes—a purely inward logic of his own, not a mental discipline, but a logic nevertheless governing the action of painting. Instead of surrendering to arbitrary impulses, he acts directly on the texture of his picture, on its highly refined stratifications, concretized in real forms, like a new object that has come within the ken of the conscious mind, which never handles it automatically but carefully builds it up and matures it until it effectively amounts to a well-defined reality. This texture accordingly embodies its own figuration; in itself it realizes an image divested of the values

Jean Fautrier (1898). Swirls, 1958. (31 ½ × 51 ¼ ") Giuseppe Panza di Biumo Collection, Milan.

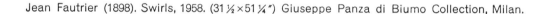

attaching to anthropomorphic representation. The **Hostages** for example, a series of pictures painted between 1942 and 1944, and among the finest Fautrier ever made, are allusive figurations; the title answers exactly to their content. But their representational significance lies entirely in the form of their thickly clotted texture. Have we here, perhaps, just such a concurrence of form and image as Klee had already achieved? Points of contact between the two men there may well be, but their methods and aspirations are utterly different. In Fautrier, image and texture coincide, not **a posteriori,** but in the very moment in which texture models the image in accordance with inner necessity; it is texture, and not the traditional formal or compositional schema, that determines both image and dimension, so that in effect the image identifies itself with the stratifications of color and loses any definition in terms of horizontal or vertical. Its rhythms are organic and have no need of directional indications: Fautrier's pictures can thus only be described as two-sided or four-sided.

Fautrier stands as far from the drip technique of Jackson Pollock, with its implied extensions beyond the canvas, as he does from the urgent physical vitality of Alberto Burri's compositions or from the ironic contrasts of image and texture by which Jean Dubuffet sets so much store. Fautrier makes a point of elaborating his texture, of making it yield subtle shades of color which come almost like a faint, distant echo of impressionist chromatism. Even when signs are inserted in it—and these are always Fautrier's characteristically non-calligraphic color-signs—that texture retains what might be called its mineral quality and loses none of the impact of its immediate presence; at the same time, its organic character sets up the relationship with nature and reality. The building up of the impasto in superimposed layers, modulated both in depth and on the surface by waves and undercurrents of pigment, represents the gradual characterization of the textured image. The wide margin Fautrier often leaves around the central nucleus has the value of a negative space, isolating the positive features of the images and throwing them into focus by contrast. In the stratifications of pigment lies the new spatial significance of this painting—

Jean Fautrier (1898). "Anything else but love", 1960. (34⅞×57⅝") Private Collection, Paris.

118

a space which is still the medium of memory and therefore of **real duration,** but which has nothing in common with the real duration of cubist space, limited as it was to the dislocation of objects on the plane surface in accordance with a time sequence.

While Wols ignored the world or set it in abeyance, Fautrier accepts it for what it is, while often reacting against it more or less vehemently. External stimuli exert a constant pressure on him which the artist accepts without any attempt to sift or select those stimuli qualitatively; what he does carefully select and consider, however, are his pictorial means, his colors and signs. So there is an underlying logic in his compositional procedure, though it does not precede the effort of composition but goes hand in hand with it. The result is that in the last analysis Fautrier transcends informal painting and creates well-defined forms which, within the pictorial organism, are not meant to differ in meaning from what they actually represent, and which are not an adumbration either. A friend of writers and poets like André Malraux, Giuseppe Ungaretti, Jean Paulhan and Francis Ponge, who were among the earliest and most perceptive interpreters of his painting, Fautrier—much like Ungaretti in fact—willingly elaborates on a sentiment of time, whether a memory or present participation in the realities of the human condition dear to André Malraux.

The pressure of stimuli essentially poetic and literary in character—which are therefore already transfigurations of reality before becoming signs—counts for a great deal in the elaboration of Henri Michaux's drawings. "Instead of one particular vision excluding others," he writes, "I should like to record the moments which, one by one, add up to life. I should like to make you see the inward phrase, the phrase without words, the thread endlessly and sinuously spun within ourselves, which connects us with everything that comes along from both outside and inside." [45] With Michaux there is no question of logic, either before, during or after the composition. Everything is surrendered to calligraphic rhythms, to a picture space in continuous transformation which eludes definition, even though a structure is present in his drawings. Stimuli impinge on him rapidly and are committed to paper with equal rapidity in a flurry of signs, while space is continually broken up by the intervals between one streak and another or by the meandering paths between tiny clusters of penstrokes. Yet there is nothing fragmentary about the final drawing; the result is a well constructed organic whole consisting not of definite forms, but of a continuously shifting pattern of potential shapes. Everything is ambiguous and indeterminate, a lyrical outpouring tantalizingly suggestive of the adventure of being in its flights beyond the pragmatic definitions of the prosaic mind.

Mediterranean landscapes, fishing nets and boats, iridescent colors playing over regular forms —all this characterized the painting of Antonio Corpora for a time. Then, reluctant to identify self-expression with the pictorial transformation of actual phenomena, he moved on to other things. In Italy, immediately after the war, Corpora stood in the forefront of the struggle to renew the painter's means of expression. In Rome he helped to found the neo-cubist group which was among the first to take a firm stand in a controversial question and to urge a radical departure from the outmoded norms of pre-war painting. The logical consequence of the position Corpora took up—one very close to that of the Painters of French Tradition—was that he exhibited at the 1952 Venice Biennale as a member of the group of Eight Italian Painters. But this apparent community of ideas was only momentary. Corpora's restless personality and original turn of mind made the constraints imposed by a group intolerable to him, the more so as his temperament prompted him to turn aside into any tempting byway and follow it up on the spur of the moment. After 1952 the light in his pictures became less and less localized and more and more autonomous; gradually it ceased to act as illumination, as it came to form a concrete part of the surface texture, enriching it and heightening its dramatic presence within the structural organization of his painting—light, in a word, had become a spatial element. This meant that he renounced a certain order and faith, the better to establish a new relationship with the reality of his own work. "All I have to begin with," writes Corpora of his working methods, "is an intuition and a general idea. My forms are nothing, informal color patches and lines, and my texture is a clotted mass, until a **revelation** intervenes and enables me to make the most of the color patches and lines which are the outgrowth of style, the raw material of my craft, the echo of emotions. Hence the rule of moderation. Order, moderation, and texture which apply only to one work, and are challenged in the next." [46]

Once he became alive to the value of informal investigations, Corpora resolutely directed his efforts toward this solution. But his **art autre** has preserved a moral principle, which serves him as a reminder not to forget the relation necessarily existing between the artist and society. His automatism is projected into the logical sphere of a mental order. From "other" necessities, then, he proceeds to still "others," in a continually reattested liberation from convention which says much for his vitality and original creative power. "Corpora's esthetic," as G.C. Argan has written, "is not primarily that of **art autre**: it is a demonstration of the fact that every esthetic is always **autre,** always different, because present reality is not a stream of forgetfulness into which we sink with loss of memory, but a concourse of tensions which, on the contrary, sharpens memory." At this level passions stand out and take form, they organize themselves in the concrete medium of the pictorial image. Space, being luminous, emotive and non-physical, is real and not illusionistic: it is itself form, it teems with life, with gleams of light that are neither ornaments nor references, but scintillations from the depths, radiations of the will to communicate. Rhythms surge impetuously over the canvas or crystallize as if suspended in the cycle of time, bodying forth the painter's vision and its moral, real and human implications. New compulsions drive the artist on: he infuses his painting with the fever of action, but frees it from the

Luigi Spazzapan (1889-1958). High Noon, 1956. (23¾×31½") Galleria Pogliani, Rome.

Antonio Corpora (1909). "Drawing," 1959. (45×57½") Galleria Pogliani, Rome.

bondage of determinism; he stabilizes it on the peak of aspiring tensions, thus securing it from the pitfalls of facile academicism. The mere will to achieve some sort of **art autre** was not enough to arrive at a new formulation: it was imperative for him to ignore the end in view and to conceive of painting as an unlimited continuum of vibrations.

Action and gesture had been released from contingencies; henceforth they formed part of experience. The magic moment of intuition was renewed again and again, welling up from the unconscious and being systematized in a more conscious, more logical zone of the mind. So that instead of pauses and literary caesuras in the paintings, we find a dynamism of consistent, structuralized rhythms; and light is present, particularly in some of Corpora's latest works, not only as a new dimension irresolvable into the continuity of space and time, but as the fruit of a confident plenitude and felicity of expression of which the painter now stands in concrete possession. Light issues from a surface texture no longer limited in any way, it streams out and modulates forms to the full extent of their surfaces or seems to shatter them at a blow into a thousand iridescent motifs, conferring a real and palpable presence on the most elusive figments of intuition and imagination. Light ultimately becomes the most suitable means of satisfying that will to communication which motivates and justifies Corpora's art, and implementing that complex moral commitment of his which is by no means limited to his artistic activity alone. Hence, as Pierre Restany has noted, "the coherence and slow progression of

Georges Mathieu (1921). The Capetians, 1954. (112¼ × 236½″) Musée d'Art Moderne, Paris.

his style, so strangely contrasting with the volte-faces of our captains of the art industry...
Beyond the pale of frivolous passions and passing crazes, his work constitutes one of the most
authentic testimonies of contemporary art."

Luigi Spazzapan is a case apart in Italian art. A painter of long experience, he was in contact
as a young man with the Futurists and then studied for a time at Kandinsky's art school in
Munich. He was painting abstract pictures as early as 1925, but he subsequently reverted to an
original form of figurative painting torn by dynamic rhythms further intensified by expressionistic
colors. Magnificent draftsman that he was, however, he always maintained a firm control over
form, often adapting it to geometric patterns. But it was only after the war that Spazzapan's
painting acquired its subtlest, most penetrating color magic, whose effect was, first, to heighten
the figurative quality of images embedded in a thick, grainy impasto, then gradually to flush
out of this textural richness any perceptible reference to the figurative. Spazzapan died in 1958,
at the height of an extremely interesting phase of development, the logical outcome of a lifetime's experience, during which every modification of style or approach had come as the fruit
of constant growth. His handling of color and his condensed and virulent light were never conditioned by any arbitrary **tachisme**; they effectively reified an idea and a train of thought, with
no interference tolerated on the part of instinct. "I believe only in verve and inspiration. I believe
so little in instinct, the most abominable superstition of this first quarter of the century, as to
identify verve as much with the consciousness as with the intelligence." So wrote Spazzapan
in 1935, and to this credo he remained faithful to the end.

Beyond the surfaces on which his forms evolve, a suggestion of space is conveyed by the quality
of the lighting, by the steady sweep of the brush which almost seems to incise the surface texture,
and by the turbulent contrast of forms. Rhythms interweave and join forces, forms expand and
are contorted in the dynamism of the structural organization. Everything goes to reveal an
unquiet state of mind in the artist—but a mind complex and prone to dramatic expression.
Color on color, black on black, red on red, rule out facile effects of transparency; their superposition is always designed in view of surface enrichment, and always yields brilliant results.
Spazzapan's career was long and the roots of his art lie deep. His signs, in the earlier works,
were steeped in a light that not even his expressionistic vehemence could dim. The same

luminosity glows through the thick impasto of his last works. In these, more impalpable and timeless than ever, light is no longer a pleasing ornament but an intimate sharer in the dramatic vicissitudes of man's life. Indeed, in light, as Spazzapan himself once said, "everything regains its form: joy, rage, fear, and so on, to the very end."

After showing leanings toward Surrealism (in 1953 André Breton organized a one-man show of his work in the Galerie l'Etoile Scellée), Simon Hantaï resolutely turned his back on evocations of reality, even of a purely fantastic order. Influenced by the trend toward informal painting, he ceased to feel any need to conjure up hallucinating visions of an imaginary world; he broke up forms, while bearing in mind the principle of their automatic associations, and reassembled them in decorative rhythms not devoid of elegance.

There is a characteristic graciousness about the painting of Georges Mathieu, an elegance born not only of form and color but implicit in the attitude of the artist himself toward his work.

Simon Hantaï (1922). St Francis Xavier in the Indies, 1958. (90¼×84¼″) Galerie Kléber, Paris.

Not that his images are lacking in driving power and even violence, indeed they almost seem to be assailed and their very existence threatened by the dynamic inroads of black and colored signs and surging impastos. Violence there is, but violence with a difference—it is, rather, a literary conception of violence somehow embodied in pure painting thanks to the saving grace of the means employed. With Mathieu, the action and gesture of painting has none of the willfulness characteristic of American art, for example. The distribution of color areas and the superposition of black signs on red forms are intuitive, dictated by instinct.

Very different is the painting of Jean-Paul Riopelle. Born in Montreal, he founded the Automatism group in 1940 with Paul-Emile Borduas. In 1947 he settled in France. For Riopelle, too, instinct is the determining factor in building up the composition, in the automatic transfer of his impulses on to canvas. But once he has fairly set to work on a canvas, he brings to bear on it the vigilant, active presence of his whole being—with the result that a logical order is in the end imposed on those impulses. Although his forms appear to have burst into countless fragments, and his color textures split wide open, he nevertheless keeps clear of the free-flowing rhythms and overall vagueness of informal painting, thanks in large measure to a dramatic intensity approximating in some ways to the esthetic of abstract expressionism and action painting. On the other hand, his colors have gained a richness and refinement which seem to stem from the best tradition of French painting.

Jean-Paul Riopelle (1924). Country, 1959. (25½×31⅞″) Owned by the Department of External Affairs of Canada.

JACKSON POLLOCK - MARK TOBEY - SAM FRANCIS
BRADLEY WALKER TOMLIN - MARK ROTHKO

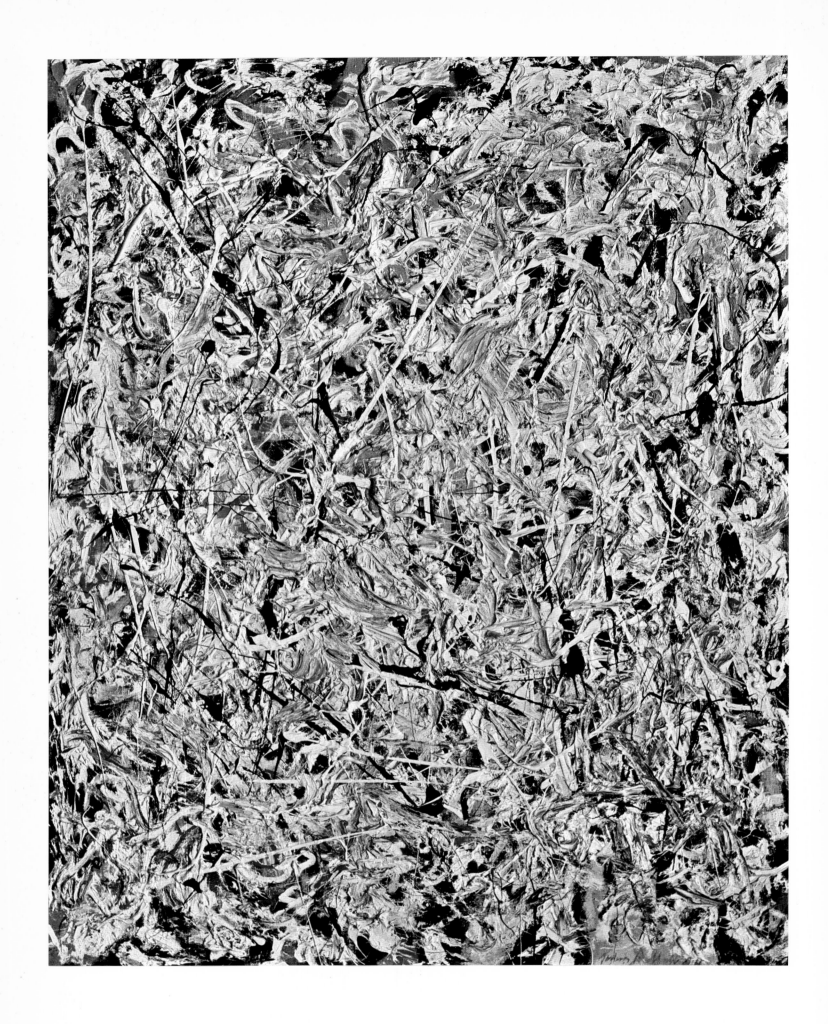

Jackson Pollock (1912-1956). White Light, 1954. (48¼×38¼″) Sidney Janis Collection, New York.

8

We have already said how pointless it is today to speak of national, regional or local styles of painting, in a world where ideas are exchanged with a facility that makes light of distance. The fact remains that certain distinguishable characteristics still prevail in certain places within the ambit of an international culture and style. Nowhere is this truer than in the United States, and it must be borne in mind in studying the rise of American painting in the years immediately after the war, when, for the first time in art history, it commanded attention by genuinely original achievements.

Does modern painting in the United States, then, represent a native product, an isolated phenomenon? No, of course it does not. American art, for all its originality, takes its allotted place within a larger context: that of world art today and the community of endeavor sponsored by the best artists of all countries. True, when we speak of action painting and abstract expressionism, what we mean here, for the sake of definition, is something specifically American; similarly, when we speak of informal painting, what we mean, again for the sake of definition, is something specifically European. But there is no hard-and-fast dividing line between them; any sharp distinction we try to draw will always prove too restrictive; in a word, it fails to fit the facts. The give-and-take between artists of all tendencies and outlooks is too close and constant for it to be otherwise. Indeed, the interpenetration of all forms of expression is probably deeper and more fruitful than many of us realize, because the artist today works out a style, a vehicle of expression, under the stress of many different stimuli emanating from what is, fundamentally, and irrespective of distinctions, the worldwide condition of modern man. Only on these terms is it possible for the artist to affirm certain national characteristics, which, logically enough, partake of the same condition. Even so, there is no denying that American painting represents an original achievement, and one that definitely stands apart from European art in general and from the French tradition in particular, on which it so long relied for its inspiration, from the days of the American impressionists like John Twachtman, George Metcalf and Childe Hassam, until it took over some of the formulations of Surrealism.

The new factor that has changed the face of the American art world is this: American artists of the present day, having assimilated such major influences as Expressionism, Picasso and Surrealism, have at last succeeded in going well beyond them on their own initiative, and one reason for their success is that they have evolved a different conception of the artist's function and of the relationship between the artist and his work. As Harold Rosenberg, one of the theorists of action painting, has observed, the American artist accepts reality only in so far as it enters into the act of creation. It is important to understand this point of view—which, to some extent, tallies with the conception of pictorial reality exemplified on the other side of the Atlantic by Hartung or Fautrier. There is, however, an essential shade of difference which makes it clear that their attitude toward reality is by no means the same: while the European artist tends to objectivize the work of art, to affirm it, that is, as a reality in its own right, the American artist recognizes a real value in his self-participation in the making of the work of art. So that while

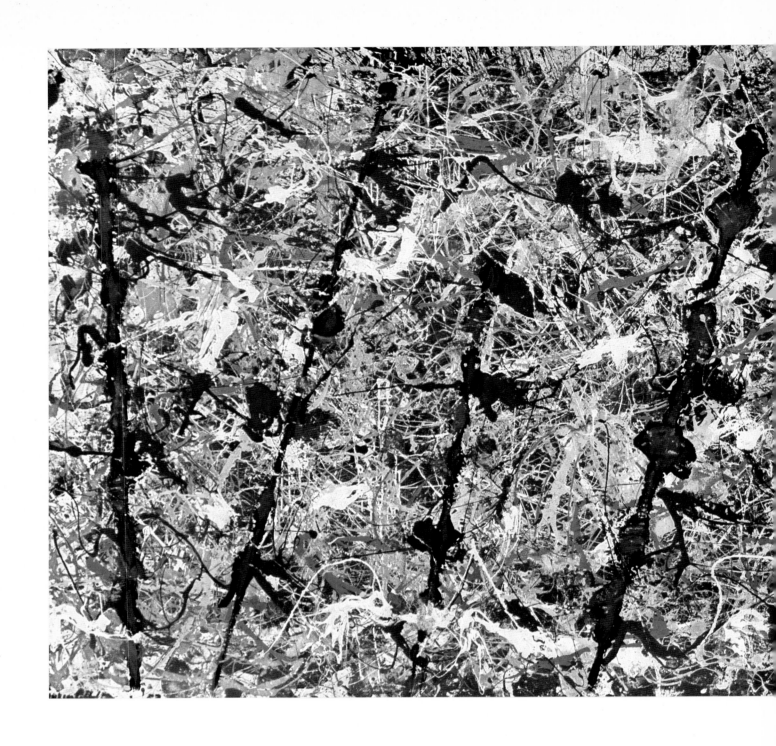

Jackson Pollock (1912-1956). Blue Poles, 1953. (83½×192½″)

Mr and Mrs Ben Heller Collection, New York.

Jackson Pollock (1912-1956). One, 1950. (110×211″) Mr and Mrs Ben Heller Collection, New York.

abstraction may result in both cases, the compulsion behind it is very different, almost as if the American painter were trying to reconcile the two opposing stimuli postulated by Worringer: the abstract impulse and empathy.

What chiefly characterizes American art to begin with—anyhow to the European mind—is the absence of any presiding body of theoretical or general intellectual principles. The lack of a long national tradition, indeed the impatience he feels with the binding ties of tradition, leaves the American painter free to forge ahead with an unbiased formulation of his own style. While in the case of the European artist a definite effort is required to overcome an inherited bias, whether academic or social, his American counterpart of today runs little risk of getting sidetracked in this way. Yet, now that it has taken its place in history, action painting, or whatever one chooses to call it, has come to represent a precedent which might in the near future become a prejudice, and which in many cases has already become an academic discipline. This was inevitable and in no way detracts from its achievement. And though American painting may be relatively free of intellectual preoccupations, it has nevertheless developed in a certain climate, against a certain background. To speak of the artist's participation in the construction of the work of art is not enough; the "action" it calls for must be based on ethical principles for the painter to find a reality in this action. He finds it, in other words, not in pure esthetic contemplation, but in the moral implications of his work. And if this is so, one reason for it lies in the peculiar position of the American artist with respect to the society he lives in.

It cannot be said that American society unreservedly accepts the artist and welcomes his activity. The fact is, furthermore, that the flowering of American painting came at a time when all intellectual activity, every venture of the free mind, was regarded as subversive, owing to an unfortunate conjunction of political circumstances. Such is the logic of things, and the words of the greatest of American philosophers have thus proved to be truer than ever: "Because art is wholly innocent of ideas derived from blame and praise, it is looked upon with the eye of suspicion by the guardian of custom... Yet this indifference to praise and blame because of preoccupation with imaginative experience constitutes the heart of the moral potency of art." [47] It is evident, however, that this moral outlook peculiar to art constitutes in itself a social principle.

Artistic activity and the sense of its importance and its ethical validity hold out the possibility of a closer relationship between the artist and society. There is no overlooking either the essential pragmatism of American society or the fact that American artists share that pragmatism. The resulting experience has been of fundamental importance, for it is one in which ethical principles count for more than esthetic qualities. This explains why it is that Surrealism, with its reliance on the unconscious mind and procedures designed to lay bare the stratified depths of memory and emotion, was so warmly welcomed by American artists, whose conception of their calling presupposed some such analysis of unconscious impulses. But it also explains why they had to go beyond Surrealism when they came to work out a new relationship with society on the strength of active participation.

The rise and breakthrough of American painting stem logically from the historical development of American society. A culture tending toward a particular type of social organization, with the requisite material wealth and intellectual ferment, necessarily reaches a point where its artistic production becomes a factor to be reckoned with. That production, however, must contribute not only to the American way of life but also to the artistic language of all countries. Such is now the case with American painting, to a quite unprecedented degree. The American discovery of the value of experience in artistic creation is a forward step of capital importance, to which not only the artists have contributed but also some notable thinkers. One of the most penetrating studies of esthetic problems ever published in the United States is John Dewey's **Art as Experience.** For Dewey, "expression, like construction, signifies both an action and its result." [48] Art is thus conceived as beginning with an analysis of its connection with the facts of ordinary experience, and thereby justifying, without any appeal to transcendence, the transformation of an ordinary product into an artistic product. Determinant in this transformation is the intervention of the artist and his power of thought—but not necessarily of abstract thought. For "the artist does his thinking in the very qualitative media he works in, and the terms lie so close to the object that he is producing that they merge directly into it." [49]

The fundamental concept of esthetic activity is to be sought for in continuous experimentation with the means at the artist's command, and lies above all in the relationship between man and his immediate environment. This should be kept in mind when we read the rare statements made by Pollock which reveal his attitude toward the work of art. Pollock's painting is as direct as painting can be; preliminary sketches were entirely dispensed with. The artist's experience, which often reflects to a remarkable degree the strata of consciousness with their various contents, takes on its active meaning at the very moment when the gesture of painting renders form concrete; its expressive power is heightened by a synthesis of the successive moments in which the creative experience takes place. What the painter never forgets—and this cannot possibly be determined by an unconscious or instinctive impulse—is the value of his action; this action is a reality deriving from experimentation and it is the only concrete datum which the artist recognizes. This is why Pollock needed to lay his canvas out flat on the floor, to walk around it, to get **into** it, and thereby identify the picture as closely as possible with the physical act of painting. Rather than a mere exteriorization, a projection of his personality on to canvas, this method enabled him to achieve something more: the unification of an external entity, material and mechanical, with an intellectual and emotional condition.

Pollock's declared intention was to express his feelings, not to describe them. And because the material means employed to that end were so closely identified with his mental and emotional life, there was no need to assimilate them to any traditional technique; such a technique, in any case, could only have served to express a contemplative outlook wholly foreign to his temperament. But at the same time—and in this he had no choice—he had to assume the entire validity of his material means before transforming them into valid forms of expression. From brushwork Pollock moved on to sheer colorwork, as he invented his famous drip technique. For the traditional pigments mixed on the palette, he came to substitute ordinary commercial paints such as Duco. Sometimes he worked on a metal support, scratching and hacking it as if to impress the mark of violence on it—a temperamental violence identified with that of the material itself.

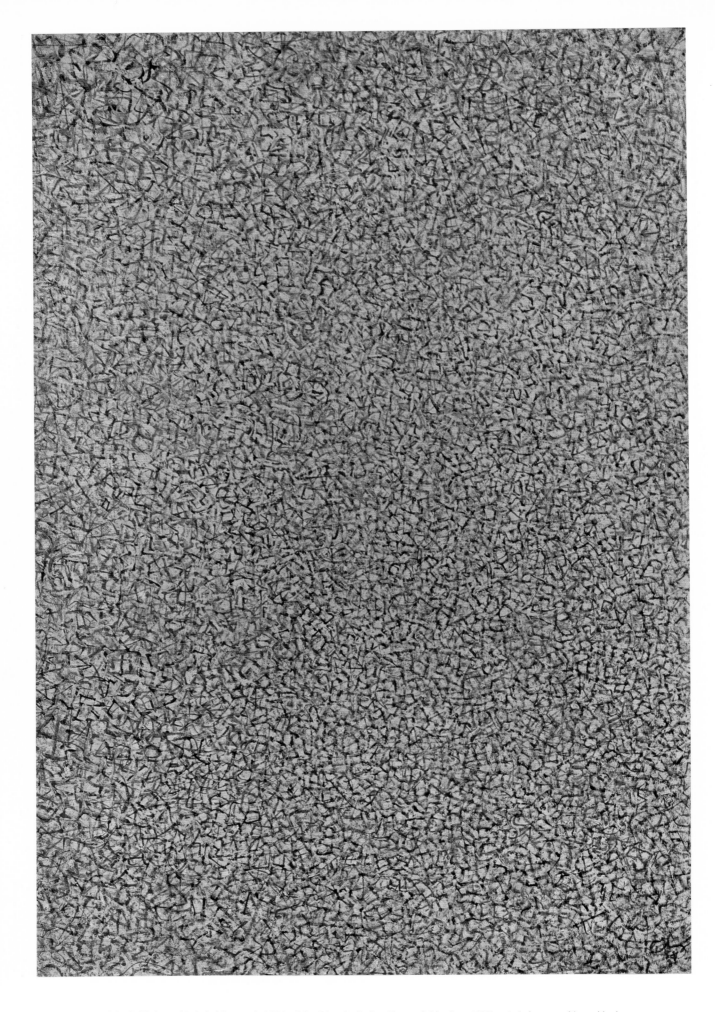

Mark Tobey (1890). Harvest, 1958. (36×24¼″) Collection of Marian Willard Johnson, New York.

Mark Tobey (1890). City Radiance, 1944. (19⅜×14¼″) Collection of Mrs Julia Feininger, New York.

Immediate sensations were thus translated into terms of immediate experience. Under these conditions, it was only natural at a given moment for Pollock to feel a closer bond of sympathy with Surrealism than with any other modern movement—but only for a time. And even then he recast and adapted whatever he took over from Surrealism, stripping it of whatever was alien to his purpose, before finally breaking free of it altogether and mastering a style of his own, fashioned by a concrete experience of life approximating to a materialistic ideology. It was a style compounded, in the last analysis, of an intensely personal vehemence, an expressionistic strain typical of a whole aspect of American painting.

Jackson Pollock was born at Cody, Wyoming, in 1912 and was killed in an automobile accident in 1956. He grew up in Arizona and California and attended the Manual Arts High School in Los Angeles. He then moved to New York City and began his training in earnest at the Art Students League under Thomas Hart Benton. Looking back on his schooling there in later years, Pollock recognized how important his classes with Benton had been, because they touched off a violent reaction against his teacher's ideas. Benton had started out from a vaguely avant-garde position, but by the time Pollock came to him in 1929 he had become one of the staunchest representatives of that revolt against modern art which so curiously coincided with the Great Depression; he was one of the painters of the "American Scene." After 1930 that revolt was headed by a "triumvirate" composed of Benton, John Steuart Curry and Grant Wood. This movement in the direction of regional realism—unlike the movement typified by Hopper, which was actuated by social ideals—was thoroughly reactionary, and not in painting alone. Its guiding aims were predominantly chauvinistic. Thomas Craven, one of the leading spokesmen of American Regionalism, has described it as at last breaking free of the "emasculated tradition of the French modernist movement." According to him, the Triumvirate put an end to "American subservience to foreign cultural fashions." [50]

Benton, then, had passed from his early experiments in near-abstraction—he had studied in Paris—to an American imitation of the Old Masters, of Tintoretto for example, in the name of a reactionary movement which aimed at steeping everything in a typically American atmosphere. Benton, however, was unquestionably a strong personality. "My work with Benton," said Pollock, "was important as something against which to react very strongly, later on; in this, it was better to have worked with him than with a less resistant personality who would have provided a much less strong opposition. At the same time, Benton introduced me to Renaissance art." [51] To Benton, too, Pollock owed a particular mode of composition, clearly visible in some of his early works, like **The Flame** of 1937; this consisted in inserting objects in a kind of curved space animated with a certain vibration. The same picture also testifies to Pollock's early interest in Mexican painting, which after 1935 had shown considerable power and originality, thanks largely to José Clemente Orozco. Unlike Benton, Orozco—and nearly all the Mexican painters—practised a vivid form of realistic Expressionism which served as an extremely effective vehicle of social ideas. No wonder that Pollock found the Mexican idiom of expression to his liking and used it to arrive at a progressive distortion of form which, with him, as it so happened, was steadily carried further and further away from the representation of visual reality.

It was probably through Expressionism that Pollock intuitively grasped the significance of Picasso's painting as it developed after 1937. **Guernica** taught him to dominate a dramatic urge, while channeling its full force into the picture; it showed him above all the possibilities inherent in the psychological expression of form; it taught him, that is, to make the most of the dramatic repercussions of emotional experience on the consciousness. What he then learned from Picasso became the point of departure of his subsequent work, which owed at the same time an appreciable debt to Surrealism. Something has already been said in an earlier chapter of the probable influence of Masson, but the painter he always admired most, together with Picasso, was Miró; for this we have Pollock's own word. There was another living example, nearer at hand, which he also took to heart; that of Arshile Gorky, who had arrived at an automatic delineation of the image which may have been helpful to him. At the same time, the persistence of an expressionistic type of formal modulation, now evolving in a wholly abstract direction, may well have had an influence on Pollock, through the medium, for example, of Willem de Kooning's work. By now, of course, Pollock's own personality had come into play with the full force of its originality, and these outside influences must not be magnified into anything more than what they actually were: momentary exchanges between several contemporary artists whose cultural background had a good many points in common, but whose later lines of development tended to diverge more and more.

By about 1944 Pollock was showing a lively interest in the density and richness of texture, in pictures like **Gothic,** where he seemed to be testing it out as a medium of emotional concentration. From 1947 on, his interest in the texture of his materials was unflagging; on those materials, on their textures, he founded the autonomy of his pictorial language. Going beyond Surrealism, which by now was no more to him than a superseded cultural influence, through a masterly intensification of surfaces Pollock succeeded in creating a new kind of painting—painting with a new meaning. After the relatively small-sized pictures of his early maturity (for example **Shimmering Substance** of 1946), with their essentially pictorial effects of texture, Pollock gradually increased the range and emphasis of his expressive power in really large-scale compositions, whose magnitude gave full scope to the compulsion that drove him to create, within the greatly extended dimensions of the picture surface, something astonishingly new: an autonomous object, constituted not only by the work itself but by the identity established between the artist and the work. And the seemingly informal construction of the surfaces is in reality organized along the strictest lines, determined of course not by a geometric schema or a rigorous distribution of forms, but by an order created by the gesture and movement of the hand, by a technical skill which, though anything but orthodox, is nevertheless accurate and precise. Indeed it is difficult to realize the full extent of Pollock's skill and precision in the handling of his materials until one has taken the trouble to examine his intricate signwork and superimposed coats of paint from close at hand.

Mark Tobey (1890). Calligraphic, 1959. (7½×13″) Galerie Jeanne Bucher, Paris.

The violence with which these great surfaces were created—though sometimes with an intimate felicity in the handling of color—reflects the human condition of the artist himself, restless and tormented, yet at bottom still a romantic. The repudiation of an abstract ideal of beauty, to make way for the organic presence of the materials, indicates both a revolt and an aspiration—and of course implies a new attitude toward painting. "My painting," wrote Pollock, "does not come from the easel. I hardly ever stretch my canvas before painting. I prefer to take the unstretched canvas to the hard wall or floor. I need the resistance of a hard surface. On the floor I am more at ease. I feel nearer, more a part of the painting, since this way I can walk around it, work from the four sides and literally be in the painting." [52] The painting, as Pollock was well aware, has a life of its own in which it is up to the painter to participate. "It is only when I lose contact with the painting that the result is a mess. Otherwise there is pure harmony, an easy give-and-take, and the painting comes out well." [52] It is a whole world teeming with life in which the artist participates—not a projection but an identification of his being. He covers the support with drippings and splashings of color, enriched with enamel and aluminum paints. The state of mind here is still a romantic one, and the concept of the image, in its rhythmic fragmentation, is still expressionistic. The painter fills every void with his active presence, and that excited presence vitalizes the physical structure of the materials with molecular energy.

Some of his black-and-white pictures of 1951 and 1952 show the transition toward a more fully realized constructive synthesis, successfully transcending both automatism and calligraphy. Then color made its reappearance, intense as never before, and yet controlled, notwithstanding the seething turmoil of the texture. And pure molecular vitality gave way, as in **Blue Poles** for example, to a kind of evocative figuration, an allusion to something external, fleetingly glimpsed but nevertheless present. It is not an appearance, however, reproduced in **trompe-l'œil** beneath the textural vibrations of the picture surface, but rather an insight into the possibility of recasting certain elements in such a way as to signify a new manner of participation. Pollock's premature death at the age of forty-four may well have interrupted his career at a point particularly rich in promise. But the body of work that remains is a magnificent achievement in itself. Its influence has not been limited to the United States alone, but has stimulated artists of all countries, helping them to broaden their outlook and enrich their expressive means.

Nothing could form a greater contrast to Pollock's painting than that of Mark Tobey. It is, first of all, the outcome of an appreciably longer evolution (Tobey was born in 1890, Pollock in 1912); secondly, of an esthetic essentially different from that of any other American painter. Tobey cannot be described as either an abstract expressionist or an action painter. He is supposed to be the leader of a so-called Pacific School; actually no such school exists. It is true that he teaches in an art school at Seattle; but an art school is not an art movement, nor has Tobey himself ever had any intention of launching a movement. The fact is that his painting defies classification; his style and his aims are wholly personal. When we come to appraise Pollock's work, we realize that it is—so to speak—the quality product of a particular conjunction of cultural and social forces which are thoroughly American, even though his painting has its rightful place, as we have said, in an international context. This is not the case with Tobey. His painting is undefinable in strictly national terms; given the same influences (and these are not American influences), it would probably have followed much the same line of development in any other part of the world. Yet it did in fact develop in the United States and the circumstance cannot be left out of account. "Without appealing to any common symbol or familiar shape," as Thomas B. Hess has written of Tobey, "the artist invites us into a mystical contemplation of pure action, not for its sake alone, but to realize an almost religious duality of microscopic strength and giant frailty." [53] Pure action, that is, taken as a value, but not objectivized nor even engaged in a violent effort of participation. Tobey attaches importance to the act of painting, but only in so far as it enables him to exteriorize his sensory impulses which, for all their mystical savor (and their attachment, therefore, to a type of reality), are not automatic; they are, rather, the projection of what the artist himself calls the secret unity and reciprocity of everything that goes to make up the inner life.

What conception of time and space is implied by a painting which aims at the exteriorization of these impulses? Time and space as conceived here obviously do not depend on any chronological or physical distribution of picture elements. Obviously too, for Tobey as for so many of the American and European artists of whom we have spoken, the picture space can no longer be assimilated either to the time sequence of the Cubists, to the psychological dimension of the Surrealists, or to the emotional agitation of the Expressionists. Tobey himself has experimented with a space of his own, quiescent but traversed by movement and steeped in color vibrations; a space which does not have any logical pattern and which, in some ways, might be likened to that of Henri Michaux, were it not so much more organic than his, a vivid presence necessary to the life of forms and their metamorphoses, their transformation into signs, into pictorial calligraphy.

Tobey has traveled widely and has lived outside the United States for long periods of his life. While on the one hand he has always looked to Europe, like his fellow artists, and has lived in France and made a long stay in England before the war, on the other he graphically expressed his peculiar outlook when he once said that America should be like a two-faced Janus, with one face turned toward Europe and the other toward the Orient. His own travels in the Far East have been decisive in the formation of his mature style. In 1934 at Shanghai the dynamic felicity of Oriental calligraphy made an impression on him which has never worn off. For Tobey, however, it is well to repeat what has already been said in connection with Franz Kline (though of course no parallel can be drawn between the two artists): if he takes an interest in Oriental calligraphy, it is only because of the pictorial equivalents it can give him, and not because of the literary

Bradley Walker Tomlin (1899-1953). Number 10, 1953. (72×102″) Munson Williams Proctor Institute, Utica, N.Y.

concepts implicit in Chinese signs. The fact remains, nevertheless, that he has gone into the matter more deeply perhaps than any other modern Western painter. He has not only mastered the external techniques of Chinese sign-writing, but has penetrated into the space-creating rhythms of those signs. "More than mere technical procedures," as Leon Kochnitzky has said, "China has given him an ethical philosophy of painting." [54] From a Chinese painter, Teng Kwei, Tobey gleaned some of the secrets not merely of calligraphy but of Chinese painting itself. He learned how to handle Oriental brushes; above all, his eyes were opened to the hidden meanings of Oriental painting.

Tobey came back from the Far East to England and there, in 1935, painted one of his most famous works, **Broadway Norm,** resorting in it for the first time to what has been called "white writing." A variety of experimental work followed thereafter, and other influences may have affected him; his interest, for example, in the painting of the Eskimoes and the North American Indians has been remarked on. **Broadway Norm** was a wholly abstract work. It was followed by the government-sponsored figurative painting with a social bias which Tobey, like many other American artists, did in the thirties for the Federal Art Project. Gradually, however, he pursued the path opened up by **Broadway Norm,** reaffirming the full pictorial autonomy of the sign and arriving at the magnificent paintings of recent years, with their gorgeous tissue of vibrant colors, no longer suggestive, however, of lurking mysteries. For in Tobey's work today everything conveys a real and tangible meaning, nothing is left to the vagaries of sensations; his brushwork is not automatic and responds compliantly to the artist's intentions. Light too is a real and tangible element, serving not to enlarge the confines of an unknown space but to intensify the organic structure of signs and forms. If symbols and allusions linger on at times, they act as references to an initial theme, to a motif of inspiration which may have stemmed from visual reality and may, in its pictorial transposition, preserve its original significance, but not its original appearance. What counts is the sincerity and truthfulness of the artist's attitude, his will to communicate, his inquiry into a spiritual reality which tends to absorb and unify all other realities, even that of action, which Tobey, unlike many other American painters, is unwilling to regard as the only concrete reality; he regards it, rather, as a possibility or means of expressing the adventure of life in pictorial terms.

Bradley Walker Tomlin also held aloof from Expressionism of any kind. His painting too has been called calligraphic. In reality his formal modulations are utterly different from those of calligraphy, because, for one thing, he develops a rhythm of positive and negative forms both on the surface and in depth. His signs—white, black, green or blue—are more than a superadded calligraphy; they form an integral part of the composition and of a sequence of spatial elements which, in many of his works, allow an underlying cubist structure to show through unmistakably. Tomlin had studied at the Académie Colarossi in Paris and was thoroughly familiar with Cubism and its possibilities of development. This in no way detracts from his originality. Tomlin in fact contributed much to the breakthrough of post-war American painting, up to his death in 1953. From 1946 on, discarding every figurative reference, he pointed the way toward the integration of signs into space, giving them movement and animation not by any show of violence but by their dislocation and directioning on the picture plane. Violence, or anything approaching it, was absolutely foreign to Tomlin's attitude toward painting, nor did he place any faith in action as a means of cementing the artist's relationship with his work. He trusted rather to the steady control of form, to the possibilities of organizing it logically within a network of interrelated lines and colors. His colors indeed seem almost traditional, with their delicate refinements of texture and flashing gleams of light, which convey a satisfying sense of real depth and enhance the linear rhythms of their intricate surface patterns.

A long stay in Paris has unquestionably influenced the color handling of Sam Francis, one of the outstanding American painters of the younger generation. Space in his painting is not organized on cubist lines, but develops quite otherwise out of a maze of forms which always lead the eye on to fresh discoveries. The painter seems to take a peculiar delight in abandoning himself to the adventure of the moment, as his hand and brush trace out its devious path.

Sam Francis (1923). Blue and Black, 1954. (77×51½″) E.J. Power Collection, London.

Mark Rothko (1903). White and Greens in Blue, 1957. (102×82″) Private Collection, New York.

Mark Rothko (1903). Red, White and Brown, 1957. (99½×81¾″) Kunstmuseum, Basel.

And his delight seems to reach its peak in an exhilarating shower of color cascading over the whole surface of the picture, sparkling with vagrant lights, with transparent eddies of blue, red and yellow. This art exemplifies the modern will to participate in the life of the painting itself, in the vibrant glitter of the colors. Appearances notwithstanding, these colors are not a pictorial transposition of naturalistic lighting (and the parallels drawn with Impressionism are absurd); these are inward colors, never without a certain tremulous delicacy even when in the grip of emphatic textural rhythms and fragmented forms. It is a delicacy, however, which has nothing traditional about it, for these color-forms are ceaselessly disintegrated and modified by the impact of irresistible rhythms and successive waves of color. Sam Francis studied under Clyfford Still, but his painting seems to retain nothing of his master's rigor or indeed anything of his teaching. Today he seems to have grown less violent, less aggressive, perhaps because he is unconcerned with expressing any convictions or laying down any rigorous principles. His painting is meant to demonstrate nothing but its own felicity.

Mark Rothko and Adolph Gottlieb were together the founders, in 1935, of the group known as The Ten. Today their work has little or nothing in common, yet both are actuated by the desire to present the painting, built up wholly in terms of surfaces, as a reality that cannot be eluded. Gottlieb studied under John Sloan and Robert Henri, two of the leading representatives of American realism in the first decade of this century. After a period of expressionistic realism, Gottlieb worked out for himself an art of forms devoid of naturalistic references—forms intended not as an equivalent of reality but as a true and actual reality in their own right. A statement of his aims, written by the artist himself, figures in the catalogue of the New Decade exhibition held in New York in 1955. "I am... concerned with the problem of projecting intangible and elusive images that seem to me to have meaning in terms of feeling. The important thing is to transfer the image to the canvas as it appears to me, without distortion. To modify the image would be to falsify it, therefore I must accept it as it is. My criterion is the integrity of the projection." [55] And since these images convey an emotion, they have a significance of their own, which they would lose if they represented anything else besides those emotions.

The painting of Mark Rothko is very far removed from both action painting and abstract expressionism, which he regards as a romantic outpouring; and any such thing is foreign to his character and temperament. His robust originality, the new problems he has raised and solved, make him one of the unquestioned leaders of contemporary American painting. The subtle complexity of his color handling also differentiates him from those European tendencies which concentrate expression in the physical properties of the painter's medium. However, as Sam Hunter has noted, "it is the paradox of Rothko's paintings, as with all serious modern art, that they achieve their maximum spiritual tension at those moments when they most strongly assert their material existence." [56] Rothko arrives at the complete identification of himself and his spiritual world with the elaboration of his color surfaces, whose intensity is increased by the very freedom with which he handles them; they are never compressed or locked in a schema, but flow freely, vitally, rhythmically over his great forms. These surfaces are not color patches; they are not punctuated with signs or reduced to their organic essentiality, but are skillfully determined in a certain way, with a regular beat, which gives them a simple, sturdy architecture from which every superfluous element and movement have been eliminated, with all emotion concentrated in a uniform luminosity.

Rothko's painting is the outcome of an unremitting process of purification. Born in Russia, he came to the United States at the age of ten, later studied art and has shared in all the vicissitudes of American painting in the past few decades. Figurative to begin with, leaning frankly toward Expressionism, he then passed on to a free interpretation of certain aspects of Surrealism, which in his case acted rather as a cultural tonic than as a purely formal lesson. With Motherwell, Gottlieb and Newman, he helped to found the Subjects of the Artist School in New York, whose activities contributed to the flowering of mid-century painting in the United States. Gradually, as he got into his stride, Rothko simplified every external and every compositional element in the extreme, exploring the possibility of working out a pure luminous form. "The progression of a painter's work," he declared in 1952, "as it travels in time from point to point, will be toward clarity: toward the elimination of all obstacles between the painter and the idea, and between the idea and the observer. As examples of such obstacles, I give (among others) memory, history or geometry, which are swamps of generalization from which one might pull out parodies of ideas (which are ghosts) but never an idea in itself. To achieve this clarity is, inevitably, to be understood." [57] Since then he has set great store by this will to clarity and communication. His painting cannot dispense with the values of a human presence, even though it creates a kind of heraldic mythology which rules out certain human conventions like geometry, memory with its host of lingering echoes and associations, and even history when regarded as a general succession of events.

Mark Rothko (1903). Brown and Black on Plum, 1958. (80×82″) Franz Meyer Collection, Zurich.

The purifying order of Rothko's art, standing as it does at the opposite pole to action painting, might tend to resolve itself into a picture space conceived entirely in terms of two-dimensional surfaces, were it not for the clean separation of one form from another, which ensures recession in depth. So that even when the artist seems to reach a constant plane of emotive reality, actually—notwithstanding the apparent regularity of his rhythmically ordered surfaces—he remains very far from any immutable, crystallized reality of the Neo-Plastic type. Forms are regular and well defined, but orchestrated and delimited by the gesture, deliberately marked off by the hand that lays them in, and not structuralized in a closed space. They are repeated, in the vertical plane of his large-scale pictures, but varied in their chromatic quality and in the intensity of their lighting, and susceptible to every impinging force and contact. The artist's presence in the work, in the material elaboration of form, is not instinctive (Rothko has left automatism behind), but is pondered over and nurtured through his technical mastery of his medium, which enables him to individuate the quality of light in its most emotive dimension, corporeal but not atmospheric, not only in bright and vivid blues, reds and yellows, but in darker tones of brown and even black. Bathed in this light, forms expand to the limit the gesture imposes on them and imply even then a possible extension beyond that limit.

Nothing could be further from the reckless exuberance of abstract expressionism. The novelty of Rothko's painting in the American art world lies above all in the peculiarity of his attitude: it is possible to express anything when the definition of forms is carried to such a pitch of pristine clarity and purity. From vitality of texture, the artist passed on to vitality of form, reasserting its structural and emotive validity, re-exploring the innermost veins of emotional expression, and re-establishing contact with the world. With Rothko the art of painting has come again to draw aside the veil and communicate, to accept and reject as in every human exchange, to sort out and order, and to lift itself to the level of a mythic monumentality, irresistibly appealing in the beauty of its colors and perfect in the metrical harmony of its language.

HANS HOFMANN · WILLEM DE KOONING · PHILIP GUSTON
CLYFFORD STILL · JAMES BROOKS · ASGER JORN
ERNST WILHELM NAY · KAREL APPEL · GER LATASTER

Hans Hofmann is the dean of American abstract painters. Born in Germany in 1880, he studied art in Munich and then accepted a teaching post there. He moved in the avant-garde circles of the Munich art world in the days before the First World War and made several stays in Paris which counted for much in the formation of his style. In 1930 he went to the United States, where he has carried on his teaching work; for him, in fact, teaching has always gone hand in hand with the practice of his art. Hofmann, then, both by background and schooling, has close ties with German Expressionism, and above all with the transition from figurative to abstract Expressionism brought about in Germany by the Blaue Reiter group. It is tempting to link up his intense colors with those of the Fauves; actually, the relations that determine his color modulations are those of German Expressionism in its second, non-figurative phase. Perhaps the closest tie is with Kandinsky. Yet, stimulating though these contacts and influences have been, Hofmann has successfully assimilated them and created a style of his own.

Hofmann today is one of the major representatives of American Abstract Expressionism. But this designation has come to embrace too wide a field of experiment, too various and even conflicting in its results, for it to indicate any clearly defined line of research. Neither Pollock nor De Kooning, for example, owes any particular debt to Hofmann; nor is the latter in any way beholden to them. Hofmann's abstractionism has developed on an entirely different plane; unlike them, he shows little concern either with the molecular vitality of the materials employed or with the rugged violence of color textures. His technique, or anyhow the general handling of his medium, seems to be largely traditional. His really revolutionary departure lies in his way of breaking up the usual conformation of planes and abolishing the restrictive limits of the canvas; above all, in the "push and pull" (as Hofmann himself calls it), the drives and counter-drives, which do away with perspective recession and create a new kind of spatial depth correlative with mass. So that the painter is no longer able to delineate this space, he can only intensify it emotionally. And emotive expression with Hofmann being based entirely on color, the result is that depth is indicated solely by color vibrations and the clash of colored forms.

The connection with visual reality is by no means broken off altogether. He is conscious of its presence and value, but never allows it to interfere in the modulation of form, which always remains autonomous. Nor does he allow it to affect his colors, which fall in line with the modern tradition of abstract and arbitrary color handling that goes back to Van Gogh.

This knack of achieving violent clashes and outbursts of color (and achieving them with a finesse of technique that says much for his sensitive control of his medium), combined with his consistent efforts to overcome the cramping physical limits of the painter's art, represents one of Hofmann's most fruitful contributions to the post-war flowering of American painting. And here too his teaching activity has been a factor of prime importance; his painting classes are famous, and undoubtedly, both from the practical and theoretical points of view, Hofmann has shared decisively in defining the new idiom of artistic expression that has come to the fore in the United States. The general problem of Abstract Expressionism, however, is highly

Hans Hofmann (1880). The Magician, 1959. (59½×44⅞″) Owned by the Artist.

complex and exceeds the scope of a single artist's work. The term itself is misleading, for the new Expressionism has nothing in common with German Expressionism; it is, on the contrary, a typically American phenomenon. Rather than indicating any common line of research, it merely denotes a general similarity of outlook, a common attitude toward painting, a common desire to push beyond its traditional limits into unexplored territory.

There came a time when the conflict of Figurative versus Abstract ceased to be a real problem. De Kooning could build up his **Women** through violent distortions of form and texture; yet the resulting images cannot be called either symbols or descriptions. Clyfford Still felt the need to reduce forms to their bare essentials and to emphasize the simplest relationships of reds, blacks and grays, without any trace of a figure or any digression into light effects. Philip Guston, on the contrary, dissolved the physical aspect of his materials into beautifully sustained rhythms of color and light. We have already touched on the distinction to be drawn between the objectivization of the work of art, characteristic of the European artist, and the resolute and active participation in it which is characteristic of the American artist. The latter attitude may be said to stem from a deep sense of moral values; this is by no means lacking in European artists but in American art it is tinged with a latent Puritanism that makes it much more compelling.

Hans Hofmann (1880). Rising Sun, 1958. (59⅞×72″) Kootz Gallery, New York.

Willem de Kooning (1904). Gotham News, 1955. (78¾×118¼″)
Albright Art Gallery, Buffalo, N.Y. Gift of Seymour H. Knox.

Sometimes, as with Barnett Newman, the more rigorous American approach results in clean-cut surface patterns which, while recalling the geometric order of Neo-Plasticism, actually derive from an expressionistic accentuation of textures and tones.

These artists have gone so far as to deplore the "decline" of Western art, which set in, we are told, with Monet. This contention may seem like mere bravado, but from their standpoint it is comprehensible. They regard painting as charged with a higher mission than hedonism and the gratification of the senses; contemplation and introspection are not enough, the work of art calls for a total engagement of the moral conscience. This is the point of view—certainly a valid one—adopted by the artists representative of the movement usually referred to as Abstract Expressionism. This credo of theirs is not of course an end in itself and has already been variously interpreted, especially by the younger men. It is in fact the youngest adherents to Abstract Expressionism who have taken the most drastic and rigorous line of approach, and made the most brutal assault on texture and images. But they do not seem as yet to have made any really original contributions of their own. Or perhaps it is too early to pass judgment on men whose lot it has been to succeed a generation of artists of the stature of Pollock and De Kooning.

Willem de Kooning (1904). Merritt Parkway, 1959. (89¾×80⅜″) Courtesy Sidney Janis Gallery, New York.

Philip Guston (1913). To Fellini, 1958. (68⅞×74″) Private Collection, New York.

To many observers the most valid contribution of the new generation of American painters is to be sought for not among those who emulate the established masters of action painting but in the Neo-Dadaism of Rauschenberg, Jasper Johns and other members of a group which has little in common with the Expressionists.

In any case, it would be a grave mistake to underestimate either the quality of the works created by what may now be considered the great generation of contemporary American artists, or the impact of their painting in Europe. Many of the younger European artists have welcomed the lesson to be learned from America. A new dimension had to be given to history, and American painting has succeeded in creating one which reflects the artist's abiding sense of the moral implications of his activity. The quest still continues today, now that informal painting has developed along parallel lines. It too is pregnant with new meaning and has taken up a position outside every pre-existing tradition of painting. These investigations have never resulted in any uniformity. Abstract Expressionism stands above all for an attitude toward painting, a moral attitude; it is not a school with a well-defined program. All the artists who have taken part in it have sought and found personal solutions to the problems of form and space. The great lesson of Abstract Expressionism has been this possibility of individualizing a work of art, even if it shares a moral imperative and a sense of history common to many.

One of the outstanding personalities of contemporary American painting is Willem de Kooning; the importance of his achievement is perhaps only surpassed by that of Pollock's. Born in Rotterdam, he studied art in Holland and Belgium and emigrated to the United States as early as 1926. It is difficult to decide whether the expressive violence he cultivates today stems from European Expressionism in general or from Dutch and Belgian Expressionism in particular. The scrupulous care he lavishes on color and color contrasts, even when his textural effects are at their most tumultuous, together with his ability to step up the tonal value even of his blacks, would seem to invalidate the latter hypothesis; the more so in view of the somber, earthy tonalities, so different from his own, of the Dutch and Belgian Realists and Expressionists. The same is true of his monumental vision: the grandeur of his images, straining the physical limits of the canvas, whether recognizable figures or forms unrelated to visual reality, have nothing in common with the bleak monumentality of Permeke's figures. If De Kooning brought with him from Holland anything instrumental in the rise of American painting, it is something that present-day painting has now completely absorbed and transformed: the precise formulation of time and space in the composition, precise in spite of the apparent (and necessary) disorder of the formal rhythms. It is not for nothing that Holland was the birthplace of Mondrian, of the painter who proved capable of destroying spatial depth and recreating it entirely on the surface. Even though he stands almost at the opposite pole to Mondrian, De Kooning has made the most of this radical reversal of the traditional conception of pictorial space. Certain works of his executed about 1930, representing eggs suspended in a silent, abstract and, in the last analysis, metaphysical space, not only bring to mind the problems of order tackled by Neo-Plasticism but even suggest a comparison with a much earlier Dutch painter: with the corporeal yet abstract form-light of certain cathedral interiors of Pieter Saenredam. De Kooning's artistic temperament, however, keeps him from lapsing into geometric patterning; the moral principle implicit in his art is incompatible with any rigid adherence to a pre-determined schema.

A friend of Gorky, De Kooning has undoubtedly been influenced by him. It is only fair to add, however, that that influence was reciprocal. While Gorky taught him how to transform a picture space of cubist origin into a psychological space, De Kooning opened Gorky's eyes to the full possibilities of intensifying the movement of colored forms and showed him how to render the dynamism of images autonomous. De Kooning's space, moreover, has always been more organic, more tangibly physical, because materializing, as it were, directly out of the real experience of the man himself. The transformation of his figurative style proceeded slowly, and the influences discernible in his painting are more or less the same as those to be found in that of Gorky, who, with his cultural preoccupations, advanced with a more cautious step. De Kooning is the bolder of the two, always ready to launch into an experiment, seizing on an idea and transmuting it into a personal vehicle of expression, even at the cost of trial and error.

After a frankly figurative period, during which he carried out various works for the Federal Art Project, he gradually stepped up his colors and departed from realistic imagery. The imaginative element increasingly prevailed. In some pictures executed even before 1940, probably under the influence of Miró as transmitted through Gorky, his images came to seem like projections of an inner world, of the unconscious mind; modulated psychologically, they seemed to grow with a primordial, independent life of their own. But it was only after 1944 that De Kooning fully mastered his style. Every trace of realism had vanished and so had the psychological allusions of his recent work. He had succeeded in making his painting real: anthropomorphic images lost the characterization of appearances and became the living forms of an immediate presence, indifferent to any systematic order of logic or narrative. A similar change came over his color: imaginative before, very much in the surrealist tradition, it now grew rampageous and violent, not so much suggesting space as creating it physically in the density and clash of

Clyfford Still (1904). Untitled, 1957. (113¾×160¼″) Kunstmuseum, Basel.

textures and forms. De Kooning never lost sight of the problem of reality: he proceeded to transform reality, not by adapting it to any particular formal rhythm, but by subjecting it to an aggressive violence which overthrew and recast its established order. For De Kooning too the experience of **acting** on the canvas, of bringing the full force of his will to bear on the elaboration of the work of art, has been of capital importance in fixing the meaning of this new reality. If Pollock's onslaught was directed at the painter's materials, leading him to substitute new products for the traditional pigments, De Kooning's onslaught, no less violent, has been directed at the image and, by the same token, at the space surrounding it. The action of painting has become identified with this break-up of form, and with the conviction that it is now possible to shatter and transform the accepted framework of reality.

Once he had worked out a non-figurative style, De Kooning set out to apply its principles, and the same methods of elaboration, to a figurative image. Something tragic, and at the same time deliberately ironical, seemed to preside over the creation of the series of **Women** which he began about 1950. The gigantic size of these figures gives them an exciting dynamism and monumentality, full of violence and contrasting movement. They have been called Michelangelesque, but there is nothing transcendent about them. They have the **terribilità,** the awfulness, inherent in emphatic textural effects, in thick black signs and color marks undescoring convulsive volumes, and in the arbitrary dislocation of anatomical features. Such painting as this, carried to so high a pitch of tension and contrast, reveals the precariousness of the human situation, the futility of idealization, and the impossibility of continuing to act on the human figure—even in this way—without running the risk of stifling the artist's inspiration.

James Brooks (1906). Loring, 1958. (78×66″) Collection The Chase Manhattan Bank, New York.

So after 1955 De Kooning's painting grew progressively less figurative. Massive forms embedded in the color texture came to stand for the sole reality of presence and experience, though he did not abandon the dramatic violence of his contrasts and the emphatic caesuras of rhythms obtained not by linear elements but by impetuous surges of color governed by the gesture of the hand that set them down. Intense blues, greens, reds and yellows clash and interpenetrate, dynamic forces arise on all sides and flash across the canvas; color overflows the outlines of forms with a flagrant disregard for the old principles of "finish" and "beauty." But the expressionistic drive and counter-drive of these galvanized forces differs markedly from the "push and pull" characteristic of Hans Hofmann's work, because with De Kooning texture itself is recast and its chromatic qualities are brought to light at the very moment of their elaboration, made compellingly real by their brutality and immediacy.

To Philip Guston the act of **seeing** matters more than anything else; it is realer than any reproduction of appearances. The resistance of his materials to the painter's efforts to cope with them already represents a dramatic element that cannot but make itself felt in the finished work. But the drama implicit in Guston's painting is an inner one, not so vividly exteriorized as that of De Kooning; the luminous quality of Guston's colors, moreover, is a sufficient safeguard against any excesses. His forms develop within an unfaltering rhythm of harmonies and contrasts, shaped rather by a modulation than by an opposition of color textures, which, instead of being convulsed and lacerated, are coolly intensified in depth upon depth of pigment—never thickened, however, to excess. In some ways this painting might seem closer to the informal experiments of the Europeans than to the vivacity of American Abstract Expressionism, but such is not really the case; the moral principle behind it, bespeaking presence as against objectivization, sets it apart from the Europeans.

After a period of figurative painting with a social message, Guston moved into the non-objective sphere as a result of long meditations on ways and means of intensifying form and light. He thus came to steep his pictures in an almost impressionistic luminosity, or better, in a luminosity which melts and blurs the outlines of forms, much as it does in Monet's last works. The parallel must not be pressed too far, however. Guston uncompromisingly repudiates not only appearances but "preassumed images or ideas of picture structure." [58] Sensations offer, he feels, unlimited possibilities of development, and he embodies them continuously in the rhythm and movement of color texture—rhythms worked out afresh in each picture on an abstract plane where memory and the present moment become one, as they do to a certain extent in the work of the European informal painters. This presence, which is also that of memory, represents Guston's most original contribution to American painting; and for the artist himself, as he has said, it is a means of regaining his identity anew in each work, of re-experiencing the presence of his ego in a unique moment of time.

The painting of Clyfford Still reflects an altogether different aspect of Abstract Expressionism. A firmer control over form and content and a greater detachment, once the artist's presence has been asserted and the picture finished, give his work a peculiar rigor admitting of no evasions. Here too the clash of dynamic forces quickens the canvas, but these rhythms fail to set up a surface tension; they seem, on the contrary, to well up from within, from the substance of the texture itself, from harshly wrought tracts of pigment, through which other images and other color textures show through. Still's approach to painting may be instinctive, but in the elaboration of the work he leaves nothing to chance. Even more important to him than the act of seeing, as he has said, is the sense of feeling himself within the picture, which he regards as a self-revelation. Everything about it is therefore concrete, for he identifies the painting with his own sense of responsibility with respect to history; the time for "illustrating outworn myths or contemporary alibis" [59] is past.

De Kooning's handling of color probably influenced the early work of James Brooks, who for a long time delighted in rich, full-bodied tonalities. Then a change came over them: progressively attenuated and simplified, they were made to emphasize a more dramatic flow of movement. In Brooks too, however, it is possible to detect a certain objectivization, a certain detachment

Ernst Wilhelm Nay (1902). Yellow and Purple, 1959. (63¾×51¼″) Eberhard Kemper Collection, Essen.

from the work, while his rhythms are left to evolve freely; indeed, sometimes they are left entirely to chance, for, as the artist says, "the painting surface has always been the rendez-vous of what the painter knows with the unknown, which appears on it for the first time."[60]

These artists so strikingly different from one another in many ways, yet all representative of what Clement Greenberg has so aptly called "American Type Painting," have made a genuinely original contribution to the enrichment of the painter's means of expression. Men like Tworkov, Stamos and Marca-Relli, in addition to those already mentioned, and not forgetting such younger artists as Grace Hartigan, Joan Mitchell and Helen Frankenthaler, have done more than produce works of the highest quality, comparable to the best being done today; they have created, for the first time in American history, a new art consciousness.

Asger Jorn (1914). Unlimited, 1959-1960. (18⅛×21⅝″) Galerie Rive Gauche, Paris.

When we turn from the United States to Europe, we see that there the recent developments of Expressionism have retained many features of the German and Nordic Expressionism of pre-war days: violent distortions of form, intensification of color and light, and the "literary" program that often goes with them. There has, of course, been an effort in some quarters to break with the past and explore the new paths that have been opened up. Nay's forms, for example, juxtaposed in the guise of colored disks, while preserving a vivacity with intimations of violence, are altogether autonomous with respect to the forms of the visual world. After being influenced by German Expressionism—as was only natural—Nay moved on to an organization of space in which the lessons of Post-Cubism certainly counted for something. But once he had ceased to reproduce real elements, this space lost its descriptive character and his painting acquired an evenness of rhythm which is utterly foreign to the spasmodic violence of Expressionism. The artist carefully controls the disposition of his forms, always assembling them with an eye to harmony and heightens their effectiveness by intensifying their colors.

The working out of an abstract idiom of expression has unquestionably been one of the master-strokes of modern art. But the results, in the case of some artists who have adopted this idiom, are not necessarily non-figurative. In many sectors of European painting today there is talk of a new figuration. Actually the terms under discussion are not clear enough. If by a return to figuration is meant something similar to the experiments of Dubuffet, well and good; this may be the right path. But if, on the other hand, such a return is to be made by way of Expressionism pure and simple, in a realistic key, then obviously we are being led astray; this would be going entirely against the grain of contemporary painting. There are, admittedly, cases which show that a new figurative art based on Expressionism, but shaped above all by surrealist influences, can achieve valid results; the fact remains that the evolution of pictorial taste today seems to be oriented in an entirely different direction.

Jorn, Appel, Corneille and Alechinsky numbered among the founders of the Cobra group; the name is composed of the sigla denoting Copenhagen, Brussels and Amsterdam, Jorn being a Dane, Appel a Dutchman, and Corneille and Alechinsky Belgians. The group has undoubtedly represented a positive element in the post-war European art world, even though its four leading members can no longer be said to have anything in common. Corneille, who lives in Paris, now practises a sophisticated type of abstract painting with an objective distribution of forms, as if they were real objects, rhythmically patterned on the picture plane and in depth, in a way that connotes a study of cubist space. Alechinsky seems to lean toward the solutions of informal painting, but does so with an originality that lies above all in his faculty of intensifying his color textures; his most recent works betray no hint or trace of the figurative. Karel Appel, on the other hand, has by no means rejected figurative painting; but his are experimental figurations, worked out anew in each successive picture. A congenital violence of temperament charges his colors and textures with an almost physical bulk and energy; densely caked pigments build up anthropomorphic images, horror-stricken faces bathed in sanguinary hues. Yet his compositional procedures are wholly abstract, the more so in view of the primordial importance he attaches to texture. Some of the same strenuous concern for physical energy is present in the

Karel Appel (1921). Bright Sunshine, 1960. (51¼×76¾″) Collection of Madame Niomar M. S. Bettencourt, Paris.

color textures of Ger Lataster, which dissolve every semblance of real images. His dynamic rhythms and violently clashing blues, blacks, reds and yellows might seem to approximate to the work of certain American painters like De Kooning and Brooks, were it not that his forms are more frankly objectivized, more external than internal, and very definitely stem from a European tradition which, by way of Expressionism, goes back as far as Delacroix.

Surrealism, automatism and the psychological formulation of images have been all-important for Asger Jorn, yet at the same time he owes a debt to Expressionism in general and, by virtue of a certain intellectualism, to Munch in particular. His painting, while at first sight it may seem fairly similar to Appel's, is more intensely charged with myths, with the figments of an unreal world, and is also more automatic. His monstruous figurations, however, are always built to the human scale, or anyhow to the normal scale of human perception. Jorn has recently gone in for some curious experiments, repainting or touching up old pictures in the naturalistic or academic vein, mostly landscapes, of no artistic value, picked up in bric-à-brac shops. He christened them **Modifications,** and in a recent showing of them he wrote as follows in the catalogue: "With this exhibition I propose to raise a monument in honor of bad painting. Personally I enjoy it more than good painting..." The humor and whimsy of the Surrealists have not died out.

Ger Lataster (1920). La côte se défend, 1959. (55⅛×45¼") Paul Facchetti Collection, Paris.

JEAN DUBUFFET · ALBERTO BURRI · ANTONIO TÁPIES

10

In a chapter of his fundamental study, **Painting and Reality,** the French philosopher Etienne Gilson examines what he calls the "material cause" of the work of art and shows how the evolution of a form in a certain way corresponds to the use of a particular material. And just as there is no such thing as pure material, so there is no such thing as pure form; all the picture elements in fact are interdependent. So it is that Byzantine mosaics—always according to Gilson—took the form peculiar to the material of which they are composed, whereas Giotto's **Navicella** in St Peter's, though executed in mosaic, is actually conceived as a painting. Though it was published in 1958, Gilson's study was written several years earlier and delivered in 1955 as a series of lectures at the National Gallery of Art in Washington. So he makes no mention of the latest trends of informal art or action painting, which might have led him to amplify his principle of the "material cause" of art forms and extend its application. If it is true that Giotto's **Navicella** marks the end of mosaic art, what about Burri's burlap bags and plastics? Do they perhaps mark the end of painting? There is no ready answer to this question, because it is always hard to fix the limits of this or that form of expression in a work of art. Burri's most recent works, executed entirely in iron, seem to cross the frontiers of painting and become sculptures or bas-reliefs; yet, in reality, they are always "pictures," their spirit and dimensions are those of painting. After all, Giotto's **Navicella** is still and always the manifestation of an artistic expression, and the same is true of the materials employed by Burri. And just as Giotto dealt the death blow to mosaic art, because for the form adequate to the mosaic he substituted that of painting; so Burri, by resorting to non-traditional materials, by brazing and soldering instead of plying the painter's brush, is thereby compelled to modify both the elaboration of his forms and their mutual relationships. The expressive possibilities of matter have been explored more intensively than ever before by the artists in the forefront of the latest trends of painting. When he says, "strictly speaking there are no colors, only coloring matter," Jean Dubuffet exemplifies a whole new attitude current among artists today, who are alive as never before to the new meanings matter can acquire when the role it plays becomes so preponderant as to modify forms in the sense indicated by Gilson. From informal painting to action painting, this inquiry into the possibilities of matter has been of capital importance; it has imparted an entirely new significance to forms and to painting; formal, compositional and structural elements have been transformed, now that matter has come to play no longer a passive but an active and determinant part in the work of art. This need of a new language—of which we have already spoken at length—has also transformed what used to be considered a mere support, a mechanical medium for the transposition of ideas, and has assigned a new function to it. These are radical changes, not to be confused with the problem of enriching the picture surface solved by the Cubists in their own way, or with the shock of incongruously assembled materials which the Dadaists intended more than anything else as a means of representing a given object out of its logical context.

For the artist today matter is a present reality: it gives its measure and dimension to the gesture —and the gesture, as we have seen, is a token of reality. When matter resists, it exalts the will to action; when it gives way and recedes, it shatters the traditional limits of space and time; when it clots and coagulates, it lends a new power and effectiveness to colors. In contemporary painting matter has neither the value of an invented object nor that of an abnormal image which shocks and thus, by its very strangeness, establishes a relationship with the spectator. The images of Dubuffet, for example, are neither abnormal nor strange. They are not transformations or hoaxes, as with the Surrealists; they are forms determined by a concretion of matter answering to a principle of elaboration which, while remote from logic, is equally remote from automatism. The esthetic of informal painting—like that of any art dependent on actual materials for its expression—is not concerned with establishing a schema in which to make those materials move and act. The actual results, moreover, from one painter to another, are very different, and sometimes are even based on opposing principles. The painting of Dubuffet, for example, is unlogical, both in his **hautes pâtes** and in his subtle **Célébrations du Sol**; while underlying Burri's iron, rags and plastics is a geometrical division of surfaces, a known compositional order serving to emphasize the unknown efficacity of the materials.

But what does this extraordinary interest in matter mean? Sometimes, in lesser artists, it has a naturalistic significance; for them matter is an equivalent of representation. In contemporary painting, of course, his abstract conception of style prevents the artist from reproducing appearances outright; for a "literal" reproduction of the object, it enables him to substitute the formless presence of matter which, with its suggestive power and molecular vitality, may well retain a naturalistic significance. With other artists, matter seems to be at war with itself, with its physical qualities, almost as if trying to overcome the qualities that define it; in its extreme tenuities, in its rents and lacerations, it seems to seek its own negation. Such is the way a painter and sculptor like Fontana handles matter; he knocks holes in the paper or canvas, tears open his surfaces, leaving slits that are almost like wounds. Still other artists, disregarding the claims of a naturalistic sensibility, use matter to create a void, for the sake of its expressive value, to achieve a metaphysical indifference ruling out any clash or contrast in the picture.

This investigation into the possibilities of matter, this objectivization of a picture element on which all others depend (and even Burri's sacks, plastics and iron are still picture elements), is indicative of an outlook common to a great many artists of all countries, in Europe, Asia and America. The esthetic of informal painting and action painting owes its success to this: that it not only sets the artist free from all previous canons of form, space and time, but affords almost unlimited possibilities of acting on this old material element in a new way, of structuralizing it in surfaces, or better, even from within. To rediscover fresh possibilities of expression in matter is tantamount to establishing a parity between intuition and realization, and thus resolving the dilemma as to which has priority over the other. By attaching equal importance to unlogical premonition and to logical formal structure; by setting the same value on imaginative intuition and technique; in a word, by unifying the successive moments of time in which he acts, matter has enabled the artist not only to work back to a unique and indivisible space, i.e. a space of memory, but also to overcome the inferiority complex felt by the artist when he had to idealize his initial intuition in an image.

There is another factor to be borne in mind: contemporary painting, contemporary art in general, has increasingly stressed—has perhaps overstressed—the technics of the artist's craft. And the investigations into matter cannot help being affected by this circumstance, even though, in reaction against it, the solutions arrived at tend to be very different from those resulting from industrial techniques. While in the rationalistic period of European culture a direct relation could exist between painters and designers, today it no longer plays any part in the determination of forms. But on a deeper level designer and artist are equally affected by historical conditions; both lay increasing stress on the technical side of esthetic activity.

Because it cannot escape the predominance of technique, the painting of matter transforms its function, isolating it in a state of indifference in which logic and unlogic no longer have any meaning. Perhaps what we have here—as has been suggested in the case of Dubuffet—is a pre-logical stage, out of which everything might successively grow and evolve, the fantastic

Jean Dubuffet (1901). The Beard of Computations, 1959. (55⅛×38⅛″) Private Collection, Paris.

and anthropomorphic image peculiar to Dubuffet's painting, and also the well-nigh Neo-Plastic order of Burri's sacks. With time, then, everything may evolve out of it: such is the heritage handed down by Paul Klee, whose importance bulks larger every day. For Dubuffet, in fact, Klee is the greatest painter of the century. For the younger generation he represents a long-awaited corrective to the unrestrained extroversion of Picasso—though needless to say the younger men continue to appreciate Picasso's wonderful power of transmuting the idea immediately and directly into form, without any lag between the two moments.

Through matter the sense of visual reality still remains and justifies itself in Dubuffet's work, even though this reality gradually loses the aspect it presents to those who look at things with a superficial eye. In speaking of his **Texturologies,** the artist had this to say: "When people tell you about their liking for this or that, don't you believe a word of it. They don't know their own minds. Take the floor of the room, the landing on the stairs; they'll tell you they've never noticed them, are almost unaware of their existence. In the field of their consciousness this may be so. But how about everything that goes on outside that field? What do they know about that? Nine-tenths of the psychic phenomena that condition our being take place outside this narrow, intermittent field." Emerging as it does from an incalculable stratification of motifs which have been deposited unconsciously in the mind in the course of a lifetime, the image is wholly irrational and liable at any moment to lose the regularity of natural or anthropomorphic definition, which is blurred and dissolved in the vibrations of matter. Starting out from the unreality of the mind, from a mysterious landscape, from a figurative extravaganza, Dubuffet

Jean Dubuffet (1901), Landscape with a Bear, 1952. (35⅞×48″) Private Collection, Paris.

Jean Dubuffet (1901). Texturology, Marmalade-Matter-Light, 1958. (38⅝×53⅝″) D.B.C. Collection, Paris.

proceeds to crystallize the image, shorn of its apparent significance and left in a state of pristine fullness that might be called organic owing to its internal mobility; then he drapes it in a serenity beyond the sphere of logic or narrative.

The terrible image of De Kooning's **Women,** as we have seen, almost succeeded in overwhelming the artist, in thwarting his voluntary participation in the life of the work. Dubuffet resolves the problem of figurative representation in an altogether different way. He never lets himself be overpowered; above all, he never lets the image stand in the way of his intentions. "Those who talk about psychological insight in connection with my portraits have failed to understand the first thing about them. These portraits were anti-psychological, anti-individualistic. The idea behind them is, that if you want to paint what is important, then even in a portrait you needn't worry much about the trivial accidents—a chubby face, a snub nose—which may make one person unlike another, nor much either about character, whether one man is sour-tempered or another more sprightly. It seemed to me that by **depersonalizing** my models, by placing them all on a very general plane as elementary human figures, I was helping to set in motion, for the picture fancier, some indefinable mechanism of imagination or stimulation, and so greatly increasing the power of the effigy." [61] Surely the real importance of a painting lies in this efficacity of the image, freed from every connection with the original visual moment which inspired it. These figures may be ironical, they are certainly not caricatural. The artist's indifference to the dramatic aspects of character excludes any possibility of the moral indictment we should inevitably expect in a caricature.

The ethic of Dubuffet's painting is of a different order: it lies in his confidence in the material capacity of painting to define an unknown world, to follow up an adventure continuously diversified. And if Dubuffet does this so successfully, the reason is that he builds up his image without relying on any preconceived ideas, without ever pausing to ask himself what it was like before or what it may become afterwards. Anything can happen, at any moment, in the process of elaborating the picture. Dubuffet's figures, which always exist, bring to mind the very changeable Trouscaillon, bogus policeman, satyr and a hundred things besides, in Raymond Queneau's novel, **Zazie dans le Métro,** an indefinable personage, sure to be present whenever the plot thickens. Banking as he does on this perpetual availability of the image, Dubuffet might seem to be in danger of falling back on literary inspiration; but his greatness as a painter, and indeed the whole ethic of his painting, lie precisely in his ability to exclude every literary reference from the work in progress. By identifying the fantastic, which may appear at any moment in a man's life, with the unforeseen developments of form and matter in the elaboration of the picture, Dubuffet creates a poem, but an exclusively pictorial poem inconceivable in any other medium of artistic expression. The only causality he accepts is that of painting and the matter that goes to its making, for his images are always "closely connected with the specific behavior of the materials employed." [62]

There might almost seem to be a contradiction between the care he lavishes on the stratification and elaboration of matter—which, logically, is a technical preoccupation—and his total indifference to any over-cultivated tradition and classification of artistic facts. In reality, his technique is never made to comply with preconceived ideas or rational schemata; his procedures, as we have said, are the very antithesis of those of industrial technology. In the picture, in the actual body of his textures, between the emotive pauses of the colors, there sometimes appear what Dubuffet himself calls "flaws." But it is precisely these elements that represent the antithesis of a pragmatic and functional technique, the negation of a definitive stabilization of pictorial procedures. "It is up to every artist to perfect his techniques," says Dubuffet; it is also the artist's duty to reject whatever comes to him at second hand, whatever has already been tried, tested and made safe. Not only techniques, but also the space and time elements of the painting, together with the antinomies inherent in the work of art, have to be worked out in compliance with the individual needs and impulses of the artist. The fact that Dubuffet has brought together a collection of "**art brut,**" of art in the raw, is significant; it testifies to his keen interest in the primordial facts of art, in artistic expression fully attained without passing through that cultural filter which all too often, without his even being aware of it, stands between the cultivated artist's imagination and his style.

By refusing to conform to any kind of system, Dubuffet's painting overcomes the antithesis between figurative and abstract which has divided modern art into two opposing camps; and in this respect it has an important lesson to bring home. Since the image, and form as well, develop in close conjunction with the material medium, and since the artist's eye and consciousness seek at the same time to grasp the value of all the things involved, whatever the extent to which they may be visible, the figurative representation of them may exist or may not exist; but the presence of the things and objects, stripped of any logical determinism, is nevertheless always perceptible, whether in the shape of a human image embodied in a kind of hieroglyph, in vague crystallizations of certain landscapes, or in the minute expansion of color patches in the **Texturologies.** In the end everything is common and everything is real, because it is all vividly spontaneous; this art is not the revelation of an extraordinary world, but the extraordinary realization of ordinary and natural phenomena. By virtue of this tranquilizing conception, Dubuffet's painting rises above the convulsive anguish which has characterized, and still characterizes, the most recent trends of art; it rises above the metaphysics and mysticism of the image, and points the way toward other, still unforeseeable solutions.

In Germany, in the recent past, as we have seen in some of Willi Baumeister's works and in the signs of Fritz Winter, painters have been concerned with acting on the body of the color textures. Today, with results squarely opposed to those of Baumeister and Winter, a whole

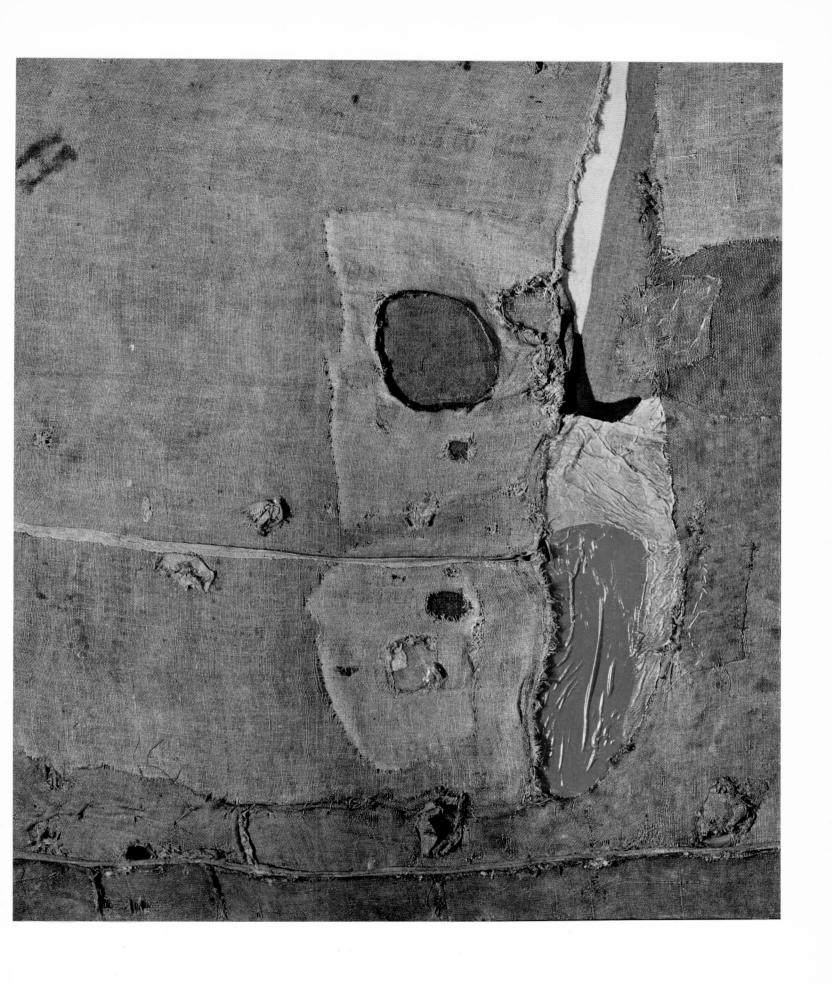

Alberto Burri (1915). Sack No. 5, 1953. (59⅛×51¼″) Owned by the Artist.

group of German informal painters has assigned the determinant role in the construction of a picture to the free elaboration of textures. One of the leading exponents of this tendency in Germany is Bernard Schultze, who has exerted an influence on several other painters. While employing intense colorations, he mixes extraneous materials with his pigments in order to heighten the effectiveness of the picture and to increase the tension of his relief surfaces. Among the younger men, mention should be made of Hans Platschek; together with Sonderborg —who, however, cannot be numbered among the **tachistes**—he seems to be the most receptive to new cultural elements, and the one best equipped to solve the problems of informal painting. The outstanding personality, however, among these painters concerned with textural elaboration and with expression more dramatic than a purely informal vision can convey, is Emil Schumacher. His painting, unlike that of Schultze, with its violent outbursts, flows rather in a vein of lyrical introspection, a lyricism that does not represent an evasion of reality but seeks to keep in permanent contact with the real presence of things and substances. For a time Schumacher relied for his expression on the negative relationship set up between different materials; such are his **Tastobjekte,** his tactile objects, made of colors and paper. His awareness of a possible reality thus originated in the tactile factualness of matter, above and beyond any figurative representation, which for him is impossible. This negative relationship ultimately became a positive one, ordering the picture surfaces and constructions in such a way as to convey a deeper will to communicate. Textures are hollowed out and incised with signs; they represent a physical equivalent of the painter's lyrical emotion, to which they give a structure without in any way lessening its imaginative impact.

We must take care not to misconstrue Alberto Burri's work: it is neither a complex of naturalistic symbols carried to their extreme limit by the use of **real** materials, nor the decadent expression of a contemplative esthetic. His painting—for painting it is, notwithstanding the absence of any reference to traditional painted surfaces—is not a phenomenon of introspection or lyricism. It simply repudiates an outworn, much-abused technique and, in its compositional process, goes beyond every known relationship of space and time. Appearances notwithstanding, and in spite of the influences readily discernible in it, Burri's work has nothing whatever to do with the experiments on materials made by the Dadaists, with the **objets trouvés** of the Surrealists, or with **collage.** It has been pointed out that his technique is similar to that of **collage:** his gunny sacks and pieces of wood, plastics and iron, require a surface to sustain them. But in the **collages** and plastic objects of the Cubists and Futurists, the materials were laid out and arranged like painted forms, and their interdependent elements created a spatial order. This is not the case with Burri. His sacks are not substituted for colors; his charred wood and plastics, with their incisions gaping like wounds, are neither symbols nor references to the unconscious. The thick stitches holding his sacks together and the bolts clinching his sheets of iron are not graphic elements: they are simply bolts and stitches, and retain their original meaning as such.

Burri's aim in employing matter as he does is to propose a reality for which there is no alternative —the only possible reality. Had he sought to invest his materials with a subversive power, had he meant them as a substitute for the traditional colors and impasto, had he aimed at building up an anti-painting, then the significance of his researches could have been discounted at the outset and the results would only have repeated results achieved before; from Picasso to Schwitters the use of shock materials has been fully exploited by modern painting. The vast possibilities of renewal opened up by Burri, however, stand on an altogether different basis. His guiding aim is to attain to the painting, to the picture, in its precise dimension, by organizing it in such a way that a free handling of matter and a free flow of compositional rhythms are accompanied by a rational scansion of space—these three elements being all of equal value, one never being subordinated to another. In one and the same work two cultural traditions coexist: on the one hand, the tradition of order, savoring of Neo-Plasticism, never preconceived and immutable however, but always elaborated in the very act of creation, and therefore never schematic; on the other, the tradition of the irrational, which leads to the unlimited opening up and repetition of forms. Burri overcomes the antinomy of these two cultures simply by

Alberto Burri (1915). Large Iron, 1960. (78¾×118¼″) Private Collection, Rome.

attaching very little importance to it, by allowing them to coexist side by side, so that their relationship in effect gives rise to a new dimension above and beyond the standard dimension of space-time.

While this is the main compositional problem, which he solves in a unique moment of time —memory uniting the past to the present and matter indicating the possibility of a future existence—the significance of the different materials employed is logically connected with this problem. His rags and sacks are not intended to voice a protest: they simply propose a reality. Burri was born at Città di Castello, a small Umbrian town where the young Raphael did one of his early works. History has its significance even for the most revolutionary of artists; to act as Burri does on such disparate materials obviously sharpens his sense of that reality of action which has been so important for contemporary art. With Burri too, then, the gesture is determinant, though he never indulges in the impetuous gesticulation of action painting; he regulates the gesture and keeps an eye on it, sustained in this by the long experience which a centuries-old tradition has stratified in his consciousness. Yet the dynamic intensity of his compositions is undeniable: vertical and horizontal rhythms equalize the tension between depth and surface; a depth often neither metaphorical nor illusionistic, but actually hollowed out of the materials themselves. None of this dynamism strains or exceeds the physical limits of the picture, however; everything develops within the four sides of the frame.

Though they are not symbols, Burri's materials have a moral significance of their own. Neither refined nor common, they are deliberately chosen among forgotten or neglected things which, no longer serving any useful purpose, have been thrown aside—battered, corroded, broken open. But, as G. C. Argan points out, "this choice of materials is not guided by any morbid taste

Antonio Tápies (1923). Raw Material with Sinuous Form, 1959. (63¾×38¼") Private Collection, Paris.

for the degraded and corrupt, though there certainly enters into it the idea that abandonment and decay do not suffice to decree and sanction the end of a thing and its irremediable exclusion from the horizon of existence." [63] Burri accordingly takes them up anew; thanks to him they surmount the threat of physical destruction; he gives them a new lease of life in which the compact organization of surfaces plays its necessary part. Skeptical, to begin with, of the expressive possibilities of the traditional means of painting, Burri has thus succeeded in restoring the organic structure of form and matter, in reinvesting them with an existential power which makes them alive and pulsating, like an organism which, from its own decay, draws new cells of life in a continuous and inevitable progression.

The rise of a new generation of Spanish painters in the period extending roughly from 1955 to 1958, when they received official recognition at the Venice Biennale, has been one of the most important developments of European art in the past few years, even apart from the intrinsic quality of the works of the individual artists. The ferment of many influences has contributed to it, from Cubism to Surrealism, together with the investigations into matter carried out by certain Italian painters like Fontana and Burri, and also, to some extent, the lessons of Vedova and Moreni. One of the first avant-garde groups was **Dau al Set** at Barcelona, which took its name from a review launched there in 1948; it included Antonio Tápies and Modesto Cuixart among its members and—until it broke up in 1953—sponsored an art largely based on Surrealism with an admixture of expressionistic elements. Another avant-garde group was formed in

Antonio Tápies (1923). Double Beige Door, 1960. (38¼×51¼") Van Abbe Stedelijk Museum, Eindhoven (Holland).

Madrid in 1957: **El Paso,** with Saura, Millares, Feito and Canogar among its members. Several writers also lent their support to these new movements: Juan Eduardo Cirlot to **Dau al Set,** José Ayllon and Manolo Conde to **El Paso.** Vicente Aguilera Cerni, a critic of international renown, has also contributed to the renewal of Spanish painting. The finest achievements of the younger Spanish painters keep to the informal esthetic, but with an expressionistic and dramatic impetus of their own, and with an original definition of the image which has no counterpart in any parallel movement elsewhere. The growth and flowering of this new painting have been promoted by an international climate favorable to the free exchange of ideas. Many of the artists just mentioned have worked for long periods in Paris, thus escaping from the isolation which, after the brilliant creations of the elder Spanish masters, from Picasso to Miró, seemed to be stifling the further growth of Spanish art.

With no intention of belittling the work of artists like Saura, Millares, Cuixart and Feito, all very young, or Canogar, the youngest of them all (he was born in 1934), it is only fair to say that the outstanding personality among the new Spanish painters is Antonio Tápies, born at Barcelona in 1923. In his early works a combination of surrealist influences, symbolic and psychological equivalents of images, and biological anthropomorphism seems to clash with an essential purity reminiscent of Miró, while the picture space still retains a descriptive function. But then, from 1953 on, Tápies struck out on an original line of research, doing away altogether with figurative symbols, hollowing color and scratching textures, eliciting abstract metaphysical intimations from spaces and surfaces. His color textures became rough and uneven, taking on the grayness of drab walls, which, however, they are not meant to reproduce; they might suggest at most the idea of a weather-beaten stone slab from which every intelligible inscription has been effaced, but which still conceals hidden ancestral meanings. The organization of his pictures has accordingly departed more and more from the dynamism of informal painting: the image is unitary and suspended in time, released from the thrall of determinism, and even from that of memory.

Critics have not failed to note how indifferent Tápies is to every form of representation. There is no reference in his painting to the experience of the senses. He almost seems intent on a sweeping negation, on blotting even his own presence out of the work; it seems, anyhow, impossible for him to surrender himself to contemplation. With Tápies—unlike Burri—matter is not meant to represent a succession of vital motifs. It is immobilized, frozen in the image, cast in a form which nullifies its capacity of organic growth. The dramatic outburst—typically Spanish—which gave rise to the picture is afterwards reduced to its negative limit, suppressed so that no disorder or disturbance may intrude on the pure and unnatural poetic moment. And yet behind it all is the negative attitude of the artist, dominated by anguish: it is not a question of escaping from a literary game of skill played in this or that mood, or of reviving the negative polemics (negative but always involving participation) of Dadaism. The artist is confronted by a choice—in other words, a moral principle—which leads him to recognize the impossibility of relying on the data of everyday experience or on those of a stable organization. The negation of the world of the senses is inevitably attended by pain and suffering. It also implies the elimination of facile pictorial effects, which might throw doubt on his relationship to experience. The color textures of Tápies are highly refined. His materials, used with great delicacy, are modulated in a few tonalities only. The resonance of his color schemes owes nothing to the traditional accords and juxtapositions—which might still be effective—of primary colors and their complementaries. It lies, rather, in the very heaviness of matter itself, from which —and in this Tápies follows the true Spanish tradition—there is no release except in death.

Conclusion

Painting is a wonderful adventure that begins anew for each generation. It holds up the mirror to man's life, not only to that of the artist but to that of the spectator, whose human condition it reflects. Painting, like every form of artistic expression, like every human activity, is an integral part of history; closely bound up with the life of our civilization, it can neither fall into decay nor rise to final perfection. It can only be conditioned, at all times, by the necessary transformations of artistic language and technique. It is a reality in itself and not the equivalent of a reality; it is the untrammeled realization of a truth which no circumstance or contingency can alter and which can never deviate from the course of history. Every work of art widens the circle of human knowledge and enriches mankind. The painting of our century has nothing to envy the painting of past centuries: it is today, as it has always been, from the graffiti of the cavemen and the masterpieces of the Renaissance to the vehement outbursts of the 20th century, the expression of man's estate, of his occupations and preoccupations, of his hopes and fears for the future. As long as men feel the need to communicate with each other, in other words as long as the human race survives, painting will stand as a supreme form of expression and communication, made supreme not only by the human imagination and emotions, but by the individual capacity of each artist to cope with the world and the power of each of us to live and express ourselves.

Forming a sequel to the previous volume dealing with the rise and development of painting in the first half of the 20th century, this book surveys and studies the evolution of painting since the Second World War. These post-war trends, which naturally have their origins in earlier developments, have continually acted or reacted on each other in a rich and stimulating interchange. Though bound to be arbitrary to some extent, as we have pointed out in the preceding pages, an attempt at classification is necessary when, as with the painting of the last fifteen years, there is no possibility of an analysis taking into account the chronological sequence of artistic events. It will be clear by now, however, that we believe in the historical continuity of modern painting, a continuity implicit in the act of painting, in artistic creation. Each artist gains his own awareness of the reality at work around him, and he in his turn works, builds, creates. We have attempted here to single out the ideas and the necessities that have made present-day painting what it is; and we have done so, not by isolating it in an ivory tower secure from the conflicts dividing men and society, but by setting it in relation to those conflicts. As we bring our study to a close, we realize—what we never doubted at the start—that any conclusions we may draw are merely tentative. The younger men take over from their elders, assimilating their lessons, but modifying and enlarging on them all the while. Here and there we have mentioned the names of young painters who have already given proof of their originality; many others could be named besides these and the story of contemporary painting could be carried further afield. In Europe and America, throughout the world, the work of yesterday is followed by that of today. As they assimilate the lessons of their masters, the younger artists work out a style of their own, pursue their own aspirations, and themselves make history.

Text References

[1] Piet Mondrian, **Plastic Art and Pure Plastic Art,** Wittenborn, New York 1945, p. 47.

[2] Marcel Proust, Preface to **Propos de Peintre, de David à Degas,** by Jacques-Emile Blanche, Paris 1919, p. XXII.

[3] André Malraux, **La Création Artistique,** Skira, Geneva 1948, p. 34.

[4] Piet Mondrian, **Plastic Art and Pure Plastic Art,** Wittenborn, New York 1945, p. 10.

[5] Ibid., p. 19.

[6] G. C. Argan, **Studi e Note,** Bocca, Rome 1955, p. 120.

[7] Quoted in Michel Seuphor, **L'Art abstrait, ses origines, ses premiers maîtres,** Maeght, Paris 1949, p. 293.

[8] Léon Degand, **Langage et Signification de la Peinture,** published by **Architecture d'Aujourd'hui,** Boulogne-sur-Seine 1956, p. 95.

[9] Auguste Herbin, **L'Art non figuratif non objectif,** Paris 1949.

[10] Hans Arp, catalogue of the Magnelli exhibition, Galerie Drouin, Paris 1947.

[11] Lionello Venturi, **Otto Pittori Italiani,** De Luca, Rome 1952, p. 11.

[12] Jean Bazaine, **Notes sur la Peinture d'Aujourd'hui,** Editions du Seuil, Paris 1953, p. 58.

[13] Ibid., p. 56.

[14] A. M., **Jean Bazaine,** Maeght, Paris 1953, p. 21.

[15] Quoted in **Dictionnaire de la Peinture abstraite,** Hazan, Paris 1957.

[16] Quoted in Achille Cavellini, **Uomo Pittore,** Edizioni della Conchiglia, Milan 1960, p. 67.

[17] Quoted in Guy Weelen, **L'Aventure poétique de Singier,** in **XXᵉ Siècle,** June 1956, p. 49.

[18] René de Solier, catalogue of the Vieira da Silva exhibition, Galerie Pierre, Paris 1955.

[19] Nicolas de Staël, excerpts from his letters to Pierre Lecuire (1949), published by Antoine Tudal in his book on De Staël, Editions du Musée de Poche, Paris 1958.

[20] Quoted by J. Grenier, **Essai sur la Peinture contemporaine,** Gallimard, Paris 1959, p. 120.

[21] Ibid., p. 89.

[22] L. Landini, **Coscienza interiore e razionalità nell'opera di De Staël,** in the catalogue of the De Staël exhibition, Galleria Civica d'Arte Moderna, Turin 1960, pp. 25-26.

[23] Dora Vallier, **Poliakoff,** Editions des Cahiers d'Art, Paris 1960, p. 20.

[24] Pierre Francastel, **Estève,** Editions Galanis, Paris 1956, p. 139.

[25] Michel Tapié, **Un Art Autre,** Editions Gabriel Giraud, Paris 1952.

[26] M. Merleau-Ponty, **Eloge de la Philosophie,** Gallimard, Paris 1953, pp. 74-75.

[27] A. Perilli, **Documenti di una nuova figurazione,** in **L'Esperienza Moderna,** N° 2, 1957, p. 30.

[28] Quoted in G. Charbonnier, **Le Monologue du Peintre,** Julliard, Paris 1959, p. 70.

[29] Quoted in Michel Ragon, **L'Aventure de l'Art abstrait,** Robert Laffont, Paris 1956, p. 168.

[30] Ibid., p. 174.

[31] Jacques Lassaigne, **Réalisme de Soulages,** in **XXᵉ Siècle,** June 1956, p. 53.

[32] Hubert Juin, **Pierre Soulages,** Editions du Musée de Poche, Paris 1958, p. 51.

[33] From a statement by Motherwell during a discussion on the theme "The Creative Artist and his Public," in **Perspectives USA,** N° 9, Fall 1954. Quoted in the exhibition catalogue, **The New American Painting,** Tate Gallery, London, and The Museum of Modern Art, New York 1959.

[34] Thomas B. Hess, **Franz Kline,** in **Art News,** March 1956, p. 51.

[35] Harold Rosenberg, exhibition catalogue, **Action Painting,** The Dallas Museum of Contemporary Art, 1958.

[36] Pierre Restany, **Tal Coat,** in **Cimaise,** N° 5, May-June 1957, p. 17.

[37] From a statement by Afro, exhibition catalogue, **The New Decade,** The Museum of Modern Art, New York 1955, p. 68.

[38] U. Apollonio, **Santomaso,** Bodensee Verlag, Amriswil 1959, p. 15.

[39] Quoted in the catalogue of the 29th Biennale, Venice 1958.

[40] From a statement by Pollock in **Possibilities,** I, New York 1947-1948 (**Problems of Contemporary Art,** N° 4, Wittenborn). Quoted in the exhibition catalogue, **The New American Painting,** Tate Gallery, London, and The Museum of Modern Art, New York 1959.

[41] André Breton, **Le Surréalisme et la Peinture,** New York-Paris 1945, p. 198.

[42] From a statement by Baziotes in **Possibilities,** I, New York 1947-1948 (**Problems of Contemporary Art,** N° 4, Wittenborn). Quoted in the exhibition catalogue, **The New American Painting,** Tate Gallery, London, and The Museum of Modern Art, New York, 1959.

[43] G. C. Argan, **Materia, tecnica e storia dell'informale,** in **La Biennale,** N° 35, April-June 1959, p. 4.

[44] Pierre Volboudt, **A chacun sa réalité,** in **XXᵉ Siècle,** June 1957.

[45] Henri Michaux, **Vitesse et Tempo,** in **Quadrum,** N° 3, 1957, p. 15.

[46] Quoted in Lionello Venturi, **Pittori Italiani d'Oggi,** Rome 1958, p. 80.

[47] John Dewey, **Art as Experience,** New York 1934, p. 349.

[48] Ibid., p. 82.

[49] Ibid., p. 16.

[50] Thomas Craven, quoted in John I. H. Baur, **Revolution and Tradition in Modern American Art,** Harvard University Press, Cambridge, Mass., 1958, pp. 21-22.

[51] Published in **Arts and Architecture,** LXI, February 1944.

[52] From a statement by Pollock in **Possibilities,** I, New York 1947-1948 (**Problems of Contemporary Art,** N° 4, Wittenborn). Quoted in the exhibition catalogue, **The New American Painting,** Tate Gallery, London, and The Museum of Modern Art, New York, 1959.

[53] Thomas B. Hess, **Abstract Painting, Background and American Phase,** The Viking Press, New York 1951, p. 121.

[54] L. Kochnitzky, **Mark Tobey,** in **Quadrum,** N° 4, Brussels 1957, p. 17.

[55] Exhibition catalogue, **The New Decade,** Whitney Museum of American Art, New York 1955, and **The New American Painting,** Tate Gallery, London, and The Museum of Modern Art, New York 1959.

[56] Sam Hunter, **Mark Rothko,** preface to the catalogue of the Rothko exhibition at the American Pavilion of the 29th Biennale, Venice 1958, p. 345.

[57] From a statement by Mark Rothko in **The Tiger's Eye,** October 1949. Quoted in the exhibition catalogue, **15 Americans,** The Museum of Modern Art, New York 1952, and **The New American Painting,** Tate Gallery, London, and The Museum of Modern Art, New York, 1959.

[58] Letter from Philip Guston to John I. H. Baur, quoted in the exhibition catalogue, **The New American Painting,** Tate Gallery, London, and The Museum of Modern Art, New York, 1959.

[59] Letter from Clyfford Still, quoted in the exhibition catalogue, **15 Americans,** The Museum of Modern Art, New York, 1952, and **The New American Painting,** Tate Gallery, London, and The Museum of Modern Art, New York, 1959.

[60] Statement by James Brooks in the exhibition catalogue, **The New Decade: 35 American Painters and Sculptors,** Whitney Museum of American Art, New York, 1955, and **The New American Painting,** Tate Gallery, London, and The Museum of Modern Art, New York, 1959.

[61] Quoted in **Tableau bon levain à vous de cuire la pâte. L'art brut de Jean Dubuffet,** by Georges Limbour, René Drouin, Paris 1953, p. 91.

[62] Quoted by James Fitzsimmons, **Jean Dubuffet,** Editions de la Connaissance, Brussels 1958.

[63] G. C. Argan, in the catalogue of the 30th Biennale, Venice 1960, p. 67.

General Bibliography

In addition to the books listed below, a complete bibliography of contemporary painting necessarily includes the following categories of publications:

1. Catalogues of major international exhibitions held periodically, such as the **Venice Biennale,** the **São Paulo Bienal,** the **Pittsburgh International,** and **Documenta I** and **II** at Kassel (1955 and 1959).

2. Catalogues of certain outstanding exhibitions held in recent years, such as **Younger European Painters** (1953) and **Younger American Painters** (1954) organized by the Solomon R. Guggenheim Museum, New York; **The New Decade** (1955), an exhibition of European and American painters organized at the Museum of Modern Art and the Whitney Museum of American Art, New York; **Cinquante Ans d'Art Moderne,** at the Brussels World's Fair (1958); and **Vitalità nell'Arte,** at the Palazzo Grassi, Venice (1959). For American painting in particular, consult the catalogues issued for the exhibition **The New American Painting,** organized by the Museum of Modern Art, New York, and shown in eight European countries (1958-1959).

3. Art magazines such as **Art International,** Zurich; **Art News,** New York; **Aujourd'hui,** Boulogne-sur-Seine; **La Biennale,** Venice; **Cahiers d'Art,** Paris; **Cahiers du Musée de Poche,** Paris; **Cimaise,** Paris; **Commentari,** Rome; **Das Kunstwerk,** Baden-Baden; **Das Werk,** Zurich; **Derrière le Miroir,** Paris; **Die Kunst,** Munich; **I Quattro Soli,** Turin; **L'Esperienza Moderna,** Rome; **L'Oeil,** Paris; **Notizie,** Turin; **Phases,** Paris; **Prisme des Arts,** Paris; **Quadrum,** Brussels; **Sele-Arte,** Florence; **Ver y Estimar,** Buenos Aires; **XX° Siècle,** Paris.

Sidney Janis, **Abstract and Surrealist Art in America,** Reynal & Hitchcock, New York 1944.

André Breton, **Le surréalisme et la peinture,** 2nd edition, New York 1945.

Dorothy C. Miller, **14 Americans,** exhibition catalogue, Museum of Modern Art, New York 1946.

Abstract and Surrealist American Art, exhibition catalogue, Art Institute of Chicago, 1947.

O. Domnick, **Die schöpferischen Kräfte in der abstrakten Malerei,** Stuttgart-Bergen 1947.

Alexander Dorner, **The Way beyond Art,** Wittenborn-Schultz, New York 1947.

L. Venturi, **La peinture contemporaine,** Hoepli, Milan n.d. (1947); French and Italian editions.

J. Lassaigne, R. Cogniat, and M. Zahar, **Panorama des Arts,** Somogy, Paris 1947 and 1948.

H. Read, **Art Now,** new edition, London 1948.

J. T. Soby, **Contemporary Painters,** New York 1948.

Léon Degand, Preface, **Do Figurativismo ao Abstraccionismo,** exhibition catalogue, Museu de Arte Moderna, São Paulo 1949.

Michel Seuphor, **L'art abstrait, ses origines, ses premiers maîtres,** Maeght, Paris 1949.

A. Leepa, **The Challenge of Modern Art,** Thomas Yoseloff Inc., New York 1949; 3rd edition, 1957.

J. T. Soby, **Twentieth Century Italian Art,** The Museum of Modern Art, New York 1949.

U. Apollonio, **Pittura italiana moderna,** Venice 1950.

C. Estienne, **L'art abstrait est-il un académisme?,** Editions de Beaune, Paris 1950.

P. Loeb, **Regards sur la peinture,** La Hune, Paris 1950.

Thomas B. Hess, **Abstract Painting, Background and American Phase,** The Viking Press, New York 1951.

G. Nicco Fasola, **Ragione dell'Arte Astratta,** Istituto Editoriale Italiano, Milan 1951.

Pittori d'Oggi, Francia-Italia, exhibition catalogues, Turin, 1951, 1952, 1953, 1955, 1957, 1959.

M. Valsecchi and U. Apollonio, **Panorama dell'Arte italiana,** Lattes, Turin 1950 and 1951.

M. Ragon, **Expression et non figuration,** Paris 1951.

H. Read, **Contemporary British Art,** Harmondsworth 1951.

A. C. Ritchie, **Abstract Painting and Sculpture in America,** exhibition catalogue, Museum of Modern Art, New York, 1951.

P. Courthion, **Peintres d'Aujourd'hui,** Pierre Cailler, Geneva 1952.

L. Degand, J. Alvard, R. V. Gindertael, **Témoignages pour l'art abstrait,** Art d'Aujourd'hui, Boulogne-sur-Seine 1952.

Dorothy C. Miller, **15 Americans,** exhibition catalogue, Museum of Modern Art, New York 1952.

R. Motherwell and A. Reinhardt, **Modern Artists in America,** Wittenborn, New York n.d. (1952).

M. Tapié, **Un Art autre,** Gabriel Giraud, Paris 1952.

L. Venturi, **Otto Pittori Italiani,** De Luca, Rome 1952.

J. Bouret, **L'Art abstrait,** Club Français du Livre, Paris 1952.

Premier Bilan de l'Art actuel, Le Soleil Noir, Paris 1953.

H. Vollmer, **Allgemeines Lexikon der bildenden Künstler des 20. Jahrhunderts,** E. A. Seemann, Leipzig 1953 ff.

Younger European Painters, exhibition catalogue, Solomon R. Guggenheim Museum, New York 1953.

Europa Kunst, exhibition catalogue, Copenhagen 1954.

Younger American Painters, exhibition catalogue, Solomon R. Guggenheim Museum, New York 1954.

L. Grote, **Deutsche Kunst im 20. Jahrhundert,** Prestel Verlag, Munich 1954.

Alfred H. Barr Jr., **Masters of Modern Art,** Museum of Modern Art, New York 1954.

Carattere della Pittura d'Oggi, exhibition catalogue, Rome 1954.

Arte figurativa e arte astratta, Quaderni della Fondazione Cini di San Giorgio Maggiore a Venezia, Sansoni, Florence 1955.

P. Dorazio, La Fantasia dell'arte nella vita moderna, Polveroni & Quinti, Rome 1955.

R. V. Gindertael, Propos sur la peinture actuelle, Paris 1955.

Holländische Kunst der Gegenwart, exhibition catalogue, Berlin 1955.

R. Lebel, Chantage de la beauté, Editions de Beaune, Paris 1955.

A. C. Ritchie, The New Decade, exhibition catalogue (European painters), Museum of Modern Art, New York 1955.

A. C. Ritchie, The New Decade, exhibition catalogue (American painters), Whitney Museum of American Art, New York 1955 (traveling exhibition shown in San Francisco, Los Angeles, Colorado Springs and St. Louis).

G. C. Argan, Studi e Note, Bocca, Rome 1956.

G. Ballo, Pittori italiani dal Futurismo ad Oggi, Edizioni Mediterranee, Rome 1956.

Rudi Blesh, Modern Art U.S.A., Knopf, New York 1956.

M. Brion, L'art abstrait, Albin Michel, Paris 1956.

M. Brion and A. Neuwirth, L'abstraction, Grund, Paris 1956.

Dorothy C. Miller, 12 Americans, exhibition catalogue, Museum of Modern Art, New York 1956.

Dictionnaire de la Peinture Moderne, Hazan, Paris 1956.

El Arte Abstracto y sus Problemas, Edición de Cultura Hispanica, Madrid 1956 (texts by R. Gullón, J. L. Fernández Del Amo, M. Sánchez Camargo, L. Figuerola Ferretti, C. Popovici, S. Gasch, J. Camón Aznar, D. C. Bayón, L. F. Vivanco, A. Cirici-Pellicer, J. A. Gaya Nuño, J. de Oteiza, F. Muñoz Hidalgo, F. Escriva, J. M. Moreno Galván, C. Lesca).

H. Haendler, Deutsche Malerei der Gegenwart, Berlin 1956.

E. Lavagnino, L'Arte Moderna, Utet, Turin 1956.

A. C. Ritchie, Masters of British Painting 1800-1950, exhibition catalogue, Museum of Modern Art, New York 1956.

Junge Kunst aus Holland, exhibition catalogue, Kunsthalle, Bern 1956.

M. Ragon, L'aventure de l'art abstrait, Laffont, Paris 1956.

L. Venturi, Arte Moderna, Bocca, Rome 1956.

L. Venturi, Saggi di critica, Bocca, Rome 1956.

J. Alvard, L'art moral, Paris 1957.

W. Grohmann, Preface to the Exhibition Arte tedesca dal 1905 ad oggi, De Luca, Rome 1957.

M. Seuphor, Dictionnaire de la Peinture Abstraite, Hazan, Paris 1957.

A. C. Ritchie, German Art of the Twentieth Century, exhibition catalogue, with texts by W. Haftmann, A. Hentzen, W. S. Lieberman, Museum of Modern Art, New York 1957.

New Art in America, presented by John I. H. Baur, with texts by L. Goodrich, D.C. Miller, J. T. Soby, F. S. Wight, New York Graphic Society, Greenwich 1957.

The World of Abstract Art, published by American Abstract Artists, Wittenborn, New York 1957.

G. Carandente, Pittori moderni della collezione Cavellini, exhibition catalogue, Rome 1957.

T. Sauvage, Pittura italiana del dopoguerra, Schwarz, Milan 1957.

B. Dorival, La Peinture du XX* Siècle, Tisné, Paris 1957; English translation, Twentieth Century Painters, New York 1958.

P. Restany, Espaces imaginaires, Paris 1957.

John I. H. Baur, Revolution and Tradition in Modern American Art, Harvard University Press, Cambridge, Mass. 1958.

A. Cavellini, Arte astratta, Edizioni della Conchiglia, Milan 1958.

P. Courthion, Art indépendant, Albin Michel, Paris 1958.

G. Dorfles, Le oscillazioni del gusto, Lerici, Milan 1958.

Cinquante ans d'art moderne, catalogue of the exhibition at the World's Fair, Brussels 1958.

Neue Kunst nach 1945, presented by W. Grohmann, with texts by M. Brion, C. Bernard, G. C. Argan, N. Ponente, U. Apollonio, O. Bihalij-Merin, W. Grohmann, H. Read, H. L. C. Jaffé, J. P. Hodin, S. Hunter, Dumont-Schauberg, Cologne 1958; English and Italian editions, 1959.

Modern Art, A Pictorial Anthology, presented by C. McCurdy, with texts by A. L. Chanin, A. Drexler, S. Hunter, B. Karpel, B. S. Myers, S. Preston, H. Schaefer, The Macmillan Company, New York 1958.

N. Ponente, Saggi e Profili, De Luca, Rome 1958.

A. Schulze Wellinghausen and A. Schroeder, Deutsche Kunst nach Baumeister, Aurel Bougers, Recklinghausen 1958.

L. Venturi, Pittori Italiani d'Oggi, De Luca, Rome 1958.

The New American Painting, catalogues of the exhibition organized by the Museum of Modern Art, New York, 1958-1959, and shown at the Kunsthalle, Basel; Galleria Civica d'Arte Moderna, Milan; Museo Nacional de Arte Contemporáneo, Madrid; Hochschule für Bildende Künste, Berlin; Stedelijk Museum, Amsterdam; Palais des Beaux-Arts, Brussels; Musée National d'Art Moderne, Paris; Tate Gallery, London; Museum of Modern Art, New York.

J. Grenier, Essais sur la peinture moderne, Gallimard, Paris 1959.

H. Read, A Concise History of Modern Painting, Thames & Hudson, London 1959.

H. Rosenberg, The Tradition of the New, Horizon Press, New York 1959.

Vitalità nell'Arte, exhibition catalogue, Palazzo Grassi, Venice 1959.

J. Fitzsimmons, European Art Today, exhibition catalogue, Museum of Art, Minneapolis 1959.

M. L. Friedman, School of Paris: The Internationals, exhibition catalogue, Museum of Art, Minneapolis 1959.

Arte Nuova, exhibition catalogue, Palazzo Graneri, Turin 1959.

G. Charbonnier, Le monologue du peintre, 2 vols., Julliard, Paris 1959-1960.

R. V. Gindertael, Permanence et actualité de la peinture, Paris 1960.

J. Guichard Meili, La peinture d'aujourd'hui, Paris 1960.

J. Alvard, Antagonismes, exhibition catalogue, Musée des Arts Décoratifs, Paris 1960.

A. Cavellini, Uomo Pittore, Edizioni della Conchiglia, Milan 1960.

Biographical and Bibliographical Notices

AFRO (1912)

Born at Udine (Venetia), Italy. His real name is Afro Basaldella. Studied art in Venice. Exhibited his work for the first time in a one-man show at the Galleria del Milione, Milan, where the avant-garde Italian painters forgathered in the thirties. Executed a mosaic decoration (now destroyed) for a school in his home town in 1936; and, in 1937, fresco decorations for the Albergo delle Rose and the Villa del Profeta at Rhodes. During the war years he continued to work in a figurative style; but by the end of the war, following up the lesson of Cubism, he had arrived at complete abstraction. He worked on in seclusion and refused to join the Fronte Nuovo delle Arti formed in 1946. But in 1952 he helped to found the group of Eight Italian Painters, who exhibited together at the 1952 Venice Biennale. His first American exhibition was held in 1948. Two years later he paid a visit to the United States and exhibited at the Viviano Gallery, New York. Since 1938 he has taken part regularly in the Venice Biennale (except in 1948 and 1958); awarded the grand prize for an Italian painter in 1956. Served as a jury member at the Carnegie International in Pittsburgh in 1955 and awarded a prize in 1958. Took part in the New Decade exhibition, Museum of Modern Art, New York (1955), and Documenta I and II (Kassel, 1955 and 1959). Invited by the University of California in 1958 as artist in residence; during his stay there he executed a large decoration on canvas for the restaurant of the Unesco building in Paris. The preliminary sketches for this decoration were exhibited in several American cities in 1959. Afro has always taken a keen interest in the ballet; in 1957 he did sets for Guglielmo Petrassi's **Ritratto di Don Chisciotte** (choreography by Millos) at the Teatro dell'Opera, Rome.

Bibliography:

L. De Libero, **Pitture di Afro,** exhibition catalogue, Galleria della Cometa, Rome, April 1936. — L. De Libero, **Afro,** Rome 1946. — L. Venturi, **Afro,** in **Commentari,** No. 3, 1954. — G. Marchiori, **Afro oggi,** in **Letteratura,** No. 13-14, 1955. — L. Venturi, exhibition catalogue, Viviano Gallery, New York, April-May 1955. — L. Venturi, **Afro,** in **Arts and Architecture,** May 1955. — D. Ashton, **Synthesists,** in **Arts and Architecture,** September 1955. — A. C. Ritchie, Catalogue of the 28th Biennale, Venice 1956. — U. Apollonio, **Appunto per Afro,** in **I Quattro Soli,** May-August 1956. — M. Calvesi, **Afro,** in **Comunità,** October 1956. — C. Efrati, **Afro,** in **Arti Visive,** No. 5, 1956. — U. Apollonio, **Afro,** in **Quadrum,** No. 2, 1956. — N. Ponente, **Afro,** in **Taccuino delle Arti,** No. 15, Rome 1957. — E. Fezzi, **Afro,** in **Prisme des Arts,** March 1957. — G. Drudi, **L'œuvre murale d'Afro à l'Unesco,** in **Aujourd'hui,** No. 21, March-April 1959.

ALBERS, Josef (1888)

Born at Bottrop,Westphalia. After obtaining his license as a primary school teacher, he studied at the Royal Art School, Berlin, 1913-1915; at the School of Applied Art, Essen, 1916-1919; at the Art Academy, Munich, 1919-1920 (under Franz Stuck, who also taught Klee and Kandinsky); and finally at the Bauhaus, Weimar, 1920-1923. At the invitation of Walter Gropius, he started teaching at the Bauhaus in 1923 and moved with the school to Dessau and later to Berlin. At various times he directed the glass, furniture and wallpaper workshops at the Bauhaus. He has had frequent one-man and group exhibitions since 1927. At the closing of the Bauhaus in 1933 Albers went to the United States, and taught at Black Mountain College, North Carolina, until 1948. From 1934-1938 he was a member of the Abstraction-Creation group, Paris, and has been a member of American Abstract Artists since 1938. From 1950-1958 he was Chairman of the Department of Design at Yale University, New Haven, where he still lives. As a visiting professor he taught from 1933-1958 at universities and art schools such as Harvard, Cincinnati Art Academy, Pratt Institute, Brooklyn, Mexico City, Havana, Santiago, Lima, Honolulu and Ulm. His major exhibitions include: "Josef Albers, Hans Arp, Max Bill," Stuttgart, 1948; one-man shows at the Cincinnati Art Museum, 1949, and Yale University Art Gallery, 1956; "Josef Albers, Fritz Glarner, Friedrich Vordemberge-Gildewart," Kunsthaus, Zurich, 1956; and two seventieth anniversary exhibitions: Kunstverein, Freiburg-im-Breisgau, and Sidney Janis Gallery, New York. He participated also in Documenta, Kassel, 1955; São Paulo Bienal, 1957, and the Pittsburgh International, 1958. In 1959 he received a Ford Foundation Fellowship.

Bibliography:

Walter Gropius and L. Moholy-Nagy, **Neue Arbeiten der Bauhaus-Werkstätten,** 1925, pp. 18-21. — H. Bayer, W. Gropius and I. Gropius, **The Bauhaus 1919-1928,** Museum of Modern Art, New York 1938. — Josef Albers, **Abstract - Presentational,** American Abstract Artists, New York 1946. — Josef Albers, **The Educational Value of Manual Work and Handicraft in Relation to Architecture,** in Paul Zucker, **New Architecture and City Planning,** Philosophical Library, New York

1949, pp. 688-694. — Elaine de Kooning, **Albers paints a Picture**, in **Art News**, New York, Vol. 57, November 1950, pp. 40-43. — **Josef Albers**, in **New Mexico Quarterly**, University of New Mexico, Winter 1953. — Hans Vollmer, in **Künstler Lexikon**, Vol. 1, p. 22, Leipzig 1953. — Josef Albers, in **Spirale**, Zurich, No. 5, pp. 1-12, Fall 1955. — George Heard Hamilton, **Josef Albers, Paintings, Prints, Projects**, exhibition catalogue, Yale University Art Gallery, New Haven, April 1956. — Max Bill, **Josef Albers**, in **Werk**, Zurich, No. 145, April 1958. —Will Grohmann, **Tribute to Josef Albers on his Seventieth Birthday**, in **Yale University Art Gallery Bulletin**, New Haven, No. 24, pp. 26-27, October 1958.

APPEL, Karel (1921)

Born in Amsterdam, where he attended classes at the Art Academy, then worked on alone. Early influences: Impressionism, Picasso, the painters of the School of Paris, the primitive arts. Took part in a collective exhibition at the Stedelijk Museum, Amsterdam, in 1946. First one-man show the same year at the Beernhuis, Groningen; another in 1947 at the Het Gildehuis Gallery, Amsterdam. Founder member in 1948 of the Dutch experimental group, which in 1949 merged with the Cobra group (Copenhagen-Brussels-Amsterdam). He also contributed to the magazine **Reflex**. Exhibited in 1949 with the Cobra group at Copenhagen and at the first international exhibition of experimental art in Amsterdam. Did a decorative painting that same year for the Amsterdam Town Hall. In 1950 he settled in Paris, where in 1951 he exhibited with the Cobra group at the Librairie 73 and took part in the exhibition "Signifiants de l'Informel." organized by Michel Tapié at the Galerie Facchetti; also took part in the second international exhibition of experimental art at Liège. Executed a mural decoration for the Stedelijk Museum in Amsterdam; further decorations for the same museum in 1956 and for the Gymnasium at The Hague. Did decorative work in 1958 for the new Unesco building in Paris and for the Dutch Pavilion at the Brussels World's Fair. Awarded the Unesco Prize at the 1954 Venice Biennale. In 1956 he produced a series of large, vehemently handled portraits. One-man shows in Amsterdam (Galerie Van Lier, 1951), Rotterdam (Galerie Venster, 1952), Brussels (Palais des Beaux-Arts, 1953), Paris (Galerie Facchetti, 1954; Galerie Rive Droite, 1955, 1956, 1960; Galerie Stadler, 1957), Amsterdam (Stedelijk Museum, 1955, 1959), Milan (Galleria dell'Ariete, 1956), Rome (La Tartaruga, 1957), Zurich (Galerie Lienhard, 1959). Participated in the exhibition "Un Art Autre" organized by Michel Tapié (Paris, 1952), the Salon de Mai (Paris, 1952, 1957), the Pittsburgh International (1952), the São Paulo Bienal (1953, 1959), the Venice Biennale (1954), Europa Kunst (Copenhagen, 1954), Younger European Painters, New York (1953), Carattere della Pittura d'Oggi (Rome, 1954), the Milan Triennale (1954), Junge Kunst aus Holland (Kunsthalle, Bern, 1956), Un Art Autre (Barcelona, 1957, then Tokyo), Documenta II (Kassel, 1959), and Vitalità nell'Arte (Venice, 1959).

Bibliography:

S. S. Vskuil, **Karel Appel**, in **Zitschrift Kroniek van Kunst en Kultur**, 1949. — C. Dotremont, **Par la grande porte** and **Les artistes libres**, in **Cobra**, 1950. — H. L. C. Jaffé, **Karel Appel**, in **The Studio**, 1952. — P. Bowles, **Karel Appel**, in **Holiday**, 1953. — J. Fitzsimmons, **Karel Appel**, in **Art Digest**, 1953. — Dr Brökk-Pernedy, **Karel Appel**, in **Les Beaux-Arts**, 1953. —C. Dotremont, **Karel Appel**, in **Les Beaux-Arts**, 1953. — D. Ashton, **Karel Appel**, in **Art Digest**, 1954. — M. Tapié, **Karel Appel**, United States Lines, Paris 1954. — J. Alvard, **Karel Appel**, in **Cimaise**, 1954. — M. Tapié, **Karel Appel**, in **Cimaise**, 1954. — J. Stahly, **Karel Appel**, in **Werk**, 1954. — K. B. Sawyer, **Karel Appel**, in **The New York Herald Tribune**, 1954. — **Vogue**, 1954, special issue devoted to Appel, with photos and color plates. — C. Dolman, **Karel Appel**, **L'aventure de la sensation extasiée**, in **Quadrum**, No. 3, 1957. — M. Tapié, E. Looken, H. Claus, Presentation of the Exhibition at the Galerie Rive Droite, Paris 1955. — M. Moreni, Presentation of the Exhibition at the Galerie Stadler, Paris 1957. — H. Neuburg, Presentation of the Exhibition at the Galerie Lienhard, Zurich 1959.

BAUMEISTER, Willi (1889-1955)

Born at Stuttgart, where in 1911 he enrolled at the Art Academy as a pupil of Adolf Hölzel. Trip to Paris in 1912 where he discovered the work of Toulouse-Lautrec and Gauguin. Another trip to Paris in 1914 with Oskar Schlemmer; this time he became an enthusiastic admirer of Cézanne. From 1919 date his first **Mauerbilder** (wall pictures). A third stay in Paris in 1924, where he came into contact with Ozenfant, Le Corbusier, Fernand Léger and, some years later, the Abstraction-Creation group (1932). He taught at the Fine Arts School in Frankfort from 1928 to 1933, when he was dismissed by the Nazis and condemned as a "degenerate painter." Thereafter he lived a retired life in Stuttgart and worked on in solitude until the end of the war; earned his living during this period by working in a printing plant. Appointed to a professorship at the Stuttgart Academy of Fine Arts in 1946. In 1947 he published a book, **Das Unbekannte in der Kunst**, written four years earlier. His work has been represented in most of the major post-war exhibitions in Europe, and also at the exhibition of German Art of the Twentieth Century, held in 1957 at the Museum of Modern Art, New York. Baumeister retrospectives organized at Documenta II (Kassel, 1959) and at the 1960 Venice Biennale.

Bibliography:

W. Graeff, **Willi Baumeister**, Stuttgart 1928. — **Sélection**, special issue devoted to Baumeister, Antwerp 1931 (texts by W. Grohmann, W. George, H. Arp, C. Zervos, Le Corbusier, M. Seuphor, etc.). — E. Westerdahl, **Willi Baumeister**, Teneriffe 1934. — W. Grohmann, **Willi Baumeister**, Stuttgart 1952. — F. Roh, **Willi Baumeister**, Baden-Baden 1954. —W. Urbanek, **Willi Baumeister**, in **I Quattro Soli**, No. 5, September-October 1955. — M. Seuphor, **Exit Baumeister**, in **Aujourd'hui**, No. 5, 1955. —W. Graeff, **Willi Baumeister**, in **La Biennale**, Venice, No. 27, March 1956. — H. Hildebrand, **Willi Baumeister**, in **Prisme des Arts**, No. 6, November 1956.

BAZAINE, Jean (1904)

Born in Paris and grew up at Forges (Ile-de-France). Worked at sculpture while attending the university; after taking his degree (Licence ès lettres) he enrolled in the Ecole des Beaux-Arts, Paris. After 1924 he devoted himself entirely to painting and attended classes at the Académie Julian. His first exhibition was held at the Galerie Van Leer, Paris, in 1932; thereafter, until the outbreak of war, he exhibited at the Galerie Jeanne Castel. In 1937 he designed stained-glass windows for a private chapel: **The Instruments of the Passion**. Awarded the Blumenthal Prize in 1938.

In 1941, at the Galerie Braun, Paris, he organized the exhibition entitled "Vingt Peintres de Tradition Française." Published his **Notes sur la peinture d'aujourd'hui** (1948, 1953, 1955). Designed stained-glass windows for the church at Assy, Haute-Savoie (1944-1946), a mosaic for the façade of the church at Audincourt near Belfort (1948-1951), and wired glass walls for the baptistery of the latter church (1954). In 1958 he designed stained-glass windows for the church at Villeparisis (Seine-et-Marne) and a large mosaic for the new Unesco building in Paris. Long painting trips in Spain (1953-1954) and Holland (1956-1957). Spent the summer of 1958 at Saint-Guénolé (Finistère). From 1948 on he exhibited at the Galerie Carré, then at the Galerie Maeght, which organized three large showings of his works in 1949, 1955 and 1957. In 1950 he exhibited at the Pittsburgh International, where he served as a jury member in 1952. Took part in the São Paulo Bienal (1951, 1953), the Younger European Painters exhibition, Guggenheim Museum, New York (1954), and the New Decade exhibition, Museum of Modern Art, New York (1955), and Documenta II, Kassel (1959). Large-scale Bazaine retrospective held in 1958 at the Kunsthalle, Bern.

Bibliography:

A. Frénaud, **Bazaine, Estève, Lapicque,** Paris 1945. — A. Frénaud and H. Maldiney, **Jean Bazaine,** in **Derrière le Miroir,** November 1949. — Pierre Gérard, **Jean Bazaine,** in **Critique,** January 1949. — J. Bazaine, **Notes sur la peinture d'aujourd'hui,** Paris 1953; new enlarged edition, 1955. — A. M. (A. Maeght), **Jean Bazaine,** Paris 1953. — M. Arland, **Jean Bazaine,** in **Derrière le Miroir,** exhibition catalogue, Galerie Maeght, Paris, May 1955. — H. Maldiney, **Bazaine,** in **Prisme des Arts,** No. 7, December 1956. — G. Limbour, **Peintres de la nouvelle génération, Jean Bazaine,** in XXe Siècle, No. 7, 1956. — A. Frénaud, **Jean Bazaine,** in **Derrière le Miroir,** April-May 1957. — F. Meyer, Preface to the Exhibition Catalogue, Kunsthalle, Bern 1958. — E. de Wilde, **A Jean Bazaine,** in **Cahiers du Musée de Poche,** No. 1, March 1959.

BAZIOTES, William (1912)

Born in Pittsburgh and brought up in Reading, Pa., 1913-1933. He moved to New York in 1933 and entered the National Academy of Design, where he studied until 1936. From 1936-1938 he taught on the WPA Federal Art Project, New York, and then worked on the easel painting project from 1938-1941. He participated in the important International Surrealist Exhibition, organized by the Coordinating Council of the French Relief Societies, at the Whitelaw Reid Mansion, New York, 1942. His first one-man show was held at Peggy Guggenheim's gallery, Art of This Century, 1944. He was awarded first prize in the Chicago Art Institute exhibition of Abstract and Surrealist American Art, 1947, and the purchase prize at the University of Illinois exhibition of Contemporary American Painting, 1951. In association with Motherwell, Rothko and Barnett Newman he founded in 1948 the school, Subjects of the Artist, which was the forerunner of the informal organization of avant-garde New York artists called The Club. He has taught at the Brooklyn Museum Art School, 1949-1952; New York University, 1949-1952; People's Art Center of the Museum of Modern Art, New York, 1950-1952; and since 1952 at Hunter College, New York. He has had one-man shows in New York regularly since 1946 at the Kootz Gallery; also Galerie Maeght, Paris, 1947. His work was represented at the following exhibitions: 15 Americans, The Museum of Modern Art, New York, 1952; The New Decade, Whitney Museum of American Art, New York, circulating to San Francisco, Los Angeles, Colorado Springs, and St. Louis, 1955-1956; The Magical Worlds of Redon, Klee, Baziotes, Contemporary Arts Museum, Houston, 1957; The New American Painting, organized by The Museum of Modern Art, shown in Basel, Milan, Madrid, Berlin, Amsterdam, Brussels, Paris, London, New York 1958-1959. He has also taken part in the following international exhibitions: São Paulo Bienal, 1951, 1953; Pittsburgh International, 1952, 1955, 1958; Documenta II, Kassel, 1959. Lives in New York.

Bibliography:

Review of the Baziotes Exhibition, Art of This Century Gallery, in **Art Digest,** New York, Vol. 19, October 1, 1944, p. 12. — Margaret Breuning, **Baziotes shows Craftsmanship and Invention,** in **Art Digest,** New York, Vol. 20, February 15, 1946, p. 10. — Review of the Baziotes Exhibition, Kootz Gallery, in **Art Digest,** New York, Vol. 27, March 1, 1953, p. 15. — **Symposium: The Creative Process,** in **Art Digest,** New York, Vol. 28, January 15, 1954, p. 16.

BILL, Max (1908)

Born at Winterthur, Switzerland. Studied from 1924 to 1927 at the Kunstgewerbeschule, Zurich, then for two years at the Dessau Bauhaus. Working as an architect, sculptor and painter, he kept in close contact with the leading avant-garde movements of the day. Coined the term "concrete art" in opposition to "abstract art" in 1935, defending and illustrating it in all phases of his multifarious activities. Belonged to the Abstraction-Creation group in Paris from 1932 to 1936; then in 1937 he joined the Allianz group of Swiss artists. In 1938 he became a member of the C.I.A.M. (Congrès International d'Architecture Moderne). Gave a course of instruction (Formlehre) at the Kunstgewerbeschule, Zurich, in 1944-1945. In 1949 he was invited to give a series of lectures on architecture at the Technische Hochschule, Darmstadt, and appointed a member of the Union des Artistes Modernes, Paris. He has written and published numerous books and articles dealing with esthetic theory. In 1947 he founded the Institut für Progressive Kultur and in 1951, in collaboration with other artists, he designed and built the Hochschule für Gestaltung at Ulm, the heir in many ways of the Bauhaus; remained in charge of the school until 1956, when he resigned. A great admirer of Mondrian and Kandinsky, Bill lives and works today in Zurich; he has exerted a profound influence on contemporary art, particularly in Italy and Argentina. He has taken part in many international exhibitions, winning first prize at the Milan Triennale in 1936 and again in 1951, the international prize for sculpture at the 1951 São Paulo Bienal, and a gold medal at the 1954 Milan Triennale. He exhibited at the Sculpture Biennial, Antwerp (1955, 1957, 1959), Documenta I and II, Kassel (1955, 1959) and the Venice Biennale (1958). One-man shows at the Galerie Eaux-Vives, Zurich (1946), Galerie Bollag, Zurich (1958), the Studio, Ulm (1959), St Gall (1959) and Leverkusen (1959).

Bibliography:

G. Schmidt, **La variation d'un même thème dans les beaux-arts,** in XXᵉ Siècle, No. 4, 1938. — H. Kayser, **Continuità di Max Bill,** in **Domus,** No. 223/224/225, 1947. — G. Schmidt, **Max Bill's Kontinuität,** in **Werk,** No. 3, 1948. — W. Grohmann, **Max Bill,** in **AZ,** No. 7,

Milan, April-May 1950. — **Max Bill spiega la pittura concreta**, in **Sele-Arte**, No. 2, September-October 1952. — E. R. Rogers, **Max Bill**, in **Magazine of Art**, May 1953. — T. Maldonado, **Max Bill**, Editorial Nueva Visión, Buenos Aires 1955. — G. Schmidt, **Max Bill**, Editions du Griffon, Neuchâtel 1957. — W. Grohmann, **Max Bill und die Synthese**, in **Werk**, No. 7, July 1957. — M. Netter, **Experimente mit Form und Farbe**, in **Bilder und Plastiken von Max Bill**, in **Quadrum**, No. 3, 1957. — H. C., **Max Bill**, in **Werk**, No. 11, November 1957. — E. Gomringer, Preface to the Exhibition Catalogue, Municipal Museum, Leverkusen 1959.

BIROLLI, Renato (1906-1959)

Born at Verona, where he studied art at the Accademia Cignaroli. Moved to Milan in 1928. Paid a visit to Paris in 1936. Returning to Italy he helped to found the Corrente group, an avant-garde movement which took a strong anti-Fascist line both in art and politics. Persecuted by the authorities, Birolli served prison terms in 1937 and 1938. Joined the Italian resistance movement in 1943; while in hiding he did a series of drawings later published under the title **Italia 1944.** Made a stay in Paris after the war and then, in 1947, became one of the moving spirits behind the Fronte Nuovo delle Arti, grouping all the avant-garde elements of post-war Italian painting. When this movement began to lose its effectiveness, he broke away and helped to found the group of Eight Italian Painters. Exhibited at the 1951 São Paulo Bienal, where he won a prize; also awarded a Carnegie prize at Pittsburgh in 1955. Showed at the Viviano Gallery in New York in 1955 and 1958, and took part regularly in the Venice Biennale, where he won several prizes. He died in Milan in 1959. Birolli retrospectives at Documenta II (Kassel, 1959) and the 1960 Venice Biennale.

Bibliography:

E. Persico, **Birolli**, in **Casabella**, March 1933. — R. De Grada, **Ritratti d'artisti**, in **L'Italia Letteraria**, October 27, 1935. — S. Bini, **Premessa a Renato Birolli**, in **Corrente di Vita Giovanile**, May 15, 1938. — S. Bini, **Birolli**, Milan 1941. — G. Piovene, **Birolli**, in **Domus**, No. 158, 1951. — G. Veronesi, **Nota su Birolli**, in **Le Arti**, No. 4, 1941. — G. C. Argan, **Renato Birolli**, Preface to the Catalogue of the First Exhibition of the Fronte Nuovo delle Arti, Milan 1947. — C. Maltese, **Cultura e Realtà nella pittura di Birolli**, in **Commentari**, No. 1, 1950. — G. Ballo, **Birolli o del colore**, in **Bellezza**, Milan, March 1950. — G. Marchiori, **Renato Birolli**, in **Letteratura**, No. 2, 1954. — L. Venturi, **Renato Birolli**, in **Commentari**, No. 4, 1954. — U. Apollonio, **Pittura di Birolli**, in **Quadrum**, No. 1, 1956. — M. Valsecchi, **Renato Birolli**, Preface to the Exhibition Catalogue, Galleria Odyssia, Rome, March 1958. — M. Valsecchi, **Renato Birolli**, Preface to the Catalogue, 30th Biennale, Venice 1960. — E. Emmanuelli (editor), **Renato Birolli, Taccuini 1936-1959**, Einaudi, Turin 1960.

BISSIER, Julius (1893)

Born at Freiburg-im-Breisgau, where he studied at the university and then enrolled in the Karlsruhe Art Academy. Served in the German army during the First World War, then devoted himself entirely to painting. Won first prize at the Deutscher Künstlerbund exhibition at Hanover in 1928 and a gold medal at Düsseldorf. Took to abstract art from 1929-1930 on. About this time he met Willi Baumeister and Oskar Schlemmer; struck up a friendship with Brancusi during a stay in Paris. Taught at the University of Freiburg-im-Breisgau from 1929 to 1933, when he resigned for political reasons and withdrew into private life. Made several trips to Italy between 1935 and 1938. After the war he resumed his activities and has taken part in many major exhibitions, both in Germany and abroad, among them Documenta II (Kassel, 1959) and the Venice Biennale (1958, 1960). In 1959 he won the Cornelius Prize awarded by the City of Düsseldorf, and in 1960 a prize at the Venice Biennale.

Bibliography:

K. Leonhard, **Julius Bissier**, Stuttgart 1947. — E. Vietta, **Julius Bissier**, in **Das Kunsthandwerk**, 1950. — S. E. Bröse, **Julius Bissier**, Presentation of the Bissier Exhibition, Kunstverein, Freiburg-im-Breisgau 1954. — W. Schmalenbach, Presentation of the Exhibition at the Municipal Museum, Duisburg, 1958-1959. — F. Bayl, **Julius Bissier**, in **Goya**, No. 28, Madrid 1959. — W. Schmalenbach, **Julius Bissier**, in **Die Kunst und das Schöne Heim**, Munich 1959. — W. Schmalenbach, **Julius Bissier**, in **Quadrum**, No. 7, 1959. — W. Schmalenbach, Presentation of the Exhibition at the Gemeente Museum, The Hague, 1959-1960.

BISSIÈRE, Roger (1888)

Born at Villeréal (Lot-et-Garonne), France. Enrolled in 1905 at the Académie des Beaux-Arts, Bordeaux, in Gabriel Ferrier's class. Went to Paris in 1910 where he worked as a journalist until 1914 and twice exhibited at the Salon des Artistes Français (1910, 1911). Spent several months in North Africa in 1911. After the war he met Lhote and Favory, with whom he exhibited from 1920 on at the Salon d'Automne and the Salon des Indépendants. Became friendly with Braque and contributed to the magazine **L'Esprit Nouveau**, edited by Jeanneret and Ozenfant, publishing articles on the art of Seurat, Ingres and Corot (in Nos. 1, 4 and 9). Exhibited at the Galerie Léonce Rosenberg in Paris. Took part in the exhibition of French art organized by the Galerie L'Effort Moderne in Amsterdam in 1921, in the retrospective of 19th and 20th Century French Art in Prague, and in the exhibition **Les Cent Peintres** organized by the Société des Amateurs d'Art in Paris. Exhibited regularly at the Galerie Druet from 1923 to 1930. Taught from 1925 to 1938 at the Académie Ranson, in Paris, where his prestige was great among the younger painters who studied or forgathered there (Garbell, Szenes, Vieira da Silva, Manessier, Le Moal, Bertholle, Wacker, Seiler, Henschel, Vera Pagava, Reichel, Gruber). In 1934 he gave a course of instruction on fresco painting. In 1935 and 1936 an exhibition hall was opened at the Académie Ranson, with showings of work by Bissière, Reichel, Wacker, Henschel, Gruber (drawings) and various groups. Though Bissière was still little known to the public at large, one of his works (**Still Life with a Cello**) was acquired for the Musée du Luxembourg, Paris, in 1935 and he was invited to take part in the exhibition **Les Maîtres de l'Art Indépendant** held at the Petit-Palais, Paris, in 1937. Retired in 1939 to the family home at Boissiérette (Lot). Stricken with a serious eye disease endangering his sight and had to give up painting altogether for a period of five years; as a diversion he took to making tapestry hangings with his wife. After the war he resumed painting: bucolic scenes and visionary works of great simplicity. In 1945 the first Salon de Mai organized an "Homage to Bissière." Large one-man show of paintings and tapestries at the Galerie René Drouin in 1947. Took part in various exhibitions outside France (Stockholm,

Berlin, Düsseldorf). Showed a series of **Untitled Images** at the Galerie Jeanne Bucher in 1951, where he has since exhibited regularly; there in 1958 he showed thirty-four small paintings forming a kind of diary of the artist's life. Awarded the Grand Prix National des Arts (1952). In 1954 the Galerie Jeanne Bucher published the **Cantique du soleil** of St Francis of Assisi, illustrated with color engravings by Bissière. Exhibited at the Venice Biennale and the Kunsthalle, Basel. Participated in the third São Paulo Bienal (1955), the Salon de Mai, Paris (1957, 1958), and many exhibitions abroad in 1957-1958 (Lübeck, Hanover, Recklinghausen; retrospective at the Stedelijk Museum, Amsterdam, and at Eindhoven; World's Fair Exhibition, Brussels; the "New Religious Art" exhibition, Delft; Beyeler Gallery, Basel). Large-scale Bissière Retrospective at the Musée d'Art Moderne, Paris, in 1959.

Bibliography:

J. Lassaigne, **Bissière**, in **Panorama des Arts**, Paris 1948. — J. Lassaigne, **Métamorphoses de Bissière**, in **Revue de la Pensée Française**, May 1954. — M. P. Fouchet, **Bissière**, Paris 1956. — J. Lassaigne, Catalogue of the Bissière Exhibition, Galerie Jeanne Bucher, Paris 1956. — J. Lassaigne, **Visite à Bissière**, in **Prisme des Arts**, No. 2, April 1956. — R. V. Gindertael, **Couleurs de Bissière**, in **Quadrum**, No. 4, 1957. — G. Weelen, Preface, Bissière Exhibition, Galerie Jeanne Bucher, Paris 1958. — J. Cassou, Preface, Bissière Exhibition, Musée d'Art Moderne, Paris 1959. — R. V. Gindertael, **Bissière**, in **Les Beaux-Arts**, Brussels 1959. — A. Chastel, **Le Privilège de Bissière**, in **Le Monde**, April 9, 1959. — J. F. Jaeger, **Les très riches heures de Bissière**, in **Les Cahiers du Musée de Poche**, No. 2, June 1959.

BROOKS, James (1906)

Born in St. Louis, he grew up in Oklahoma, Colorado and Texas. He attended Southern Methodist University, Dallas, 1923-1925. He moved to New York in 1926; studied under Kimon Nicolaides and Boardman Robinson at the Art Students League, 1927-1930. During the summer of 1931 he stayed in Woodstock, New York, and shared a converted barn with Bradley Walker Tomlin. He painted murals at Queensborough Public Library, Woodside Branch, 1938, and International Overseas Air Terminal, La Guardia Airport, 1942, while working on the WPA Federal Art Project, 1938-1942. From 1942-1945 he served in the U. S. Army. He taught at Columbia University, 1946-1948; since 1948 he has taught at the Pratt Institute, Brooklyn. He was a visiting critic of painting at Yale University, New Haven, 1955-1956. His first one-man show was held in 1950 at the Peridot Gallery, New York; other one-man shows at Peridot Gallery, 1951-1953; Miller-Pollard Gallery, Seattle, 1952; Area Arts, San Francisco, 1953; Grace Borgenicht Gallery, New York, 1954; Stable Gallery, New York, 1957, 1959. His work was represented in the following exhibitions: The New Decade, Whitney Museum of American Art, New York, circulating to Los Angeles, Colorado Springs and St. Louis, 1955-1956; 12 Americans, Museum of Modern Art, New York, 1956; The New American Painting, organized by the Museum of Modern Art and shown in Basel, Milan, Madrid, Berlin, Amsterdam, Brussels, Paris, London, New York, 1958-1959. He participated also in the Pittsburgh International, 1952 (fifth prize), 1955, 1958; São Paulo Bienal, 1957; Documenta II, Kassel, 1959. He lives in New York.

Bibliography:

Brooks' Musical Abstractions, in **Art Digest**, New York, Vol. 24, April 15, 1950, p. 20. — Review of the Brooks Exhibition, Borgenicht Gallery, in **Art News**, New York, Vol. 52, February 1954, p. 45. — Bernard Chaet, **Studio Talk, Concept of Space and Expression, An Interview with James Brooks**, in **Arts**, New York, Vol. 33, January 1959, p. 33. — Herbert Read and H. H. Arnason, **Dialogue on Modern U. S. Painting**, in **Art News**, New York, Vol. 59, May 1960, p. 36.

BRYEN, Camille (1907)

Born at Nantes, France. At nineteen he settled in Paris and in 1927 published his first book of poems, **Opoponax**, followed in 1932 by **Expériences.** Executed drawings, collages and graffiti and wrote poems. In 1934 he exhibited for the first time at the Galerie Au Grenier in Paris ("spontaneous" drawings and collages). In 1935, with Arp, Magritte, Max Ernst and others, he took part in the surrealist exhibition at Louvières, Belgium. Exhibited his first **tachiste** painting, **Cire et bougie**, at the Salon des Surindépendants in 1936. In 1937 he signed the Dimensionist Manifesto with Arp, Kandinsky, Picabia, Marcel Duchamp and Robert Delaunay, and exhibited at La Cachette with Picabia, Cendrars and Duchamp. In 1945 he took part in the surrealist exhibition at Brussels. For Wols's first exhibition at the Galerie Drouin he wrote a poem for his friend, who was presented by Silveire and H. P. Roché. In 1946 he participated in the first Salon des Réalités Nouvelles, Paris, where he exhibited again in 1947 and 1948. One-man show in 1947 at the Galerie du Luxembourg, Paris, where he and Georges Mathieu also organized an exhibition of the Psychic Non-Figuration movement, entitled **L'Imaginaire.** A second exhibition of the group was held the following year at the Galerie Allendy. Participated in the Black and White exhibition in 1949 at the Galerie des Deux-Iles, where he held a one-man show the same year, presented by Audiberti (**Pierres poilées**). Took part in the exhibition of Grands Courants de la Peinture Contemporaine in Lyons. In 1950 he exhibited at the Galerie des Deux-Iles and the Galerie Pierre, Paris. Took part in the exhibition Véhémences Confrontées (1951, Galerie Nina Dausset, Paris), with Hartung, Capogrossi, Mathieu, Pollock, Wols and others, presented by Michel Tapié; Signifiants de l'Informel (1951, Galerie Facchetti, Paris); Un Art Autre (1952, Galerie Facchetti, Paris); Art Fantastique (1952, Basel); Salon d'Octobre (1953, Paris); Phase I, II, III (1954, 1955, 1956, Paris); Tendances Nouvelles (1955, Kunsthalle, Bern). A large retrospective, with over a hundred of his works, was held at Nantes in 1959.

Bibliography:

La Tour de feu, issue dedicated to the **Révolution de l'Infiguré**, No. 51, Paris, Autumn 1956. — P. Restany, **Lo spazio nell'uomo**, Presentation of the Bryen Exhibition, Galleria dell'Attico, Rome 1959. — J. Audiberti, **Camille Bryen**, All'Insegna del Pesce d'Oro, Milan 1959. — R. V. Gindertael, **Bryen**, Raymonde Cazenave, Paris 1960.

BURRI, Alberto (1915)

Born at Città di Castello near Perugia. Studied medicine and practised as a doctor until the outbreak of war, painting on the side all the while. Carried out experiments in color tonalities akin to those of Mafai and Scipione, the initiators of what has been called the Roman School. The end of the war found him a prisoner of war in Texas. Returning to Italy he gave up his medical practice and devoted himself entirely to painting. First one-man show at the Galleria La Margherita, Rome, in 1947; another at the same gallery in 1948. Paid a visit to Paris in 1948. Returning to Rome he presented his first abstract works at the Fondazione Origine, exhibiting with Capogrossi and the sculptor Colla. One-man show in 1952 at the Galleria dell'Obelisco, Rome, where for the first time he exhibited his pictures entitled **Blacks** and **Mildews.** Since then he has been recognized as one of the most daring innovators of post-war Italian painting. In 1953 J. J. Sweeney published a monograph on his work, and the same year the Frumkin Gallery in Chicago organized his first exhibition in the United States; then he exhibited in New York (Solomon R. Guggenheim Museum), Los Angeles and San Francisco. In 1955 he took part in the New Decade exhibition at the Museum of Modern Art, New York, in the São Paulo Bienal, and the Pittsburgh International, where he exhibited again in 1958 and won a prize. Exhibited at the Venice Biennale in 1956, 1958 and 1960. Burri exhibitions at the Arts Club of Chicago and the Albright Art Gallery in Buffalo (1958) were followed in 1960 by a one-man show at the Martha Jackson Gallery, New York. Participated in Documenta II at Kassel (1959) and in exhibitions in various Italian cities and at Basel and Brussels. A documentary film on his work was made in 1960.

Bibliography:

E. Villa, **Burri**, in **Arti Visive**, No. 4-5, 1953. — M. Sawin, **Burri patches a Picture**, in **Art Digest**, December 1953. — J. J. Sweeney, **Burri**, Rome n.d. (1953). — M. Gendel, **Burri "makes a Picture,"** in **Art News**, December 1954. — G. Marchiori, **Note su Burri**, in **Notizie**, Turin, April 1958. — J. J. Sweeney, Presentation at the 29th Biennale, Venice 1958. — E. Crispolti, **La Pittura di Alberto Burri**, in **Il Verri**, February 1959. — G. C. Argan, Catalogue of the Burri Exhibition at the Palais des Beaux-Arts, Brussels 1959. — L. L. Sosset, **Alberto Burri**, in **Les Beaux-Arts,** Brussels, April 1959. — U. Apollonio, **Alberto Burri**, in **Le Arti**, March-April 1959. — E. Vietta, **Alberto Burri**, in **Art international**, N° 4, Zurich 1959. — G. C. Argan, Presentation at the 30th Biennale, Venice 1960.

CORPORA, Antonio (1909)

Born at Tunis, where he studied at the local art school, then in Florence, where his first one-man show was held. In 1930 he made a stay in Paris, then in 1932 settled for a time in Milan, where he came into contact with some of Italy's leading abstract artists and also with the Galleria del Milione. He worked hard and also wrote articles defending his views on art. The outbreak of war found him at Tunis, where he remained until 1945, when he returned to Italy and settled in Rome. That same year he founded the Neo-Cubist group with Turcato, Monachesi, Guttuso and Fazzini, and in 1947 joined the Fronte Nuovo delle Arti with Birolli, Morlotti, Pizzinato, Vedova, Santomaso, Leoncillo, Viani, Franchina, Guttuso and Turcato. He took part in numerous exhibitions, in Milan (1947), at the Rome Quadriennale (1948), the Venice Biennale (1948, 1950) and the Pittori Romani exhibition at Salzburg (1949). One-man shows in 1950 at the Galleria dell'Obelisco, Rome, and the Galleria del Milione, Milan. Took part in more group exhibitions: Peintres Italiens d'Aujourd'hui (Paris, 1951), Pittori Romani (Paris, 1951), Pittori d'Oggi, Italia-Francia (Turin, 1951,

1952, 1953), and the São Paulo Bienal (1951, 1955). Won the Prix de Paris in 1951 and other prizes at the Venice Biennale (1950, 1952, 1956) and the Rome Quadriennale (1955-1956). Broke with the Fronte Nuovo in 1952 and helped to found the group of Eight Italian Painters with Afro, Birolli, Santomaso, Moreni, Morlotti, Turcato and Vedova. Participated in many of the large international exhibitions: First International Art Exhibition (Tokyo, 1952), International Exhibition of Drawing (Chicago, San Francisco, Los Angeles, 1952), Arte Astratta Italiana e Francese (Rome, 1953), Carnegie International (Pittsburgh, 1952, 1955), Documenta I and II (Kassel, 1955, 1959), and the 1960 Venice Biennale.

Bibliography:

A. Del Massa, **Corpora**, in **L'Illustrazione Toscana**, No. 3, 1930. — R. Carrieri, **Corpora alla Galleria del Milione**, in **L'Illustrazione Italiana**, June 18, 1939. — L. Venturi, **Corpora**, Rome 1948. — L. Degand, **Corpora**, in **Art d'Aujourd'hui**, 1950. — C. Zervos, **Corpora**, Paris 1952. — C. Zervos, **Corpora**, in **Cahiers d'Art**, No. 1, 1952. — P. Guéguen, **Corpora**, in **XX° Siècle**, 1952. — W. Grohmann, **Corpora**, in **Neue Zeitung**, November 5, 1953. — L. Venturi, **Corpora**, in **Commentari**, No. 1, 1955. — G. Ballo, **Corpora**, introduction by L. Venturi, Rome 1956. — G. C. Argan, Presentation at the 28th Biennale, Venice 1956. — C. Zervos, **Corpora**, with essays by L. Venturi, A. Chastel, L. Degand, G. C. Argan and P. Francastel, Paris 1957. — A. Chastel, **Corpora**, in **Le Monde**, June 28, 1957. — G. C. Argan, Catalogue Preface, Galerie Springer, Berlin 1958. — L. Venturi, Catalogue Preface, Kleeman Gallery, New York 1958. — Nello Ponente, **Recente Pittura di Corpora**, Preface to the Corpora Exhibition, Galleria Blu, Milan, April 1959. — M. Mendes, Catalogue Preface, Galleria Pogliani, Rome 1960. — Nello Ponente, Presentation at the 30th Biennale, Venice 1960.

DUBUFFET, Jean (1901)

Born at Le Havre. Went to Paris to study painting in 1918 and attended classes for a while at the Académie Julian. He soon gave up painting, however, and took a passionate interest in classical studies, palaeography, ethnology, languages, literature, music and philosophy. In 1924 he abandoned the arts altogether and decided to follow a business career. That same year he went to Buenos Aires as an industrial designer, but failing to make a success of it he returned to France six months later. He launched one or two business ventures which came to nothing. A critical period, both morally and materially. In 1930-1931 he started a small wine business in Paris, but in 1933-1934 his artistic instincts reasserted themselves: he shut up shop and took to painting again. On the side, to earn a living, he made marionettes, masks and plaster casts. He went through a fresh crisis in 1937: falling a prey to misgivings, convinced that as an artist he would always be a failure, he went back into business again. In 1942 he again felt the desire to paint and returned to art with redoubled energy, leaving his business in the hands of his partner (he sold out in 1947). He exhibited for the first time at the Paris gallery of René Drouin, the first man (together with the writer Georges Limbour) to believe in him and encourage his efforts. This 1944 exhibition created a sensation and gave rise to a good deal of controversy. He resorted to new materials and worked out new techniques of his own, making graffiti and striving for "primitive" and "childlike" linework. He began building up a collection of "art brut" (drawings, paintings and objects executed by lunatics, children and people devoid of any artistic training). He later exhibited his collection and organized a Foyer de l'Art Brut. Exhibited at the Galerie Drouin in 1946 (**Mirobolus, Macadam & Cie, hautes pâtes**). Worked on a series of gouaches entitled **Paysages féeriques** and published **Prospectus aux amateurs de tous genres**. In 1947, at the Galerie Drouin, he exhibited **Portraits à ressemblance extraite, à ressemblance cuite et reconfite dans la mémoire,** and the Pierre Matisse Gallery in New York organized an exhibition of his work. From 1947 to 1949 he traveled in the Sahara and stayed at El Golea, working hard and experimenting with new pigments and materials. Exhibited in 1949 at the Galerie Rive Gauche, Paris, and the Galerie Le Diable par la Queue, Brussels. That same year he published **L'Art Brut préféré aux arts culturels** and two sets of lithographs, **Matières et Mémoires** and **Les Murs.** Made a trip to New York where Pierre Matisse in 1952 exhibited his recent works and pictures painted in the United States. In 1953 he exhibited at La Hune in Paris; in 1954 at the Cercle Volney in Paris he showed a large selection of paintings, drawings and various works, executed since 1942, and at the Galerie Rive Gauche he exhibited **Petites Statues de la vie précaire,** made of plaster, old newspapers, coal, lava, sponges, etc. In 1955 the Institute of Contemporary Arts in London organized a large exhibition illustrating all phases of his activity. In 1956, at the Galerie Rive Gauche, Paris, he presented **Assemblages d'empreintes** (paper cut-outs and India ink) and also exhibited in Belgium and the United States. Paris exhibitions at the Galerie Rive Droite (1957) and the Galerie Facchetti (1957, 1958). A retrospective was organized in 1957 at the Leverkusen Museum (Morsbroich Castle). Further exhibitions in Milan (Galleria del Naviglio, 1958), Rome (Galleria Selecta, 1958), London (Tooth Gallery, 1959), Frankfort and Paris (Galerie Daniel Cordier, **Célébrations du Sol,** 1958-1959), New York (Pierre Matisse Gallery, 1959), Milan (Galleria Blu, 1960), Paris (Galerie Daniel Cordier, **As-tu cueilli la fleur de barbe?,** 1960), London (Tooth Gallery, **Quarante éléments botaniques,** 1960), Paris (Galerie Berggruen, series of lithographs entitled **Phénomènes,** 1960). Took part in Vitalità nell'Arte (Venice, 1959), Documenta II (Kassel, 1959) and Dalla Natura all'Arte (Venice, 1960).

Bibliography:

G. Limbour, **Révélation d'un peintre,** in **Comoedia,** July 8, 1944. — J. Paulhan, **Lettre à J. Dubuffet,** in **Poésie 44,** No. 20; reprinted as the preface to the Dubuffet exhibition at the Galerie Drouin, Paris 1944. — L. Parrot, **Jean Dubuffet,** Paris 1944. — M. Arland, **Jean Dubuffet,** in **Le Spectateur des Arts,** December 1944. — R. Raufast, **Dubuffet ou l'art primitif vivant,** in **Formes et Couleurs,** June 1945. — M. Tapié, **Mirobolus, Macadam & Cie, hautes pâtes de Jean Dubuffet,** Paris 1946. — J. Saget, **Du beau du bon Dubuffet,** in **Combat,** November 3, 1946. — C. Greenberg, **Jean Dubuffet and "Art Brut",** in **The Partisan Review,** 1949. — Thomas B. Hess, **Dubuffet paints a Picture,** in **Art News,** May 1952. — G. Limbour, **Pierres d'exercice philosophique,** in **Temps Modernes,** June 1953. — G. Limbour, **Tableau bon levain à vous de cuire la pâte,** Paris 1953. — A. Vialatte, Preface to the Dubuffet Exhibition, Galerie Rive Gauche, Paris 1954. — G. Limbour, Preface to the Dubuffet Exhibition, Institute of Contemporary Arts, London 1955. — R. Bertelé, **Empreintes assemblées de Jean Dubuffet,** in **XX* Siècle,** 1956. — G. Limbour, **Jean Dubuffet,** in **L'Œil,** January 1957. — J. Ribemont-Dessaignes, **Jean Dubuffet à la limite de l'humour,** in **XX* Siècle,** January 1957. — G. Limbour, **Description d'un tableau,** in **Botteghe Oscure,** No. 19, Rome 1957. — G. Limbour, Preface to the Dubuffet Exhibition, Galerie Rive Droite, Paris 1957. — J. Fitzsimmons, **Jean Dubuffet, A Short Introduction to his Work,** in **Quadrum,** No. 4, Brussels 1957. — G. Limbour, **Les Texturologies de Jean Dubuffet,** in **Art International,** No. 9-12, 1958. — M. Ragon, **Jean Dubuffet,** in **Cimaise,** February 1958. — M. Ragon, **Jean Dubuffet,** Paris 1958; in English, New York 1959. — W. Grohmann, Preface to the Exhibition **Lob der Erde,** Galerie Daniel Cordier, Frankfort 1958. — P. Volboudt, **Jean Dubuffet, Les métamorphoses de l'élémentaire,** in **XX* Siècle,** Christmas 1958. — P. Guéguen, **Jean Dubuffet, ou le rachat de la matière,** in **Aujourd'hui,** December 1958. — G. Raimondi, **Il lavoro di Jean Dubuffet,** in **Comunità,** Milan, January 1959; French and English translations in **Art International,** No. 5-6, 1959. — G. Limbour, Preface to the Dubuffet Exhibition, Pierre Matisse Gallery, New York 1959. — A. Pieyre de Mandiargues, **Jean Dubuffet ou le point extrême,** in **Cahiers du Musée de Poche,** No. 2, June 1959. — P. Restany, **Dubuffet au naturel,** in **Art International,** No. 5-6, 1959. — A. Pieyre de Mandiargues, Preface to the Dubuffet Exhibition, Galerie Berggruen, Paris 1960. — D. Ashton, **Le peintre malgré lui,** in **Arts and Architecture,** Los Angeles, January 1960. — Introduction to the **Cosmorama** of Jean Dubuffet, with chronology of exhibitions and bibliography, **Cahiers du Collège de Pataphysique,** No. 10-11, 1960.

ESTÈVE, Maurice (1904)

Born at Culan in the Berry region of central France. Showed an aptitude for painting very early and went to Paris while still in his teens to study at the Académie Colarossi and the Grande-Chaumière in Montparnasse. Worked in 1919 as a furniture designer while painting on the side, chiefly landscapes in the impressionist style. Made a trip to Germany. Began exhibiting at the Salon des Indépendants, then showed regularly at the Salon des Surindépendants from 1929 on. First one-man show in 1930 at the Galerie Yvangot, Paris. In 1937 he worked with Robert Delaunay at the Pavillon de l'Air et des Chemins de Fer at the Paris World's Fair, and exhibited at the Petit-Palais. Traveled for several months in Italy, England and Scandinavia. Another one-man show in 1938 at the Galerie L'Equipe, Paris; invited the same year to take part in an exhibition at Prague. Exhibited yearly at the Salon d'Automne from 1941 to 1944, and participated in group exhibitions at the Galerie Friedland (1942), the Galerie de France (1943), the Galerie Berri-Raspail (1942), the Galerie Carré (1945, with Bazaine and Lapicque), and in 1946-1947 at Amsterdam (Stedelijk Museum), Copenhagen and Stockholm. An important retrospective exhibition of his work from 1937 to 1947 was held at the Galerie Louis Carré, Paris, in 1948. He showed regularly at the Salon de Mai, Paris, and took part in major exhibitions abroad: São Paulo Bienal (1953), Venice Biennale (1954), Pittsburgh International (1955), Pittori d'Oggi, Francia-Italia, Turin (1955), and Documenta II, Kassel (1959). One-man shows have been held at the Galerie Villand-Galanis, Paris, in 1955 (Recent Works), 1956 (Watercolors and Drawings) and 1960 (Drawings). A large Estève exhibition was organized in 1956 at the Royal Museum, Copenhagen (Paintings, Watercolors and Drawings from 1929 to 1955).

Bibliography:

P. Lesbats, **Cinq peintres d'aujourd'hui (Beaudin, Borès, Estève, Gischia, Pignon)**, Paris 1943. — J. Lescure, **Estève**, Paris 1945. — H. Rostrup, Preface to the Estève Exhibitions in Copenhagen and Stockholm, 1947. — F. Elgar, **Un grand artiste de la couleur, Estève**, in **Carrefour**, April 14, 1948. — J. Lescure, **Dallo spazio alla significazione a proposito di Chastel, Estève, Lapicque**, in **La Biennale**, No. 16, October 1953. — P. Francastel, **Estève, spontanéité et construction**, in **Prisme des Arts**, No. 2, April 1956. — P. Francastel, **Estève**, Paris 1956. — G. Boudaille, **Estève**, in **Cimaise**, September 1958. — A. Frénaud, **Estève, aquarelles récentes**, Paris 1958. — F. Elgar, **Dessins d'Estève**, Paris 1960.

FAUTRIER, Jean (1898)

Born in Paris. Brought up and schooled in England, where he received a solid grounding in classical and modern languages and also in the sciences. Showed an aptitude for drawing while still at school. Enrolled at the Royal Academy in London (1912) and then at the Slade School, but the instruction was not to his liking and he soon ceased to attend classes. Called up in 1917, he served in the French army at the front and was severely wounded and gassed. Returning to Paris in 1920, he took a studio in Montmartre and devoted himself to painting. Maroon Period, 1923-1924. Paul Guillaume organized his first one-man show at the Galerie Bernheim in 1927. Became friendly with André Malraux, who got him a commission from Gallimard to illustrate Dante's Inferno. So-called Black Period. In 1928 he exhibited at the Galerie Ariel, Paris. Gray Period: he intensified his texture and stood now on the threshold of informal painting. A long stay at Chamonix in 1929, where he developed a passion for the mountains and ski-ing. Took a new interest in color and entered his Blue Period; from now on his work became increasingly abstract. Exhibited at the Galerie de la N.R.F. in 1933 (preface by André Malraux) and again in 1939 (lithograph illustrations for Dante's Inferno). When war broke out he took refuge at Marseilles, then at Aix-en-Provence and Bordeaux. Returned in 1940 to Paris where his house became a Resistance center. Hunted by the SS, he went into hiding in the mountains, then (with the help of his close friend Jean Paulhan) in Paris itself. Finally he took refuge at Châtenay, in the suburbs of Paris, where he painted his **Hostages**. An exhibition of his work was held at the Galerie René Drouin, Paris, in 1943 (preface by Jean Paulhan), followed by a showing of his **Hostages** at the same gallery in 1945 (preface by André Malraux). Trip to Holland in 1947. From 1949 to 1953 he earned his living by reproducing works of art through a process of his own invention. An exhibition of his paintings and "multiple originals," Galerie Billiet-Caputo, Paris, 1950. In 1951 he took part in the exhibition "Signifiants de l'Informel," organized by Michel Tapié at the Galerie Facchetti, Paris. Trip to New York, then to Spain (1952), to Portugal and again to the United States (1953). After 1954 he was able to devote himself entirely to painting. Exhibited a vast group of works, including "objects" and "nudes," at the Galerie Rive Droite in 1955 (preface by Jean Paulhan). Exhibited **The Partisans** in 1957 as a protest against the turn of events in Hungary. Took part in 1958 in the exhibition "Où sont les origines de l'art informel?" Exhibitions in New York (Alexander Jolas Gallery and Hugo Gallery, 1956; Sidney Janis Gallery, 1957), Milan, Düsseldorf, Bologna, Rome, Freiburg-im-Breisgau and London (1958). Trips to England, Italy, Germany, the Canary Islands and Morocco. In 1959 he traveled in Italy (Milan and Rome), Germany and England (exhibiting at the Hanover Gallery, London). Then he went to Japan for an exhibition of his work and sailed around the world. Exhibited in 1959 in Rome, Bologna, Düsseldorf and took part in Documenta II at Kassel. Awarded the International Prize for Painting at the 1960 Venice Biennale. One-man show at the Galleria dell'Immagine, Turin 1960.

Bibliography:

M. Zahar, **Fautrier ou de la puissance des ténèbres**, in **Formes**, No. 7, July 1930. — A. Malraux, **Les Arts. Exposition Fautrier**, in **La Nouvelle Revue Française**, February 1, 1933. — J. Paulhan, **Fautrier, Œuvres (1915-1943)**, Preface to the Fautrier Exhibition, Galerie René Drouin, Paris 1943 (with **Quelques opinions de 1929**, by L. Vauxcelles, P. Léonard, L. L. Martin, J. Martin, A. Tabarant, Y. Mareschal, A. Malraux, Acaste, P. Fierens). — A. Malraux, **Les Otages**, Preface to the Fautrier Exhibition, Galerie Drouin, Paris, October-November 1945; this text was reprinted in the catalogue of Fautrier Exhibitions at Düsseldorf (February 1958), Galleria Apollinaire, Milan (October 1958), Leverkusen (December 1958) and Hanover Gallery, London (June 1959). — D. Wallard, **Les Otages de Fautrier**, in **Poésie**, Paris, January 1946. — F. Ponge, **Notes sur les Otages de Fautrier**, Pierre Seghers, Paris 1946. — J. Paulhan, **Fautrier l'enragé**, Georges Blaizot, Paris 1949. — J. Paulhan, **Les Débuts d'un art universel**, Preface to the Exhibition of Fautrier's "Multiple Originals," Galerie Billiet-Caputo, Paris, November-December 1950. — R. de Solier, **Fautrier**, in **Monde Nouveau**, April 1955. — M. Tapié, **Fautrier paints a Picture**, in **Art News**, December 1955. — J. Alvard, **Fautrier**, in **Cimaise**, No. 4, March 1955. — F. Ponge, **Paroles à propos de Nus de Fautrier**, Galerie Rive Droite, Paris 1956. — R. Droguet, **Fautrier 43**, Lyons 1957. — A. Verdet, **Le tragique de l'humour chez Fautrier**, in **XX° Siècle**, No. 8, January 1957. — M. Ragon, **Fautrier**, Paris 1957. — P. Restany, **Fautrier, Trente années de figuration informelle**, Paris 1957. — M. Calvesi, Preface to the Fautrier Exhibition, Galleria dell'Attico, Rome, April 1958. — L. Alloway, **Fautrier's Form**, in **Art International**, Zurich, September-October 1958. — A. Verdet, **Fautrier**, Paris 1958. — J. Paulhan, **Jean Fautrier**, in **XX° Siècle**, 1958. — Herbert Read, Preface to the Fautrier Exhibition, Galleria Apollinaire, Milan 1958. — P. Restany, **Jean Fautrier et l'insurrection de la forme**, in **Art International**, No.1-2, Zurich 1959. — J. Lescure, **Dialoghi con Fautrier**, in **La Biennale**, No. 34, January-March 1959. — G. C. Argan, **Da Bergson a Fautrier**, in **Aut-Aut**, No. 55, January 1960. — P. Bucarelli, **Jean Fautrier**, Milan 1960 (with a complete bibliography).

FRANCIS, Sam (1923)

Born at San Mateo, California, and studied at the University of California, Berkeley, 1941-1943. After serving in the U.S. Air Force, 1943-1945, he took up painting and was instructed privately by David Parks, Professor at the California School of Fine Arts, San Francisco. He first exhibited at the San Francisco Museum of Fine Arts, 1946; first one-man show, San Francisco, 1948. Returning to the University of California, he received his B.A. degree, 1949, and M.A., 1950. He visited Paris in 1950, where he met Jean-Paul Riopelle and a group of younger American painters. The Galerie Nina Dausset held a one-man exhibition in 1952. In 1954 he returned briefly to California. The Kunsthalle, Bern, exhibited seven of his paintings in "Tendances Actuelles," 1955; in the same year he had another one-man show at the Galerie Rive Droite, Paris. In 1956 he executed a mural in three sections for the Kunsthalle, Basel (installed 1958). He traveled around the world in 1957-1958, stopping in New York, Mexico, California, Japan, Hong Kong, Siam and India. While in Japan he executed a mural for the Sofu School of Flower Arrangements, Tokyo, 1957. He made a second world voyage in 1959, again visiting India, Japan, California and New York. He executed a mural for the Park Avenue Chase Manhattan Bank, New York, 1959. His major exhibitions include frequent one-man shows in New York (Martha Jackson Gallery), London (Gimpel Fils), Bern (Kornfeld and Klipstein), 1957; Tokyo and Osaka. The Kunsthalle, Düsseldorf (1959), and the Kunsthalle, Bern (1960), have also presented one-man shows. In addition he participated in the Pittsburgh International, 1955, 1958; São Paulo Bienal, 1959; Documenta II, Kassel, 1959. He lives in Paris, and visits frequently his other studios in New York, Los Altos, Calif., Tokyo and Bern.

Bibliography:

Ecole du Pacifique, in **Cimaise,** Paris, No. 7, June 1954. — Review of the Francis Exhibition, Galerie Rive Droite, Paris, in **Art News,** New York, Vol. 54, June 1955. — **Sam Francis,** exhibition catalogue, Klipstein and Kornfeld, Bern 1957. — **Sam Francis, Shirley Jaffe, Kimber Smith,** exhibition catalogue, Centre Culturel Américain, Paris 1958. — **Sam Francis,** exhibition catalogue, Klipstein and Kornfeld, Bern 1959. — D. Ashton, Review of the Francis Exhibition, Martha Jackson Gallery, New York, in **Arts and Architecture,** Los Angeles, No. 76, February 1959. — F. Meyer, **Sam Francis,** exhibition catalogue, Kunsthalle, Bern 1960. — Yoshiaki Tono, **From a Gulliver's Point of View,** in **Art in America,** No. 2, New York 1960.

GORKY, Arshile (1905-1948)

Born at Hayotz Dzore, Turkish Armenia. The family fled Turkish oppression to Erivan, Russian Transcaucasia, during World War I. He attended the Polytechnic Institute in Tiflis, 1916-1918. He emigrated to the United States in 1920 with his sister. Worked first in a rubber factory in Watertown, Mass., then moved to Providence and studied briefly in night classes at the Rhode Island School of Design. He moved to Boston where he studied at the New School of Design, 1923, and taught in the life class, 1924. Moving to New York in 1925, he first studied, then taught at Grand Central School of Art until 1931. He first exhibited in the Museum of Modern Art in "An Exhibition of Work by 46 Painters and Sculptors under 35 Years of Age," 1930; then with the Société Anonyme, 1931. Invited to join the Abstraction-Creation group in Paris, 1932. His first one-man shows were at the Guild Gallery, New York, 1932, and the Mellon Galleries, Philadelphia, 1934. From 1935, when he was represented in the exhibition of Abstract Painting in America, he showed regularly at the Whitney Museum in New York. 1936-1938 worked for WPA Federal Art Project and executed murals for Newark Airport, New Jersey (present whereabouts unknown). In addition, he painted murals for the Aviation Building, New York World's Fair, 1939 (these have also disappeared). In 1942 he organized a course in camouflage painting at the Grand Central School of Art. From 1943 to 1948 he lived for part of each year in Connecticut, Virginia and New York. His first major New York one-man show was held in 1945 at the Julien Levy Gallery. A fire in 1946 in his studio in Sherman, Conn., destroyed many of his paintings. He committed suicide in 1948. A memorial exhibition was held at the Whitney Museum, New York, shown also in Minneapolis and San Francisco. He was also represented in " Le Surréalisme en 1947", an international exhibition presented by André Breton and Marcel Duchamp, Galerie Maeght, Paris, 1947; Venice Biennale, 1950; The New American Painting, Museum of Modern Art, New York (shown in 8 countries in Europe), 1958-1959; Documenta II, Kassel, 1959.

Bibliography:

Willem de Kooning, letter in **Art News,** New York, vol. 25, February 1, 1949, p. 19. — Aline Loucheim, **Contemporary Art in New York,** in The Atlantic Monthly, Boston, Vol. 186, December 1950, pp. 65-70. — Stuart Davis, **Arshile Gorky in the 1930's: A Personal Recollection,** in **Magazine of Art,** New York, vol. 44, February 1951, pp. 56-58. — Lloyd Goodrich, **Notes on Eight Works by Arshile Gorky,** in **Magazine of Art,** Vol. 44, February 1951, pp. 59-61. — Henry McBride, **Success at Last,** in Art News, Vol. 52, April 1953, pp. 66-67. — Meyer Schapiro, **Gorky: The Creative Influence,** in Art News, New York, Vol. 56, September 1957, pp. 28-31. — Ethel K. Schwabacher, **Arshile Gorky,** Macmillan, New York 1957.

GUSTON, Philip (1913)

Born in Montreal, Canada. He went to the United States in 1916 and grew up in Los Angeles. The only formal art training he received was during three months' study at the Otis Art Institute, Los Angeles. He visited Mexico in 1934-1935, then moved to New York in 1935, where he worked on the WPA Federal Art Project until 1940. Under WPA he executed several murals, including one in the Federal Works Agency Building at the New York World's Fair, 1939, and one at the Queensbridge Housing Project, 1940. At the same time the Treasury Department's Section of Fine Arts commissioned murals for the U. S. Post Office in Commerce, Ga., 1938, and the Social Security Building, Washington, D.C., 1942. He has taught at the State University of Iowa, 1941-1945; Washington University, St. Louis, 1945-1947, and at New York University since 1950. In 1947-1949 he traveled in Italy, Spain and France on a Guggenheim Fellowship (1947), a Prix de Rome (1948) and a grant from the American Academy of Arts and Letters. He was awarded a Ford Foundation Grant in 1959. His first one-man show took place at the State University of Iowa, Iowa City, 1944; first exhibition in New York at Midtown Galleries, 1945. Recently he has exhibited at the Sidney Janis Gallery, New York, 1956, 1958, 1960, and participated in the Pittsburgh International, 1955, 1958; São Paulo Bienal, 1957, 1959; and Documenta II, Kassel, 1959. He lives in New York and West Hurley, New York.

Bibliography:

Paul Brach, **A New Non-Objective Guston Poses Questions of Degree,** in Art Digest, New York, Vol. 26, January 1, 1952. — Review of the Guston Exhibition, Peridot Gallery, in **Art News,** New York, Vol. 50, January 1952. — Leo Steinberg, **Fritz Glarner and Philip Guston among "Twelve Americans" at the Museum of Modern Art,** in Arts, New York, Vol. 30, June 1956. — Doré Ashton, Review of the Guston Exhibition, Sidney Janis Gallery, in **Arts and Architecture,** Los Angeles, Vol. 75, May 1958. — Review of the Guston Exhibition, Sidney Janis Gallery, in **Arts,** New York, Vol. 34, February 1960. — Doré Ashton, Presentation at the 30th Biennale, Venice 1960.

HANTAÏ, Simon (1922)

Born at Bia, Hungary. Attended classes at the Academy of Fine Arts, Budapest, from 1941 to 1947. Went to Italy in 1948, then to Paris in 1949, where he settled for good. There he met André Breton, who presented his first one-man show at the Galerie L'Etoile Scellée in 1953. That same year he took part in the exhibition of Younger European Painters, organized by J. J. Sweeney at the Solomon R. Guggenheim Museum, New York. Several one-man shows in recent years at the Galerie Kléber, Paris. In 1959 he took part in Documenta II at Kassel. With Georges Mathieu in 1957 he organized the "Cérémonies Commémoratives de la Deuxième Condamnation de Siger de Brabant" at the Galerie Kléber, Paris.

Bibliography:

R. Goldwater, **These Promising Younger Europeans,** in **Art News,** December 1953.

HARTUNG, Hans (1904)

Born in Leipzig, Germany. From eight to ten he lived in Basel, Switzerland, where he developed a passionate interest in astronomy and photography, and even built himself a telescope. Classical schooling in Dresden from 1915 to 1924. Attracted to painting while still in his teens, studying Goya, Hals, El Greco, Rembrandt, then the Expressionists, and Corinth and Slevogt. Departed radically in his early work from an "objective" interpretation of reality, though Mondrian and Kandinsky were still unknown to him. Took his degree in philosophy and art history at Leipzig University in 1924, then attended the Fine Arts Schools in Leipzig and Dresden until 1926. Moved to Munich and continued his art studies there until 1930, making hundreds of copies in the museums. His eyes were opened to contemporary painting at the Dresden International Exhibition in 1926. During the summer of that year he made a long cycling tour through Italy, and in 1927 visited Paris, Belgium, Holland, Sweden and the Tirol. Spent the winters of 1927, 1928 and 1929 in Paris; stayed for a time on the Riviera in 1930 and 1931. Exhibited in 1931 at the Galerie Heinrich Kühl, Dresden, where he met Fritz Bienert and Will Grohmann, who bought a picture from him. In 1932, stricken with illness and depression after the death of his father, he settled in the island of Minorca, where he had a house built. In 1935, after a trip to Sweden, he returned to Germany; but the Nazi régime made life difficult for him. With the help of Will Grohmann and Christian Zervos he was able to leave Germany and settle in Paris, where he met Kandinsky, Mondrian, Hélion, Goetz, Domela and Magnelli. Took part in the Salon des Surindépendants (from 1935 to 1938), in the exhibition "De Cézanne à nos jours" (1937) organized by Zervos at the Jeu de Paume, and in the exhibition of Twentieth Century German Art in London (1938). An exhibition of his drawings and pastels was organized at the Galerie Henriette, Paris, in 1939. At the outbreak of war he enlisted in the French Foreign Legion and served for two years in North Africa. Discharged in 1941, he returned to France and lived in the unoccupied zone until 1943, when the Germans moved in; he then escaped to Spain, where he spent seven months in prison. Finally released, he made his way to North Africa and joined General de Gaulle's army. Took part in the invasion of France in 1944 and was badly wounded at the siege of Belfort; his left leg had to be amputated. Awarded the Médaille Militaire, the Croix de Guerre and the Legion of Honor. In 1945, in recognition of his war record, he received French nationality. He returned to Paris and began to paint again. Took part in 1946 in the Salon des Réalités Nouvelles and the Salon de Mai, where he exhibited yearly thereafter. First one-man show in 1947 at the Galerie Lydia Conti, Paris. Exhibited pastels at the Galerie Carré with Lanskoy and Schneider in 1949, and showed there regularly thereafter. Hartung exhibition at the Kunsthalle, Basel, in 1952. Participated in the exhibition of Advancing French Art, organized by Louis Carré in New York, San Francisco and Chicago; the Venice Biennale (1952); Abstrakte Malerei (Basel, Galerie Beyeler, 1956), Pittori d'Oggi (Turin, 1957), the Carnegie International, Pittsburgh (1958), New York and Paris Painting in the Fifties (Houston, 1959). One-man shows in Paris (Galerie de France, 1956, 1958, 1960; Galerie Craven, Early Drawings, 1956), Rome (Graphic Work, 1958), Munich (1958). Awarded the Rubens Prize by the city of Siegen in 1958 and the International Prize at the 1960 Venice Biennale.

Bibliography:

Madeleine Rousseau, Preface to the Hartung Exhibition, Galerie Lydia Conti, Paris 1947. — D. Sutton, Preface to the Hartung Exhibition, Hanover Gallery, London 1949. — M. Rousseau, O. Domnick, J. J. Sweeney, **Hans Hartung,** Stuttgart 1950. — R. de Solier, **Hans Hartung,** in **Cahiers d'Art,** July 1952. — M. Seuphor, **Hans Hartung,** in **Art Digest,** March 1955, No. 11, Vol. 29. — R. de Solier, **Hans Hartung,** in **Quadrum,** No. 2, November 1956. — W. Schmalenbach, **Hans Hartung,** Preface to the Hartung Exhibition, Kestner Gesellschaft, Hanover 1956. — R. V. Gindertael, **Hans Hartung,** in **Cimaise,** October 1956. — R. V. Gindertael, Preface, Exhibition of Early Drawings, Galerie Craven, Paris 1956. — G. Marchiori, Preface, Exhibition of Graphic Work, Galleria Il Segno, Rome 1958. — Catalogue of the Hartung Exhibition, Galerie de France, Paris, June 1960. — R. Cogniat, Catalogue of the Biennale, Venice 1960. — Dominique Aubier, **Hans Hartung,** in **Camera,** No. 8, August 1960.

HERBIN, Auguste (1882-1960)

Born at Quiévy, near Cambrai, France. Grew up at Le Cateau-Cambrésis, where he showed an aptitude for drawing. In 1898 he went to Lille and enrolled in the Ecole des Beaux-Arts. In 1901 he settled in Paris and began to paint, influenced by Impressionism. Sold some pictures in 1902 to Le Père Soulier, and in 1904 to Clovis Sagot. Exhibited at the Salon des Indépendants in 1905, and yearly thereafter until 1909. Stayed for a time at Bruges. From 1906 on he took an increasing interest in problems of color-form and departed more and more from "objective" representation. In 1907 he met Wilhelm Uhde, who bought some canvases from him; exhibited at the Salon d'Automne and visited Corsica and Hamburg. The pictures he submitted to the 1908 Salon d'Automne were rejected by the selection committee (Braque's work was rejected the same year). In 1909 he took a studio in the Bateau-Lavoir. From 1910 to 1912 he tackled problems closely related to Cubism, but took no part in the cubist exhibitions at the Salon des Indépendants. Stayed in 1911 at Hardricourt, Strasbourg and Andlau; in 1912 at Vadencourt. Lived and worked at Céret, near Perpignan, in 1913, combining rigorously geometric forms with brilliant color. Stayed for a while at Condé-sur-Aisne in 1914 (many of the canvases done there were destroyed in the war). First one-man show in Paris in 1917 at the Galerie L'Effort Moderne. Did frescos and geometric-abstract sculptures, in addition to painting, until 1921. Between 1922 and 1925 he reverted to figurative painting. He himself has designated the subsequent phases of his work as follows: 1925-1939, second abstract period; from 1939 on, abstract non-objective period. Exhibited at the Salon des Indépendants in 1927 and 1928, and founded the Abstraction-Creation group with Vantongerloo in 1932. Exhibited regularly at the Salon des Réalités Nouvelles, of which he served as one of the chairmen until 1955. One-man shows held regularly at the Galerie Lydia Conti (until 1947), then at the Galerie Denise René, Paris. Published a book in 1949: **L'art non figuratif non objectif.** Exhibited at Liège in 1954 (A.P.I.A.W.) and at the Palais des Beaux-Arts, Brussels, in 1956. Herbin retrospectives were organized at Freiburg-im-Breisgau in 1956 and at Turin in 1959 (at the exhibition "Pittori d'Oggi, Francia-Italia"). He died in Paris in 1960.

Bibliography:

A. Jakowski, **Auguste Herbin,** Paris 1933. — R. Massat, **Auguste Herbin**; L. Estang, **Herbin le rigoureux**; P. Peissi, **Herbin le pur**, in **Art d'Aujourd'hui** No. 4, November 1949. — P. Guéguen, Herbin, in **Art d'Aujourd'hui**, No. 3-4, February-March 1952. — L. Degand, **L'Exposition Herbin**, in **Art d'Aujourd'hui**, No. 3-4, February-March 1952. — R. V. Gindertael, **Le passage de la ligne**, in **Art d'Aujourd'hui**, No. 7-8, October 1952. — J. Alvard, **Herbin, un art inobjectif**, in **Cimaise**, August 1954. — C. H. Sibert, **Herbin**, in **Cimaise**, July 1955. — R. Bouillier, **Herbin, maître du géométrisme**, in **Arts, Lettres, Spectacles**, No. 620, May 1957. — Jacques Lassaigne, Preface to the Herbin Retrospective, Turin 1959. — D. Chevalier, **Auguste Herbin, In Memoriam**, in **Art d'Aujourd'hui**, No. 25, 1960.

HOFMANN, Hans (1880)

Born at Weissenberg, Bavaria. In 1886 he moved to Munich, where he was educated, and began in 1898 to study art. He studied under Willi Schwarz, who interested Philipp Freudenberg, a Berlin art collector, in his work. With the aid of Freudenberg, Hofmann went in 1904 to Paris where he stayed until 1914. His first one-man exhibition was shown at Paul Cassirer's, Berlin, 1910. In Munich, in 1915, he founded an art school and made a reputation as an artist-teacher. After teaching in the summer session at the University of California, Berkeley, in 1930, he moved permanently to the United States. He taught at the Chouinard Art Institute, Los Angeles, and again at the University of California in 1931, and then moved to New York, where he taught at the Art Students League, 1932-1933. In the summers of 1932-1933 he taught at the Thurn School, Gloucester, Mass. He opened the Hofmann School of Art in New York, 1934, and in 1935, a summer school in Provincetown, Mass. He became an American citizen in 1941. His first one-man show in New York took place at Peggy Guggenheim's gallery, Art of This Century, in 1944. In the same year the Arts Club of Chicago exhibited a retrospective one-man show, which was followed by similar exhibitions at the Addison Gallery of American Art, Andover, Mass., 1948: Bennington College, Vt., 1955; the Art Alliance, Philadelphia, 1956; and the Whitney Museum of American Art, New York, 1957. In addition he has exhibited almost every year since 1944 in New York, most recently at the Kootz Gallery, and has participated in the Pittsburgh International, 1952, 1958, Documenta II, Kassel, 1959, Venice Biennale, 1960. In 1956 Hofmann

executed a 1,200 foot mosaic for an office building at 711 Third Ave., N.Y., architect William Lescaze. He lives in New York.

Bibliography:

J. H. Lawson, **Hans Hofmann Exhibition at Art of This Century,** in **Arts and Architecture,** Los Angeles, Vol. 61, March 1944. — Clement Greenberg, **Most Important Teacher of Our Time,** in **The Nation,** New York, April 21, 1945. — Hans Hofmann, **Search for the Real,** Addison Gallery of American Art, Andover, Mass., 1949. — Elaine de Kooning, **Hans Hofmann paints a Picture,** in **Art News,** New York, Vol. 49, February 1950. — Paul Bird, **Hofmann Profile,** in **Art Digest,** New York, Vol. 25, May 15, 1951. — Clement Greenberg, exhibition catalogue, Bennington College, Bennington, Vermont, 1955. — Hans Hofmann, **The Color Problem in Pure Painting. Its Creative Origin,** in **Arts and Architecture,** Los Angeles, Vol. 73, February 1956. — Frederick S. Wight, **Hans Hofmann,** University of California Press, Berkeley and Los Angeles 1957. — Doré Ashton, in **Cimaise,** Paris, No. 3, January-March 1959. — K. B. Sawyer, Presentation at the 30th Biennale, Venice 1960. — See also statements by the artist in Kootz Gallery catalogues, New York.

JORN, Asger (1914)

Born at Vejrun (Jutland), Denmark. Began life as a schoolmaster, then in 1936 he went to Paris, studied painting under Fernand Léger and collaborated with Le Corbusier at the Temps Nouveaux pavilion of the Paris World's Fair in 1937. In 1938, with the architect Dahlmann Olsen, he launched the magazine **Helhesten.** From 1938 to 1948 he worked hard in Denmark and joined the Host and Spiralen groups. From 1948 to 1951 he was a prominent member of the Cobra group (Copenhagen-Brussels-Amsterdam), supported the movement for an imaginist Bauhaus, and joined the Situationist International and the Surindépendants. Held his first one-man show in 1948 at the Galerie Breteau, Paris, and took part in the first International Exhibition of Experimental Art, Amsterdam, 1949. Settled in Paris for good in 1955 and made his first trip to Italy, putting in several long stays there in the next few years and coming into contact with the members of the Nuclear Art group. One-man shows in Rome (Galleria dell'Asterisco, 1954), Milan (Galleria del Naviglio, 1955), Venice (Galleria del Cavallino, 1957), Paris (Galerie Rive Gauche, 1957, 1958, 1960). Exhibited his **Modifications** in 1959 at the Galerie Rive Gauche. His work was represented at the Fifty Years of Modern Art exhibition (Brussels World's Fair, 1958), the Carnegie International, Pittsburgh (1958), the Institute of Contemporary Arts, London (1958), Vitalità nell'Arte, Venice (1959), Documenta II (Kassel, 1959), and the traveling exhibition of European Art Today (United States, 1959-1960). Besides painting, his activities extend to engraving, sculpture and ceramics; one of his ceramics, made during the summer months at Albisola (Italy) for the high school at Aarhus (Denmark), measures 100 by 10 feet. He has also illustrated several books by Danish authors.

Bibliography:

E. Jaguer, Preface to the Jorn Exhibition, Galleria dell'Asterisco, Rome, June 1954. — E. Jaguer, Catalogue Preface, Galleria del Naviglio, Milan, October 1955. — J. Prévert, Catalogue Preface, Galerie Rive Gauche, Paris, June 1957. — R. Bertelé, Catalogue Preface, Institute of Contemporary Arts, London, May 1958. — Y. Taillandier, Catalogue Preface, Galerie Rive Gauche, Paris, May 1960.

KLINE, Franz (1910)

Born at Wilkes-Barre, Pa., and grew up in Philadelphia. He studied at Girard College, Philadelphia, and attended art classes at Boston University School of Fine and Applied Arts, 1931-1935. He lived in England in 1937-1938, studying at Heatherly's Art School in London. He went to New York in 1938; first exhibited at the Annuals of the National Academy of Design, 1942-1945. The Egan Gallery, New York, gave him his first one-man show in 1950; since then he has had frequent one-man exhibitions in the United States and Europe; in New York most recently at the Sidney Janis Gallery. He has taught at Black Mountain College, North Carolina, 1952; Pratt Institute, Brooklyn, New York, 1953-1954; Philadelphia Museum School of Art, 1954. Now lives in New York. His work was included in the following exhibitions: The New Decade, Whitney Museum of American Art, New York, circulating to San Francisco, Los Angeles, Colorado Springs and St. Louis, 1955-1956; 12 Americans, Museum of Modern Art, New York, 1956; The New American Painting, organized by the Museum of Modern Art, New York, and shown in Basel, Milan, Madrid, Berlin, Amsterdam, Brussels, Paris, London, and New York, 1958-1959; the Pittsburgh International, 1952, 1955, 1958; Venice Biennale, 1956, 1960; São Paulo Bienal, 1957; Guggenheim International Award, New York, 1958, 1960; and Documenta II, Kassel, 1959.

Bibliography:

Reviews of Kline Exhibitions at the Egan Gallery, **Art News**, New York, Vol. 49, November 1950, and **Art Digest**, New York, Vol. 26, December 1, 1951. — R. Goodnough, **Kline paints a Picture**, in **Art News**, New York, Vol. 51, December 1952. — Martica Sawin, **An American Artist in Japan**, in **Art Digest**, New York, Vol. 29, August 1, 1955. — Leo Steinberg, Review of the Kline Exhibition, Sidney Janis Gallery, in **Arts**, New York, Vol. 39, April 1956. — Elaine de Kooning, **Two Americans in Action: Franz Kline, Mark Rothko**, in **Art News Annual**, New York, No. 27, November 1957. — **Is Today's Artist with or against the Past?**, in **Art News**, Vol. 57, September 1958. — Frank O'Hara, **Franz Kline Talking**, in **Evergreen Review**, Vol. 2, No. 6, 1960. — K. B. Sawyer, Presentation at the 30th Biennale, Venice 1960.

KOONING, Willem de (1904)

Born in Rotterdam. In 1916 he was apprenticed to a decorating and commercial art firm run by Jan and Jaap Gidding. For the next eight years he studied in night classes at the Academie voor Beeldende Kunsten en Technische Wetenschappen, Rotterdam. In 1920 he began to work as an apprentice to Bernard Romein, an artist who worked also in commercial art for a department store. He moved to Belgium in 1924, where he painted and studied in Brussels and Antwerp. He returned to Rotterdam, 1925, and then went to the United States in 1926. At first he supported himself by working in New Jersey as a house painter then in New York City as a free-lance commercial artist. During the summer of 1928 he visited the artists' colony, Woodstock, N.Y. His friendship with Arshile Gorky dates from this period; they shared a studio in the late 1930s. In 1935-1936 he worked for WPA Federal Art Project on mural and easel projects, under the supervision of Burgoyne Diller. He worked under Fernand Léger on a mural for French Lines' pier, New York, and in 1937 was commissioned to design a mural for the Hall of Pharmacy at the New York World's Fair. In the early 1940s he exhibited in group shows and maintained close friendships with other New York artists. He taught at Black Mountain College, summer, 1948; and at Yale University, 1950-1951. His first one-man show, held at the Egan Gallery, New York, 1948, established his reputation. Since then he has exhibited regularly in New York, most recently at the Sidney Janis Gallery, and in museum exhibitions: The New Decade, Whitney Museum of American Art, 1955, circulating to San Francisco, Los Angeles, Colorado Springs, St. Louis; The New American Painting, organized by the Museum of Modern Art, shown in Basel, Milan, Madrid, Berlin, Amsterdam, Brussels, Paris, London, New York, 1958-1959; New Images of Man, Museum of Modern Art, New York, 1959. In 1951 he was awarded first prize at the Chicago Art Institute Annual. He has also participated in the following international exhibitions: Venice Biennale, 1948, 1950, 1954, 1956; São Paulo Bienal, 1951, 1953; Pittsburgh International, 1952, 1955, 1958; and Documenta II, Kassel, 1959. Lives in New York.

Bibliography:

Renée Arb, **Spotlight on de Kooning**, in **Art News**, New York, April 1948, Vol. 47. — Clement Greenberg, Review of the de Kooning Exhibition, Egan Gallery, in **The Nation**, New York, April 22, 1948. — **What Abstract Art Means to Me: Statements by Six American Artists**, in **Museum of Modern Art Bulletin**, New York 1951, Vol. 18, No. 3. — Thomas B. Hess, **De Kooning paints a Picture**, in **Art News**, New York, March 1953, Vol. 52. — Henry McBride, Review of the de Kooning Exhibition, Sidney Janis Gallery, in **Art News**, April 1953, Vol. 52. — **Is Today's Artist with or against the Past?**, in **Art News**, June 1958, Vol. 57. — Kenneth B. Sawyer, **Three Phases of Willem de Kooning**, in **Art News and Review**, London, November 22, 1958, Vol. X, No. 22. — Peter Selz, **New Images of Man**, Museum of Modern Art, New York 1959, pp. 88-95. — Thomas B. Hess, **Willem de Kooning**, Braziller, New York 1959.

LANSKOY, André (1902)

Born in Moscow. Grew up at St Petersburg. At Kiev in 1919 with the White Russian army. Began to paint, first with the painter Sudeikine, then alone, and became an enthusiastic admirer of Van Gogh and Matisse. Went to Paris in 1921, where for a time he attended art classes at the Grande-Chaumière in Montparnasse. Went in at first for fantastic subjects, then turned away from these as he began to experiment with color-forms inspired by nature. Painted a great many landscapes. Exhibited for the first time in 1923 with a group of Russian artists (Galerie La Licorne, Paris). In 1924 Wilhelm Uhde bought some of his pictures and introduced him at the Galerie Bing, which organized his first one-man show in 1925. From 1930 on he took a keen interest in Klee's and Kandinsky's painting and began to work out an abstract style of his own, which reached maturity ten years later. Participated in group exhibitions at Amsterdam, Utrecht and The Hague in 1938. By 1937 he had broken away for good from figurative painting; by 1941 he felt himself "liberated from the object." One-man shows in Paris in 1942 (Galerie Berri-Raspail), 1944 (Galerie Jeanne Bucher, non-figurative works), 1948 (Galerie Louis Carré), 1949 (Galerie des Garets); and in Brussels in 1948 (Galerie Ex-Libris). Took part in 1950 in the exhibition Advancing French Art, organized by Louis Carré in Paris and New York. Executed his first tapestry designs. Exhibitions and one-man shows from 1951 to

1959: Galerie Jacques Dubourg, Paris (1951); Comité d'Action Artistique, Antwerp (1952); Galerie Louis Carré, Paris (1952, 1957); Arthur Tooth Gallery, London (1953); Wuppertal and Cologne (1954); Stockholm (1955); Galerie Palmes, Paris (1956); Fine Art Associates, New York (1956, 1957); Albert Loeb Gallery, New York (1959); Galerie Raymonde Cazenave, Paris (1959). Took part in collective exhibitions in Chicago (1952), East Hampton ("What Business Men Collect," 1952), Paris (Salon de Mai, 1955 to 1960), Basel (Abstrakte Malerei, Galerie Beyeler, 1956), Pittsburgh (Carnegie International, 1958), Minneapolis (School of Paris 1959: The Internationals).

Bibliography:

R. V. Gindertael, **Lanskoy, ébauche d'un portrait** (11 portraits by A. Ostier), Carré, Paris 1957. — D. Ashton, **Lanskoy,** in **Arts,** March 1958, Vol. 30, No. 6. — R. V. Gindertael, Preface to the Lanskoy Exhibition, Galerie Raymonde Cazenave, Paris 1959. — Jean Grenier, **André Lanskoy,** Hazan, Paris 1960.

LATASTER, Ger (1920)

Born at Schaesberg (Limburg), Holland. Attended classes at the Decorative Arts School at Maestricht, then enrolled at the Art Academy, Amsterdam. In 1950 he received a grant from the French government enabling him to make a long stay in Paris. Trip to Brittany. Took part in the Premio Lissone exhibition in 1955 and exhibited with an avant-garde group of young Dutch painters at the Galerie Jahrling in Wuppertal. In 1959 he took part in the Vitalità nell'Arte exhibition, Venice, and Documenta II, Kassel. First one-man show at the Galerie Facchetti, Paris, in 1960.

Bibliography:

Lataster, in **Palaestra,** No. 2, 1948. — Sandberg, Presentation, Lataster Exhibition, Galerie Facchetti, Paris 1960.

LE MOAL, Jean (1909)

Born at Authon-du-Perche (Eure-et-Loir), France. After attending classes at the Ecole des Beaux-Arts, Lyons, he enrolled in the Ecole des Arts Décoratifs, Paris, and copied paintings at the Louvre, where he met Manessier. About 1934 he studied at the Académie Ranson, Paris, where he attended the classes in fresco painting given by Bissière. From 1935 on he traveled widely in Spain, Belgium and Holland, where his eyes were opened to color. Took part in 1937 in the first Salon des Jeunes Artistes, Galerie Beaux-Arts, Paris, presented by Jacques Lassaigne; and in 1938 in the Témoignage exhibition at the Galerie Matières opened by Breteau. In 1939 he paid a visit to the United States; with a whole group of artists he helped to decorate a ceiling at the New York World's Fair covering over 1500 square yards in area. Back in France, he began experimenting in abstraction, though he continued to produce figurative paintings until 1942, when his style became wholly abstract. Collaborated with the theatrical producer Jacquemont, executing stage sets for **Le buveur émerveillé, L'étoile de Séville, Les gueux au Paradis, Noces de sang, L'annonce faite à Marie.** Took part after the war in major exhibitions of French painting abroad, in Stockholm, Copenhagen, Turin (Pittori d'Oggi, 1957, with a room devoted to him), Milan, Tokyo. Since 1943 he has exhibited yearly at the Salon de Mai, Paris. Exhibited with Manessier and Singier first at the Galerie de France (1944), then at the Galerie Drouin (1946). One-man shows at the Galerie de France in 1956 and 1959. His work was represented at Documenta II, Kassel, 1959.

Bibliography:

C. Bourniquel, **Trois peintres : Le Moal, Manessier, Singier,** Paris 1946. — J. Lassaigne, **Le Moal,** in **XXᵉ Siècle,** N° 6, January 1956. — **Le Moal de la Galerie de France,** presentation at the Galleria dell'Ariete, Milan, March 8, 1957.

MAGNELLI, Alberto (1888)

Born in Florence, where he began painting at an early age, encouraged by a friend of the family. In 1909 he decided to make a career of painting, but attended no art school. In 1911 he sold one of his first pictures at the Venice Biennale. In 1914 he moved in the circle of painters and writers connected with the Florentine art magazine **Lacerba,** then came in contact with the Futurists. During a stay in Paris (February-June, 1914) he met Apollinaire, Max Jacob, Archipenko, Fernand Léger and Picasso. Painted a series of schematized still lifes and figures in pure, violent colors, and then, in Florence in 1915, his first abstract works in bright flat colors. While keeping in touch with the avant-garde milieus of Italian art, he pursued an independent line of research leading toward complete abstraction. In 1918 he painted his **Lyrical Explosions,** prefiguring what was later called **tachisme;** then in 1920, reverting to figurative art, he produced some highly simplified, architecturally ordered compositions. In 1931 he settled for good in Paris. In 1932 the marble quarries at Carrara inspired him to paint a series of pictures called **Stones.** By 1935 he had achieved a thoroughly abstract style based on "invented figuration," and from 1937 on he pushed further and further along the path of complete abstraction. An important exhibition of his work was held at the Galerie Drouin, Paris, in 1947. Awarded second prize at the 1951 São Paulo Bienal. He showed at the 1954 Venice Biennale and the same year a large Magnelli retrospective was held at the Palais des Beaux-Arts, Brussels. Another large exhibition at Antibes in 1955 and a one-man show at Eindhoven, Holland, in 1957. Took part in the exhibition of Artistes du XXᵉ Siècle, Liège (1958), Documenta II, Kassel (1959) and the Venice Biennale (1960). One-man show at the Galerie de France, Paris, in 1960.

Bibliography:

A. Jakowsky, **Alberto Magnelli,** in **Cahiers d'Art,** N° 5-6, 1934. — Hans Arp, **Magnelli,** Paris 1947. — C. Zervos, **Magnelli,** in **Cahiers d'Art,** 1947. — J. Lassaigne, **Magnelli,** in **Panorama des Arts,** Paris 1948. — L. Degand, **Alberto Magnelli,** in **Les Arts Plastiques,** N° 5-6, Brussels 1948. — C. Estienne, **Magnelli,** in **Art d'Aujourd'hui,** N° 2, 1949. — G. Marchiori, **Severini e Magnelli,** in **La Biennale,** N° 2, Venice, July 1950. — R. Longhi, **Visita a Magnelli,** in **Paragone,** N° 1, 1950. — R. V. Gindertael, **Magnelli,** in **Art d'Aujourd'hui,** N° 6, August 1952. — L. Degand, **Magnelli,** Edizioni del Cavallino, Venice 1952 (French and Italian editions). — R. Bordier, **Simplicité de Magnelli,** in **Art d'Aujourd'hui,** N° 1, February 1954. — L. Degand, Preface to the Magnelli Retrospective, Palais des Beaux-Arts, Brussels 1954. — A. Verdet, **Magnelli,** exhibition catalogue, Musée d'Antibes, 1955. — A. Verdet, **Thèmes de Magnelli,** in **XXᵉ Siècle,** N° 6, January 1956. — G. Huguet, **Alberto Magnelli,** in **Preuves,** N° 64, June 1956. — M. Seuphor, **Collages de Magnelli,** in **XXᵉ Siècle,** N° 9, 1957. — G. Habasque, **Magnelli,** in

Aujourd'hui, N° 16, March 1958. — J. Lassaigne, Artistes du XXᵉ Siècle, exhibition catalogue, Liège 1958. — F. Le Lionnais, Magnelli, Paris 1960.

MANESSIER, Alfred (1911)

Born at Saint-Ouen (Somme), France. Spent most of his boyhood at Abbeville, and after graduating from the Lycée, attended the Ecole des Beaux-Arts at Amiens. Enrolled in 1929 in the Ecole des Beaux-Arts, Paris, in the department of architecture and design. Spent a good deal of time at the Louvre, where he made the acquaintance of Le Moal. Exhibited at the Salon des Indépendants in 1933, 1934, 1935. At the Académie Ranson in 1935 he met Bissière, who gathered a small group of artists around him (including Manessier, Le Moal, Bertholle and the sculptor Etienne Martin). In 1937, at the Paris World's Fair, he worked at the Pavillon de l'Air et des Chemins de Fer (designed by the architect Aubley). Took part in 1938 in the Témoignage exhibition at the Galerie Matières (opened by Breteau in the Rue des Canettes), along with Le Moal, Bertholle, Verbanesco, Stahly, Martin, etc. Took part in 1939 in the second Salon des Jeunes Artistes. Lived in 1940-1941 at Bénauge (Lot), near Bissière's home at Boissiérette. Participated in the 1941 exhibition of Vingt Peintres de Tradition Française at the Galerie Braun, Paris, and in the 1942 Salon d'Automne (where he exhibited regularly until 1949). Revelation of the Faith in 1943: this was the turning point of his life and has profoundly influenced his work. He was living at the time in Normandy, at Bignon. Began building up his figures under indirect lighting. Exhibited his **Pilgrims at Emmaus** in 1944 at the Salon de la Libération. Took part in 1945 in the exhibition Jeune Peinture Française at the Palais des Beaux-Arts, Brussels, and the following year in a large-scale joint exhibition at the Galerie Drouin, Paris, with Le Moal and Singier. Showed yearly at the Salon de Mai, Paris, from 1948 on. Designed stained-glass windows for the church at Bréseux (Doubs) and in 1949 a tapestry **(Christ at the Column)** for the Dominican oratory at Le Saulchoir (Seine-et-Oise). The same year he exhibited lithographs on the theme of Easter at the Galerie Jeanne Bucher, Paris, and paintings in Toronto and Dublin. Took part in 1950 in exhibitions of French painting at Stockholm and Göteborg, and in 1952 in the Pittsburgh International and Pittori d'Oggi, Turin (1951). Designed stained-glass windows in 1952 for the All Saints church at Basel and in 1953 for Saint-Pierre de Trinquetaille at Arles. Large exhibition of religious pictures in 1952 at the Galerie de France, Paris; he exhibited in 1953 at Turin, New York and the São Paulo Bienal (awarded first prize for painting). Lived at Crotoy (Somme) in 1954 and decorated the Lycée Climatique at Argelès. Also took part in the 1953 exhibition at the Guggenheim Foundation. Exhibited in 1955 at the Palais des Beaux-Arts, Brussels, at Eindhoven, at the Museum of Modern Art, New York, and the Sacred Art exhibition, Vienna. Awarded the international prize at the 1955 Valencia exhibition (Venezuela). Exhibited works inspired by Holland at the Galerie de France in 1956 and enamels executed from his designs by Father Dupeux at the Dominican monastery of Ligugé. Collaborated in 1957 with the Swiss architect Bauer on the chapel at Hem (Nord), designing stained glass and tapestries (woven by Plasse-Lecaisne). Exhibited in 1958-1959 in Paris (Galerie de France, watercolors), Hanover, Essen, The Hague, Turin, Zurich and Kassel (Documenta II). Lived and worked for a time in Haute-Provence, at Moissac; a large exhibition of the works painted there was held at the Galerie de France, Paris. For the ballet festival at Nervi (near Genoa), in 1960, he designed sets and 330 costumes for **The Human Comedy,** based on Boccaccio's Decameron, with choreography by Massine.

Bibliography:
C. Bourniquel, **Trois peintres, Le Moal, Manessier, Singier,** Paris 1946. — L. Degand, **Lapicque et Manessier,** in **Art d'Aujourd'hui,** N° 5, December 1949. — A. Morello, **Manessier, antifigurativo,** in **La Fiera Letteraria,** March 8, 1953. — C. Bourniquel, **Oeuvres récentes de Manessier,** in **XXᵉ Siècle,** N° 4, January 1954. — R. Cogniat, **Dans l'atelier de Manessier,** in **Les Nouvelles Littéraires,** February 18, 1954. — J. Cayrol, **Manessier,** Paris 1955. — B. Dorival, **Alfred Manessier, artisan religieux,** in **L'Oeil,** N° 10, October 1955; reprinted in **The Selective Eye,** 1956-1957, pp. 158-163. — E. de Wilde, **Manessier 1955-1956, La Hollande,** Paris 1956. — J. Dupeux, **Manessier et les émaux de Ligugé,** in **XXᵉ Siècle,** N° 8, January 1957. — **Manessier de la Galerie de France,** presentation at the Galleria dell'Ariete, Milan, March 8, 1957. — W. George, **Manessier et la primauté du spirituel,** in **Prisme des Arts,** N° 8, January 1957. — W. Schmalenbach, **Manessier,** exhibition catalogue, Gemeente Museum, The Hague 1959. — J. A. Cartier, **Développement et signification de l'œuvre de Manessier,** in **Il Punto della Settimana,** V, N° 13, January 16, 1960. — A. M. Cocagnac, O. P., **Manessier cultive son jardin,** in **Signes des Temps,** Paris, February 1960.

MASSON, André (1896)

Born at Balagny (Oise), France. Took a keen interest in painting while still a boy. He first attended the Académie des Beaux-Arts, Brussels, then in 1912 enrolled at the Ecole des Beaux-Arts, Paris. Made a trip to Italy in the spring of 1914. After working for a time at Céret, near Perpignan, in 1918, he settled in Paris for good in 1919, where he went through a cubist period, influenced above all by Juan Gris. First one-man show at the Galerie Simon, Paris, 1924, presented by Kahnweiler; there André Breton bought Masson's first symbolic canvas, **The Four Elements,** which was exhibited alongside his early still lifes and landscapes. Now in close contact with the Surrealists, especially with Antonin Artaud, Joan Miró and Max Ernst, he joined the group and took part in all their exhibitions up to 1929, notably the first collective exhibition of the Surrealists at the Galerie Pierre, Paris, 1925. Illustrated **Soleil bas** by Georges Limbour (1924), **Simulacre** by Leiris (1925) and **Justine** by the Marquis de Sade (1928). Practised automatic drawing and read a number of books which have profoundly influenced his work (Blake, Sade, Kafka, Nietzsche, Chinese poetry and philosophy). Obsessed at this period by the following themes: metamorphoses, dreams, eroticism. Broke with the Surrealists in 1929 and showed no further interest in their activities. Trips to Germany and Holland in the early thirties. Joint exhibition with Miró in 1933 at the Pierre Matisse Gallery, New York. Lived at Tossa, Catalonia, 1934-1936, working in a style of almost paroxysmal expressionism and illustrating several books, among them **Sacrifices** by Bataille, **Don Quixote** and **La Tauromachie.** He returned to France in 1937 and took up with the Surrealists again, participating in the International Surrealist Exhibition in Paris in 1938. His second surrealist period lasted until 1947, when Breton openly condemned his work and he withdrew from the movement. In 1938 he illustrated **Glossaire, j'y serre mes gloses** by Leiris and finished his **Emblematic View of Toledo,** a painting begun in

1933. In 1941 he was with Breton at Martinique, then lived in the United States from 1942 to 1945. Working there in isolation, he produced a large body of graphic work and painted his **Indian Springs** and **Iroquois Landscapes.** In 1946 he returned to France, published **Bestiaire** (12 lithographs and drawings) and did stage sets for **Morts sans Sépulture** by Jean-Paul Sartre and **Hamlet** produced by Jean-Louis Barrault. Settled in the South of France in 1947, near Aix-en-Provence, and began his Aix Period, which lasted until 1956, when his art entered a new, richer, freer phase. His lithographs and illustrated books were exhibited in England in 1947 under the auspices of the Arts Council of Great Britain. **Les Conquérants,** by André Malraux, published by Albert Skira in 1949 with 35 etchings by Masson. Numerous exhibitions of his work from now on: Buchholz Gallery, New York 1949 (landscapes); retrospective at the Kunsthalle, Basel, 1950, with Giacometti (94 works); Galerie Louise Leiris, Paris, 1947 1948, 1951, 1952; Galerie Blanc, Aix-en-Provence, 1956 (works of his Aix Period); Galerie Louise Leiris, Paris, 1957 (early and recent paintings); large retrospective, Marlborough Gallery, London, 1958; Venice Biennale, 1958; Galleria L'Attico, Rome, 1959; Documenta II, Kassel, 1959.

Bibliography:

Sur André Masson, texts by J. L. Barrault, G. Bataille, A. Breton, R. Desnos, P. Eluard, A. Guerne, P. J. Jouve, M. Landsberg, M. Leiris, G. Limbour, B. Péret, Paris 1940. — M. Leiris and G. Limbour, **André Masson et son univers,** Geneva 1947. — Catalogue, Masson Exhibition, Kunsthalle, Basel 1950. — J. Lassaigne, **L'évolution d'André Masson,** in **Revue de la Pensée Française,** July 1952. — J. A. Keim, **André Masson e il piacere di dipingere,** in **Le Arti,** N° 5-6, May 1954. — Catalogue, Masson Exhibition (Aix Period, 1947-1956), Galerie Louis Blanc, Aix-en-Provence 1956. — G. Limbour, **Tableaux récents d'André Masson,** in **XXᵉ Siècle,** N° 6, January 1956. — A. Jouffroy, **Le sentiment du vertige,** in **Arts, Lettres, Spectacles,** N° 619, May 1957. — Catalogue, Masson Exhibition, Galerie Louise Leiris, Paris 1957. — A. Jouffroy, **André Masson: l'art commence où le réalisme finit,** in **Arts, Lettres, Spectacles,** N° 657, February 1958. — W. George, **Les anticipations d'André Masson,** in **Prisme des Arts,** N° 17, 1958. — W. Rubin, Presentation of the Masson Retrospective, Marlborough Gallery, London 1958. — L. Venturi, Presentation of the Masson Exhibition, Galleria L'Attico, Rome 1959.

MATHIEU, Georges (1921)

Born at Boulogne-sur-Mer. Took up painting at the age of twenty-one; his first non-figurative works date from 1944. He and Bryen launched the Psychic Non-Figuration movement in 1947; its first exhibition was held at the Galerie du Luxembourg, Paris. He took part in exhibitions of informal painting and contributed to the development of the informal esthetic both by his paintings and his writings, in which he has set forth his theories and laid down a whole program of activity in pursuance of them. Among his writings are **Analogie de la non-figuration** (1949), a note on the relation between art and Lupasco's logic of the contradictory (1952), and an article on American painting published in **Art Digest** (1953). First one-man show at the Galerie Drouin, Paris, in 1950; another at the Stable Gallery, New York, in 1952. Took part in the exhibition "Signifiants de l'Informel," organized by Michel Tapié in 1951, and in the Younger European Painters exhibition, Solomon R. Guggenheim Museum, New York, 1953.

Shot a film with Robert Descharnes in 1954. In 1958 he delivered a lecture, **From the Abstract to the Possible,** at the Palais des Beaux-Arts in Brussels; in 1959 he published an essay, **From Aristotle to Lyrical Abstraction,** in **L'Oeil,** N° 52, and in May 1960 three articles in English in **Art International.**

Bibliography:

J. Alvard, **Mathieu,** in **Cimaise,** November 1953. — M. Tapié, **Mathieu paints a Picture,** in **Art News,** February 1955. — J. Fitzsimmons, Preface to the Mathieu Exhibition, Kootz Gallery, New York 1957. — F. Russoli, Catalogue of the Collective Exhibition organized by Associazione delle Arti Figurative, in **Notizie,** Turin, March 1960. — G. Mathieu, three articles in English in **Art International,** Zurich, May 1960.

MATTA ECHAURREN, Roberto (1912)

Born at Santiago, Chile. Studied architecture at Santiago, then went to Paris, where he worked with Le Corbusier from 1933 to 1935. Then he moved to Spain, where he met Garcia Lorca and began to work at drawing and painting in earnest. Returning to Paris in 1936 he joined the surrealist movement and maintained close relations with other members of the group, with Breton and Miró in particular. In 1939 he went to the United States with Yves Tanguy and Marcel Duchamp and remained there for the duration of the war. Then he returned to Europe, settled again in Paris and worked for a time in Italy. His work has been frequently exhibited in the leading art centers of Europe and the United States, and he has taken part in the most important international exhibitions held since the war, notably Documenta II, Kassel, 1959.

Bibliography:

André Breton, **Matta,** in **Le Surréalisme et la Peinture,** 2nd edition, New York, 1945. — A. Jouffroy, **Le réalisme ouvert de Matta,** in **Cahiers d'Art,** N° 1, 1953. — E. Glissant, **Matta "Terre Nouvelle",** Preface to the Matta Exhibition, Galerie du Dragon, Paris 1956. — L. Hoctin, **Oeuvres graphiques de Matta,** in **Arts,** April 10-16, 1957. — P. Waldberg, **Matta, l'aube, le vertige,** in **Quadrum,** N° 5, 1958.

MICHAUX, Henri (1899)

Born at Namur, Belgium, where he spent his childhood and early youth, with frequent stays in the country. Then he moved to Brussels, where he lived until about 1920. Settled in Paris in 1923 and devoted himself to writing. Began to travel: worked his way across the Atlantic as a deckhand, spent a year in Ecuador, crossed the Pacific and visited India, China and the Indian Archipelago, and came back to Europe by way of Egypt. His experiences and impressions in foreign lands inspired a long series of books and poems, many of which he illustrated himself; **Ecuador** (1929), **Un certain Plume** (1930), **La nuit remue** (1931), **Un barbare en Asie** (1932), **Voyage en grande Garabagne** (1936), **Au pays de la magie** (1942), **Epreuves, Exorcisme** (1943), **Ici Poddema** and **L'espace du dedans** (1944), **Face aux verrous** (1954), **Misérable miracle** (1956), **L'infini turbulent** (1957). Devoted himself more and more to drawing and painting, and began taking mescaline, which enabled him to give the freest possible expression to emotions and sensations. Exhibited drawings in Paris at the Galerie Rive Gauche (1946), gouaches at the Galerie René Drouin (1948), and ink sketches, gouaches and drawings at the Galerie Daniel Cordier (1959). Awarded the Einaudi Prize at the 1960 Venice Biennale.

Bibliography:

R. Bertelé, **Henri Michaux, poeta, pittore, disegnatore,** in **Vernice,** N° 15, September 1947. — J. Lassaigne, **Henri Michaux,** in **La Bataille,** May 1948. — M. Tapié, **Au pays d'Henri Michaux,** Paris 1948. — H. P. Roché, **Les gouaches d'Henri Michaux,** Paris 1948. — H. Michaux, **Mouvements,** Paris 1951. — M. Tapié, **Henri Michaux et le Visuel,** in **XXᵉ Siècle,** N° 3, June 1952. — J. Alvard, **L'infini turbulent de Michaux,** in **Cimaise,** August 1957. — R. Bertelé, **Dessins turbulents de Michaux,** in **XXᵉ Siècle,** March 1958. — H. Michaux, Exhibition at the Galleria dell'Ariete, Milan 1958. — M. Bense, Preface, Michaux Exhibition, Galerie Lienhard, Zurich 1959.

MIRÓ, Joan (1893)

Born at Montroig, near Tarragona. Entered the School of Fine Arts, Barcelona, in 1907, and moved on to the Gali Academy in 1912. But soon he had had enough of official academic instruction and chose to work on independently. First exhibition of his work at the Dalmau Gallery, Barcelona, in 1919. Influenced by Van Gogh and Fauvism in his early landscapes and still lifes. First trip to Paris in 1919: there he met Picasso and came under the influence of Cubism. His first Paris exhibition was held in 1921 at the Galerie La Licorne (preface by Maurice Raynal). Painted chiefly still lifes at this time. Fell in with the Dadaists, then with the Surrealists. Greatly struck by Miró's work, André Masson brought it to the attention of André Breton and Max Ernst. Finished **The Farm** in 1922 after nine months' work. From 1924 dates **Plowed Earth,** his first really non-objective canvas. Exhibited at the Galerie Pierre, Paris, in 1925. That same year Miró and Ernst did sets and costumes for Diaghileff's **Romeo and Juliet** (Russian Ballet). His work was represented at the first surrealist exhibition at the Galerie Pierre, 1925. Discovered and admired the work of Paul Klee. From this period dates **Harlequin Carnival.** Trip to Holland in 1928, where he admired Vermeer and painted a series of **Dutch Interiors.** First American exhibition at the Curt Valentin Gallery, New York. Took part in an exhibition of collages at the Galerie Goemans, Paris, 1930 (preface by Aragon). Sets and costumes in 1931-1932 for **Jeux d'Enfants** (Ballets Russes de Monte Carlo). A special issue of **Cahiers d'Art** devoted to Miró in 1934. Executed a large mural painting for the Spanish Pavilion at the Paris World's Fair in 1937. After the German invasion of France in 1940 he returned to Barcelona with his family. The following year he settled for the duration at Palma, Majorca, where he painted, drew, did lithographs and decorated pottery fired by Artigas. After the war, in 1947, he traveled to the United States, where he executed a mural painting for the Terrace Plaza Hotel, Cincinnati. Returned to Europe in 1948 and settled down at Barcelona, making frequent trips to Paris. In 1950 he illustrated Tristan Tzara's **Parler seul** with 75 color lithographs. Has exhibited at the Galerie Maeght, Paris, since 1953. Awarded first prize for engraving at the 1954 Venice Biennale. Exhibited at Brussels and Amsterdam in 1956. Produced two large ceramics, **Wall of the Sun** and **Wall of the Moon,** for the new Unesco building in Paris; these two works earned him the Guggenheim International Award for 1958. Lives and works today at Majorca.

Bibliography:

A. Breton, **Le Surréalisme et la Peinture,** Paris 1928; 2nd edition, New York 1945. — David Gascoyne, **A Short Survey of Surrealism,** London 1935. — A. H. Barr, **Fantastic Art, Dada, Surrealism,** Museum of Modern Art, New York 1936. — J. Levy, **Surrealism,** New York 1936. — J. Miró, **Je rêve d'un grand atelier,** in **XXᵉ Siècle,** N° 2, Vol. I, May 1938. — Miró, **Sur le Carnaval d'arlequin,** in **Verve,** N° 4, January-March 1939. — J. J. Sweeney, **Joan Miró,** Museum of Modern Art, New York 1941 (with an extensive bibliography). — J. Miró, **Jeux poétiques,** in **Cahiers d'Art,** Vol. 20-21, 1945-1946. — Michel Leiris, **The Prints of Joan Miró,** Curt Valentin, New York 1947. — Clement Greenberg, **Joan Miró,** Quadrangle Press, New York 1948. — A. Cerici-Pellicer, **Miró y la imaginación,** Omega, Barcelona 1949. — J. E. Cirlot, **Joan Miró,** Cobalto, Barcelona 1949. — Raymond Queneau, **Joan Miró,** Paris-New York 1952. — J. Prévert and J. Ribemont-Dessaignes, **Joan Miró,** Maeght, Paris 1956. — S. Hunter, **Joan Miró: His Graphic Work,** London-Milan 1959. — W. Erben, **Miró,** Silvana, Milan 1959. — J. T. Soby, **Miró,** Museum of Modern Art, New York 1959 (with bibliography and complete documentation). — Guy Weelen, **Miró,** 2 vols., Hazan, Paris 1960.

MORTENSEN, Richard (1910)

Born in Copenhagen and grew up in Denmark. In 1934 he joined the Linien group at Copenhagen, with which he exhibited for the first time; then, in 1936, he joined the Groenningen group, also at Copenhagen. He took part in the first International Exhibition of Abstract and Surrealist Art, Copenhagen, 1937, and made a long stay in Paris that same year. From 1942 to 1947 he exhibited regularly at various Copenhagen galleries and from 1944 on took part in the exhibitions of the Groenningen group. He settled in Paris for good in 1947 and participated in the following group exhibitions: Galerie Breteau, 1948; Tendances de l'Art Abstrait, Galerie Denise René, 1948; Génie Français, Pavillon de Marsan, 1950; Aspects de l'Art d'Aujourd'hui and Espaces Nouveaux, Galerie Denise René, 1950; Galerie Denise René, 1954. His work was also represented at Klar Form, a traveling exhibition grouping twenty artists of the School of Paris (Copenhagen, Oslo, Stockholm, Helsinki, Liège, 1951-1952). In 1951 he competed for the Prix Kandinsky and exhibited at the Cercle Volney, Paris (Danish Artists in France) and at the School of Paris exhibition, Kunsthaus, Zurich. Exhibited tapestries (1952) and lithographs (1953, with Salto and Soendergaard) at the Galerie Denise René, Paris, and took part in a traveling exhibition of tapestries in the United States. Represented at the International Exhibition of Abstract Art (Galleria d'Arte Moderna, Rome, 1953), Europa Kunst (Denmark, 1953-1954), Seven Artists of the School of Paris (Kunsthalle, Bern, 1954), Documenta I and II (Kassel, 1955 and 1959), and international exhibitions of abstract art at Leverkusen (1954), in Brazil (Museum of Modern Art, São Paulo, 1954), Venezuela (Valencia, 1955), Cuba (1955), Brussels (with Deyrolle and Vasarely, 1955), Stockholm (with Baertling and Jacobsen, 1956). Painting trips to Corsica in 1959. Large exhibition of his work at the Danish Pavilion of the 1960 Venice Biennale.

Bibliography:

L. Degand, **Richard Mortensen,** in **Art d'Aujourd'hui,** No. 1, 1950. — J. Dewasne, **Richard Mortensen,** in **Art d'Aujourd'hui,** No. 6, 1950. — L. Degand, **Klar Form, Richard Mortensen,** in **Art d'Aujourd'hui,** No. 1, 1951. — K. G. Hulten, **Artistes danois vivant en France: Mortensen, Jacobsen,** in **Art d'Aujourd'hui,** No. 7, October-November 1953. — J. Alvard, **Mortensen,** in **Cimaise,** January 1954. — R. Bordier, **L'art et la** manière (une conquête sur la technique; automatisme et méthode chez Mortensen), in Art d'Aujourd'hui, No. 4-5, May-June 1954. — O. Baertling, **Richard Mortensen**, in Art d'Aujourd'hui, No. 3, 1955. — L. Degand, Presentation of the Mortensen Exhibition, Galerie Denise René, Paris 1956. — R. V. Gindertael, **Richard Mortensen**, in **Journal du Palais des Beaux-Arts**, Brussels, February 1956. — J. Dopagne, **Mortensen et Deyrolle**, in XX° **Siècle**, No. 9, 1957. — Lars Rostrup Boyesen and Jorn Rubow, Presentation at the 30th Biennale, Venice 1960.

MOTHERWELL, Robert (1915)

Born at Aberdeen, Washington, and grew up at Salt Lake City, 1919-1924, Beverly Hills, 1924-1928, and San Francisco, 1928-1938. In his teens he studied painting at the Otis Art Institute, Los Angeles, and the California School of Fine Arts, San Francisco. He graduated from Stanford University in 1936 and studied philosophy at Harvard Graduate School in 1937-1938. After visiting Paris (1938-1939) and studying at the University of Grenoble, France (summer 1938), he taught at the University of Oregon, 1939-1940, and then went to New York in 1940 to study under Meyer Schapiro in the Department of Fine Arts and Archaeology at Columbia University. In 1941 he studied engraving under Kurt Seligmann. Visited Mexico, 1941, 1943. He first exhibited in the International Surrealist Exhibition, organized by the Coordinating Council of the French Relief Societies, Whitelaw Reid Mansion, New York, 1942. His first one-man exhibition was held at Art of This Century, New York, 1944; it was followed by exhibitions at Kootz Gallery, New York, 1946-1953; Arts Club of Chicago, San Francisco Museum of Art, Galerie Jeanne Bucher, Paris, 1946; and in New York, more recently, at the Sidney Janis Gallery. He has taught at Black Mountain College, North Carolina, summers 1945, 1951; Colorado Springs Fine Arts Center, summer 1954; and at Hunter College New York, since 1951. In 1948 he founded "Subjects of the Artist" school, New York, with Baziotes, Rothko and Barnett Newman. He was co-editor of **Possibilities**, in New York with Harold Rosenberg, 1947-1948; edited **The Documents of Modern Art** series, 1944-1951, and **Modern Artists in America**, No. 1, New York, 1952. The Congregation B'nai Israel, Millburn, New Jersey, commissioned a mural for its Synagogue, 1951. In addition he has participated in the Pittsburgh International, 1952, 1955, 1958; São Paulo Bienal, 1955; and Documenta II, Kassel, 1959. He lives in New York.

Bibliography:
Review of the Motherwell Exhibition at Art of This Century, in **Art News**, Vol. 43, November 1, 1944. — **What Abstract Art Means to Me: Statements by Six American Artists**, in **The Museum of Modern Art Bulletin**, New York 1951, Vol. 18, No. 3. — **The Painter and the Audience**, in **Perspectives U.S.A.**, No. 9, September 1953. — James Fitzsimmons, **Robert Motherwell**, in **Design Quarterly**, No. 29, Minneapolis 1954. — J. Lanes, **Reflections on Post-cubist Painting**, in **Arts**, Vol. 33, May 1959. — E. C. Goossen, **Robert Motherwell and the Seriousness of the Subject**, in **Art International**, Zurich, No. 1-2, 1959.

NAY, Ernst Wilhelm (1902)

Born in Berlin. From 1925 to 1928 he studied at the Berlin Art Academy in the classes of Carl Hofer. Lived and worked for a time in Paris (1928) and Rome (1931-1932). One-man show in 1933 at the Galerie Flechtheim, Berlin. After 1936 he was forbidden by the Nazis to exhibit his work; it figured, however, at the exhibition of "degenerate art" organized by the Nazis at Munich in 1937. All the pictures by Nay which had been acquired by German museums were confiscated by the government in 1938. He made a stay in Norway in 1937-1938 at the invitation of Edvard Munch. Called up in 1940 Nay served in the German army until 1945. Resumed painting immediately after the war and exhibited in 1946 at the Galerie Günther Franke, Munich. Took part in the Premio Lissone in Italy, 1953, and was awarded a gold medal. Awarded the Lichtwark Prize by the city of Hamburg in 1955. One-man shows at the Kleeman Gallery, New York (1955, 1958, 1959), and the Galerie Les Contemporains, Brussels (1958). His work has been represented at the major international exhibitions of recent years: São Paulo Bienal, 1955; Venice Biennale, 1956; German Art of the Twentieth Century, Museum of Modern Art, New York, 1957; Documenta I and II, Kassel, 1955 and 1959. Large exhibitions of his work at the Kunsthalle, Düsseldorf (1959), and the Kunsthalle, Basel (1960, with Willi Baumeister). Nay is at present a member of the Zen group of artists.

Bibliography:
E. W. Nay, in **Das Kunstwerk**, No. 8-9, 1950. — W. Grohmann, **E.W. Nay**, in **Cahiers d'Art**, No. 2, December 1952. — E.W. Nay, **Vom Gestaltwert der Farbe-Fläche, Zahl und Rhythmus**, Munich 1955. — W. Hess, **E.W. Nay**, in **Die Kunst und das Schöne Heim**, April 1956. — W. Grohmann, Catalogue Preface, Nay Exhibition, Galerie Les Contemporains, Brussels 1958. — A. Rüdlinger, Catalogue Preface, Nay and Baumeister Exhibition, Kunsthalle, Basel 1960.

NICHOLSON, Ben (1894)

Born at Denham, England. He studied art at the Slade School in London, then traveled extensively in Europe: in France, where he met some of the cubist painters, and in Italy and Switzerland. He also visited the United States and lived for a time at Pasadena, California, in 1917-1918. From 1925 to 1936 he was a member of the " 7 and 5 " group. In 1933 he joined Unit One and from 1933 to 1935 was a member of the Abstraction-Creation group in Paris, where he met Mondrian in 1934. When Mondrian took refuge in England in 1938 (before going to the United States), he and Nicholson were neighbors at Hampstead. In 1937, in collaboration with J. L. Martin and Naum Gabo, he published **Circle**, an international review of constructivist art. Exhibited at the Venice Biennale (1934), Thesis, Antithesis, Synthesis (Lucerne, 1935) and Cubist and Abstract Art (Museum of Modern Art, New York, 1936). Published **Notes on Abstract Art** in **Horizon** (October 1941), reprinted the following year in **Art of This Century**, New York. Since the war he has participated in the major international exhibitions both in Europe and America, notably at Documenta II, Kassel, 1959. A large Nicholson retrospective was held in 1952-1953 at the Art Institute of Detroit, the Dallas Museum of Contemporary Art, and the Walker Art Center of Minneapolis. Another retrospective in 1955 at the Musée d'Art Moderne, Paris. In 1958 he executed a decorative painting for the Unesco building in Paris. Awarded the Carnegie Prize at the Pittsburgh International (1952), the Prix des Critiques de Belgique (1954), the Premio Ulisse at the Venice Biennale (1954), the Governor of Tokyo Prize (1955), first prize at the International Exhibition of Lugano (1956), and the Guggenheim Award (1956).

Bibliography:

H. S. Ede, **Ben Nicholson, Winifred Nicholson and William Staite Murray**, in **Artwork**, No. 16, 1928. — Herbert Read, **Ben Nicholson's Recent Work**, in **Axis**, No. 2, 1935. — Jan Tschichold, **On Ben Nicholson's Reliefs**, in **Axis**, No. 2, 1935. — Herbert Read, **Ben Nicholson and the Future of Painting**, in **The Listener**, October 9, 1935. — Herbert Read, **The Development of Ben Nicholson**, in **London Bulletin**, No. 11, 1939. — John Summerson, **Ben Nicholson**, in **The Burlington Magazine**, August 1949. — Herbert Read, Preface to Vol. I, **Ben Nicholson, Paintings, Reliefs, Drawings**, Lund Humphries, London 1948; new edition, 1955; Vol. II, 1956. — Herta Wescher, **Ben Nicholson**, in **Art d'Aujourd'hui**, March 1953. — J. P. Hodin, **Ben Nicholson, Il Pitagoreo**, in **La Biennale**, October 1954. — Gillo Dorfles, **Ben Nicholson**, in **Aut-Aut**, No. 22, 1954. — Herbert Read, Preface to the Catalogue, Nicholson Retrospective, Musée d'Art Moderne, Paris, January 1955. — Herta Wescher, **Ben Nicholson**, in **Cimaise**, No. 6, May-June 1956.

OKADA, Kenzo (1902)

Born in Yokohama, Japan. He studied in 1923 at the Tokyo Academy of Fine Arts, then went to Paris, where he lived from 1924 to 1927. Returning to Tokyo, he exhibited in one-man shows at the Nichido Gallery, Tokyo, 1929-1935, and the Hokuso Gallery, Tokyo, 1944-1950. He has taught at the School of Fine Arts, Nippon University, 1940-1942; Musashino Art Institute, 1947-1950; Tama Fine Arts College, 1949-1950. He went to New York in 1950 and was first exhibited there by the Betty Parsons Gallery, 1953. Since then he has had frequent one-man shows at the Parsons Gallery in New York, and also at the Corcoran Gallery, Washington D.C., 1955. Besides winning prizes in Japanese competitions, he has won prizes at the Art Institute of Chicago, 1954; Pittsburgh International, 1955 (Garden Club Prize); purchase prize at the Columbia Museum of Art Biennial, South Carolina, 1957. In 1960 he was awarded a Ford Foundation grant. His work was shown at the Pittsburgh International in 1958, and in the Japanese section at the Venice Biennale, 1958. He lives in New York.

Bibliography:

Review of the Okada Exhibition, Betty Parsons Gallery, in **Art Digest**, Vol. 28, October 15, 1953. — Review of the Okada Exhibition, Betty Parsons Gallery, in **Art News**, Vol. 54, March 1955. — Sam Hunter, **New York, Art Capital of the East**, in **Art in America**, No. 43, February 1955. — **Laurels for New Talent Artists of 1954 and 1955**, in **Art in America**, Vol. 44, February 1956. — Robert M. Coates, **East is West and West is East**, in **The New Yorker**, Vol. XXXII, October 27, 1956. — A. Imaizumi, **Recent Work of Kenzo Okada**, in **Mizue**, No. 638, Tokyo, August 1958. — Review of the Okada Exhibition, Betty Parsons Gallery, in **Art News**, Vol. 58, November 1959.

PIGNON, Edouard (1905)

Born at Bully (Pas-de-Calais), France. He attended the Ecole Communale at Marles-les-Mines, then at the age of fifteen he went to work as a miner, as his father had done before him. Soon he left the mines, however, and became a house painter, drawing and painting in his spare time. Called up for military service in 1925, he served for two years in a French air force unit in Syria, but continued to paint on the side. Discharged in 1927, he went to Paris and found a job at the Citroën Works. Attended evening classes in a Montparnasse art school and discovered the painting of Van Gogh, Gauguin and Matisse. From 1928 to 1934 he took all sorts of odd jobs to earn a living and attended sculpture classes at the Ecole des Arts Décoratifs, Paris, where he met Dayez and worked with the sculptors Wlérick and Arnold. He exhibited for the first time in 1932 at the Salon des Indépendants and again in 1933 at the Salon des Artistes du Travail, Galerie Billiet, Paris. Took part in 1934 in the A.E.A.R. exhibition (Association des Ecrivains et Artistes Révolutionnaires) at the Porte de Versailles, where he met Adam, Estève, Fernand Léger, Vieira da Silva, Frans Masereel and André Lhote. By 1936 his work had attracted the attention of the critics and he was able to devote himself entirely to painting. At this time he painted chiefly views of the working-class districts of Paris. Exhibited in 1937 at the Salon du Temps Présent (Galerie Durand-Ruel). Called up at the outbreak of war, he returned to Paris in 1940 and thereafter played an active part in the Resistance movement, though he went on painting all the while. In 1941 he participated in the exhibition of Vingt Peintres de Tradition Française, Galerie Braun, Paris, then exhibited with Bazaine and Chauvin at the Galerie Jeanne Bucher. Commissioned to do a decorative painting for the Ecole Professionnelle des Jeunes Filles at Creil, near Paris. In 1942 he took part in the exhibition of Six Jeunes Peintres at the Galerie de France, then exhibited at the Galerie Friedland with Bazaine, Estève, Gromaire, Gischia, Lapicque, Lhote and Tal Coat; took part in 1943 in Douze Peintres d'Aujourd'hui, Galerie de France, with Bazaine, Estève, Lapicque, Le Moal, Manessier, Singier, Robin, Villon, Gischia, Fougeron and Desnoyer. Showed at the 1944 Salon de la Libération and was one of the founders of the Salon de Mai, where from now on he exhibited regularly. Painting trip to Collioure, south of Perpignan, in 1945. Exhibited the same year at the Palais des Beaux-Arts, Brussels. Large one-man show in 1946-1947 at the Galerie de France, Paris. After a long stay at Ostend, where he found an inspiring theme in the life of the fishermen, and a trip to Sweden, he returned to Paris in 1948 and produced a series of pictures on mining themes. Designed sets and costumes for **Schéhérazade** by Jules Supervielle, produced by Jean Vilar. In 1949-1950, at the Galerie de France, he exhibited the pictures painted at Ostend and a series of miners. Made a trip to Italy and on the way back stopped at Sanary, near Toulon, where he took an interest in naturalistic themes inspired by work in the fields. In 1951 he won a prize at the São Paulo Bienal and spent a holiday at Vallauris as the guest of Picasso. Worked on a series of drawings and paintings in which he reverted to the themes nearest his heart at the time of the Liberation (**Dead Workman, Maternity,** etc); these were exhibited in 1952. Designed sets and costumes in 1952 for **Mère Courage** by Berthold Brecht, produced by Jean Vilar. Took an interest in ceramics and made another stay at Vallauris in 1953. Large exhibition of his recent work at the Galerie de France. Sets and costumes for Vauthier's **Nouvelle Mandragore**, produced by Jean Vilar. The Maison de la Pensée Française, Paris, organized in 1954 a vast exhibition of his watercolors, ceramics, drawings, and the lithograph illustrations for **Noir et Blanc** and **Massacre des Innocents** by H. Parmelin. Recent works exhibited in 1955 at the Galerie de France. Exhibited in 1955 and 1957 at Pittori d'Oggi, Francia-Italia, Turin; in 1956 at the French Pavilion of the Venice Biennale and at Cinq Peintres et le Théâtre, Galerie de France, Paris, along with Coutaud, Léger, Gischia and Labisse. In 1957 he took part in exhibitions of French art in Japan and at Edinburgh. One-man shows held at the Galerie de France, Paris (1958, 1960), Perls Gallery, New York (1958) and Galleria II Segno, Rome (1960).

Bibliography:

L. Degand, **Edouard Pignon** (and others), in **Le Point,** XXXVI, December 1947. — J. F. Michelet, **Edouard Pignon,** in **Kunsten Idag,** Oslo, No. 2, 1949. — G. Marchiori, **Continuità di Pignon,** exhibition catalogue, Galleria Sandri, Venice 1950; reprinted in **Pittura Moderna in Europa,** Venice 1950. — F. Arcangeli, Pignon, in Paragone, No. 31, 1952. — A. Cardinali, **Edouard Pignon, ceramista a Vallauris,** in **Realismo,** III, October 1954. — P. Descargues, **Pignon, peintre des espaces colorés,** in **Prisme des Arts,** No. 4, 1956. — F. Elgar, **Edouard Pignon,** in **XX° Siècle,** No. 7, 1956. — H. Lefebvre, **Edouard Pignon,** Paris 1956. — R. Cogniat Presentation in the Catalogue of the Biennale, Venice 1956. — H. Parmelin, **Cinq peintres et le théâtre,** Paris 1956. — H. Parmelin, Preface to the Pignon Exhibition, Galleria II Segno, Rome 1960. — H. Parmelin, **Edouard Pignon,** published by the Galerie de France, Paris 1960.

POLIAKOFF, Serge (1906)

Born in Moscow. Grew up in Moscow and St Petersburg, with occasional holiday trips to the Caucasus. A talented musician, he became an expert guitarist while still a boy and later earned a living at various times with his guitar. He left Russia in 1919, after the revolution. For several years, with an aunt who sang to his accompaniment, he drifted from Constantinople to Belgrade, Vienna, Berlin, and finally to Paris, where he settled for good in 1923 and found a steady job with an orchestra. He took to painting in 1930, worked for a time on his own, then attended classes at the Académie Frochot in Montmartre and the Grande-Chaumière in Montparnasse. He took part in an exhibition for the first time in 1931 at the Galerie Drouant-David; he exhibited in 1932 at the Salon des Artistes Français, in 1935 at the Salon de la Nationale des Beaux-Arts. He moved to London in 1935 and enrolled at the Slade School, haunting the museums and developing a passion for the Italian Primitives and the Egyptians. He returned to Paris in 1937, met Kandinsky, and exhibited his first abstract painting at the Galerie Le Niveau in 1938. He now met Otto Freundlich and became friendly with Sonia and Robert Delaunay. Exhibited yearly at the Salon des Indépendants up to 1945. First one-man show in 1945 at the Galerie L'Esquisse, Paris. Took part in the 1946 Salon de Mai and continued to exhibit there yearly. Awarded the Kandinsky Prize in 1947. He saw some pictures by Malevitch for the first time in 1952 and was greatly struck by them. Numerous exhibitions of his work have been held since the war: Copenhagen (1948); Galerie Denise René, Paris (1948, 1949); Galerie de Beaune, Paris (1951, gouaches); Galerie Dina Vierny, Paris (1951); Galerie Ex-Libris, Brussels (1952); Galerie Bing, Paris (1954); Amsterdam and Cologne (1954); Lille (1955); Knoedler Gallery, New York (1955); Galerie Creuzevault, Paris (1957, paintings); Galleria del Naviglio, Milan (1957); Galerie Berggruen, Paris (1957, 1959); Kunsthalle, Basel (1958); Kunstverein, Hamburg (1958); Statens Museum for Kunst, Copenhagen (1958); Kunsthalle, Düsseldorf (1958); Hanover Gallery, London (1959); Galerie Knoedler, Paris (1959); Kunsthalle, Bern (1960). He has taken part in many group exhibitions: Tendances, Galerie Maeght, Paris (1951); School of Paris, Royal Academy, London (1951); Klar Form, Stockholm (1952); Kunsthaus, Zurich (1952); Musée de Verviers (1953); Palais des Beaux-Arts, Brussels (1953); A.P.I.A.W., Liège (1953); Tendances Actuelles de l'Ecole de Paris, Kunsthalle, Bern (1954); Documenta II, Kassel (1959); Awarded the Lissone Prize in 1955.

Bibliography:

R. Vrinat, **Portrait d'artiste, Poliakoff,** in **Actualité Artistique Internationale,** 1952. — R. V. Gindertael, **Poliakoff, peintre naturel,** in **Les Beaux-Arts,** Brussels, March 1953. — C. Estienne, **De Poliakoff à Matta,** in **Combat,** November 1954. — C. Zervos and R. V. Gindertael, **Poliakoff,** in **Cahiers d'Art,** II, 1954. — L. Degand, **Poliakoff,** in **Art d'Aujourd'hui,** 1954. — R. de Solier, **Poliakoff,** in **Nouvelle Revue Française,** December 1954. — F. Elgar, **Poliakoff,** in **Carrefour,** October 17, 1956. — M. Ragon, **Poliakoff,** Paris 1956. — R. Butler, **Poliakoff,** in **Arts,** New York, December 1956. — G. di San Lazzaro, Preface to the Poliakoff Exhibition, Galleria del Naviglio, Milan 1957. — M. Valsecchi, **Poliakoff,** in **Oggi,** April 1957. — J. Lassaigne, Prefaces to the Poliakoff Exhibitions, Galerie Berggruen and Galerie Creuzevault, Paris 1957. — P. Guéguen, **Poliakoff,** in **Aujourd'hui,** No. 15, 1957. — D. Vallier, **Espaces de Poliakoff,** in **Cahiers d'Art,** 1957. — J. P. Aron, **La réalité picturale de S. Poliakoff,** in **Prisme des Arts,** No. 10, March 1957. — R. Cogniat, **Poliakoff,** in **Le Figaro,** November 21, 1957. — Jean Grenier, **Poliakoff,** in **L'Oeil,** No. 39, March 1958. — H. Gasser, **S. Poliakoff,** in **Werk,** No. 11, November 1958. — F. Meyer, **La technique de S. Poliakoff,** in **XX° Siècle,** No. 12, May-June 1959. — J. Russell, Preface to the Poliakoff Exhibition, Hanover Gallery, London, May-June 1959. — D. Vallier, **Poliakoff,** Paris 1959. — C. Zervos, Preface to the Poliakoff Exhibitions, Galerie Berggruen and Galerie Knoedler, Paris 1959. — F. Meyer, Preface to the Poliakoff Retrospective, Kunsthalle, Bern, April-May 1960.

POLLOCK, Jackson (1912-1956)

Born at Cody, Wyoming, and grew up in Arizona and California. He attended the Manual Arts High School, Los Angeles, and studied sculpture and painting. In 1929 he went to New York, where he studied until 1931 at the Art Students League under Thomas Hart Benton. He returned to the West on visits in 1930, 1931, 1932, 1934, but finally settled in New York, 1935. From 1938 to 1942 he worked on the WPA Federal Art Project. He first exhibited in a group show of French and American artists at the McMillan Gallery, New York, 1942. Peggy Guggenheim gave him his first one-man show at the Art of This Century in 1943 and also made a contract with him which lasted until 1947 and enabled him to devote all his time to painting. He moved to Easthampton, Long Island, 1946, where he lived for the rest of his life. He exhibited regularly in New York, at the Betty Parsons Gallery after Peggy Guggenheim returned to Europe, and later at the Sidney Janis Gallery (from 1952). In 1950 Peggy Guggenheim organized his first one-man show in Europe, at the Museo Correr, Venice, and the Galleria del Naviglio, Milan. After exhibiting at the 1950 Biennale in Venice with Gorky and de Kooning, he was shown frequently in both America and Europe: 15 Americans, Museum of Modern Art, New York, 1952; The New Decade, Whitney Museum of American Art, New York, circulating to San Francisco, Los Angeles, Colorado Springs and St. Louis, 1955; The New American Painting, organized by the Museum of Modern Art and shown in Basel, Milan, Madrid, Berlin, Amsterdam,

Brussels, Paris, London and New York, 1958-1959. Major one-man shows were presented by the Kunsthaus, Zurich, 1953; the Museum of Modern Art, New York, 1956, and the Galleria d'Arte Moderna, Rome, 1958. His paintings were shown in the São Paulo Bienal, 1951, 1957; Pittsburgh International, 1952, 1955; Venice Biennale, 1956, and Documenta II, Kassel, 1959. He was killed in an automobile accident in 1956.

Bibliography:
James J. Sweeney, **Jackson Pollock,** exhibition catalogue, Art of This Century, New York, November 1943. — Jackson Pollock, in answer to a questionnaire, in **Arts and Architecture,** Los Angeles, February 1944. — Peggy Guggenheim, **Out of This Century,** Dial Press, New York 1946. — Jackson Pollock, **My Painting,** in Possibilities, I, New York, Winter 1947-1948. — Alfred H. Barr, **Gorky, de Kooning, Pollock,** in **Art News,** Vol. 49, June 1950. — P. Tyler, **Jackson Pollock: The Infinite Labyrinth,** in **Magazine of Art,** March 1950. — Robert Goodnough, **Pollock paints a Picture,** in **Art News,** Vol. 50, May 1951. — B. H. Friedman, **Profile: Jackson Pollock,** in **Art in America,** Vol. 49, New York, December 1955. — Sam Hunter, **Jackson Pollock: The Maze and the Minotaur,** in **New World Writing, Ninth Mentor Selection,** 1956. — Sam Hunter, Jackson Pollock, catalogue preface, Museum of Modern Art, New York 1956-1957. — Clement Greenberg, **Jackson Pollock,** in **Evergreen Review,** Vol. 1, No. 3, 1957. — E. Crispolti, **Appunti su Jackson Pollock,** in **I Quattro Soli,** January-February 1957. — P. Tyler, **Hopper and Pollock,** in **Art News Annual,** 1957. — N. Ponente, Catalogue of the Pollock Exhibition, with prefaces by Palma Bucarelli and Sam Hunter, Galleria Nazionale d'Arte Moderna, Rome 1958. — William Rubin, **Notes on Masson and Pollock,** in **Arts,** Vol. 34, November 1959. — Frank O'Hara, **Jackson Pollock,** Braziller, New York 1959.

RIOPELLE, Jean-Paul (1923)

Born in Montreal. There, at the age of seventeen, he helped to found the Automatism group of painters. First experiments in non-figurative painting in 1944. In 1946, after traveling across the United States and through Italy, he settled in Paris. Took a keen interest in surrealist theories. The Galerie Nina Dausset organized a showing of his works and he took part in the International Exhibition of Surrealism at the Galerie Maeght in 1947 and, with Wols, Mathieu and Hartung, in the exhibition entitled **L'Imaginaire** at the Galerie du Luxembourg, Paris. One-man shows in Paris (Galerie Pierre, Galerie Craven, Galerie Dubourg), New York (Pierre Matisse Gallery) and London (Gimpel Gallery). His work has been represented in the following exhibitions: São Paulo Bienal (1951, 1955), Younger Painters of the School of Paris in London, Glasgow and Edinburgh (1952), Younger European Painters, Solomon R. Guggenheim Museum, New York (1953), the Venice Biennale (1954), the Kunsthalle, Bern (1955), the Kunsthalle, Basel (1959), Documenta II, Kassel (1959), and School of Paris 1959: The Internationals, Minneapolis (1959).

Bibliography:
Aparté entre Elisa, André Breton, Benjamin Péret, on the Riopelle Exhibition, Galerie Nina Dausset, Paris 1949. — G. Duthuit, **A Painter of Awakening: Jean-Paul Riopelle,** catalogue preface, Pierre Matisse Gallery, New York 1954. — G. Duthuit, Preface, Riopelle Exhibition, Galerie Rive Droite Paris 1954. — P. Schneider, **Jean-Paul Riopelle,** in **L'Oeil,** No. 18, 1956. — B. P., **Riopelle,** in **Art Digest,** New York, June 1956. — P. Heron, **Riopelle and the Controlled "Accident",** in **Art Digest,** New York, June 1956. — P. Restany, **Riopelle à la Galerie Dubourg,** in **Cimaise,** Paris, June-August 1956. — P. Schneider, Preface, Riopelle Exhibition, Galerie Jacques Dubourg, Paris 1960, and Galleria dell'Ariete, Milan 1960.

ROTHKO, Mark (1903)

Born at Dvinsk, Russia. He emigrated to the United States in 1913 and lived in Portland, Oregon. He attended Yale University from 1921 to 1923. Taking up painting in 1926, he studied under Max Weber at the Art Students League, New York. His first one-man show (drawings and watercolors) was held at the Portland Art Museum, 1933; later in the same year he exhibited again at Contemporary Arts, New York. In 1936-1937 he worked on the WPA Federal Art Project in New York. Peggy Guggenheim presented another one-man show at Art of This Century, 1945, and in 1946 both the San Francisco Museum of Art and the Santa Barbara Museum of Art devoted exhibitions to his work. He was co-founder of the school "Subjects of the Artist" with Baziotes, Motherwell and Barnett Newman in 1948. He taught at the California School of Fine Arts, San Francisco, summers 1947 and 1949, and at Brooklyn College, 1951-1954. He has exhibited frequently at the Betty Parsons Gallery and the Sidney Janis Gallery in New York and been included in the Museum of Modern Art exhibitions: 15 Americans, 1952, and The New American Painting, 1959. He has also participated in the São Paulo Bienal, 1951; Pittsburgh International, 1958; Venice Biennale, 1958; Guggenheim International Award, New York, 1958 (National Section Award); and Documenta II, Kassel. He lives in New York.

Bibliography:
Review of the Rothko Exhibition, Art of This Century, in **Art Digest,** Vol. 19, January 15, 1945. — Clement Greenberg, **American Type Painting,** in **Partisan Review,** Vol. XXII, New York, Spring 1955. — Dore Ashton, **Mark Rothko,** in **Arts and Architecture,** Vol. 74, Los Angeles, August 1957. — Elaine de Kooning, **Mark Rothko,** Catalogue Preface, Contemporary Arts Museum, Houston, Texas, 1957. — Elaine de Kooning, **Two Americans in Action: Kline and Rothko,** in **Art News Annual,** No. 27, 1958. — Dore Ashton, Review of the Rothko Exhibition, Sidney Janis Gallery, in **Arts and Architecture,** Vol. 75, April 1958. — Sam Hunter, Presentation at the 29th Biennale, Venice 1958.

SANTOMASO, Giuseppe (1907)

Born in Venice and attended classes at the Academy of Fine Arts (where he now teaches). While still very young he took part in exhibitions at Ca' Pesaro. In 1937 he made a long trip to Holland and France. One-man shows in Amsterdam (1937), Paris (1939), Genoa (1940), Florence and Milan (1942), Rome (1943). He also took part in the Rome Quadriennale of 1943. In 1945 he illustrated Paul Eluard's **Grand Air,** published in Milan, and in 1947 joined the Fronte Nuovo delle Arti. Since the war his work has figured in nearly all the major exhibitions of avant-garde art both in Italy and abroad. Exhibited at the Venice Biennale in 1948, 1950 (awarded the Incom Prize), 1952, 1954 (awarded first prize for an Italian painter), 1960. Participated in an exhibition at Cairo in 1949, in a traveling exhibition of contemporary Italian art in Germany in 1950-1951, and in the São Paulo Bienal in 1951, 1953 (awarded Second Prize), 1955, 1959. Exhibited in Scandinavia and Paris in 1951. Withdrew from the Fronte Nuovo delle Arti and in 1952 joined the group of Eight Italian Painters (Afro, Birolli, Corpora, Moreni, Morlotti, Santomaso, Turcato, Vedova). Took part in group exhibitions of Italian art in Berlin, Hanover, Zurich and La Chaux-de-Fonds (1953), in Documenta I and II (Kassel, 1955 and 1959) and the exhibition at the Palais des Beaux-Arts, Brussels (1959). Awarded the Marzotto Prize for painting in 1959. One-man shows in Munich (1955), New York (1957), Amsterdam (1960) and St Gall (1960).

Bibliography:

G. Marchiori, **Galleria: Santomaso**, in **Il Corriere Padano**, November 9, 1938. — G. Marchiori, **Santomaso**, in **Corrente di Vita Giovanile**, April 30, 1939. — A. Podestà, **Bepi Santomaso**, in **Domus**, March 1940. — R. Pallucchini, **B. Santomaso**, in **Emporium**, May 1942. — U. Apollonio, **Sul pittore Santomaso**, in **Paesaggio**, April-May 1946, No. 1. — M. Valsecchi, Preface, First Exhibition of the Fronte Nuovo delle Arti, Milan 1947. — G. Dell'Oro, **L'arte ceramica di Giuseppe Santomaso**, in **Il Gazzettino Illustrato**, June 3, 1949. — H. Read, Preface, Santomaso Exhibition, Hanover Gallery, London, November-December 1953. — G. Marchiori, **Santomaso**, Venice 1954. — G. C. Argan, **Santomaso**, Catalogue of the 27th Biennale, Venice 1954. — G. Breddo, **Santomaso**, in **La Biennale**, 1954, No. 19-20. — L. Venturi, **Bepi Santomaso**, in **Commentari**, 1955, No. 2. — H. von Heilmaier, **Giuseppe Santomaso und die Wandlungen der italienischen Malerei**, in **Die Kunst und das schöne Heim**, May 1955. — G. Marchiori, Preface, 7th Quadriennale, Rome 1955-1956. — U. Apollonio, **Elementi della natura in un pittore astratto**, in **Quadrum**, No. 3, 1957. — G. Marchiori, **Tempere di Santomaso**, Preface, Santomaso Exhibition, Galleria Il Segno, Rome 1957. — U. Apollonio, **Santomaso**, Bodensee Verlag, Amriswil 1959 (text in German, English and French). — Giuseppe Mazzariol, Preface, Santomaso Exhibition, Galleria Pogliani, Rome 1960.

SCHNEIDER, Gérard (1896)

Born at Sainte-Croix (Vaud), Switzerland. He grew up at Neuchâtel, where he studied decorative art with the painter Alfred Blailé. Moving to Paris, he attended the Ecole des Arts Décoratifs from 1916 to 1919, and the Ecole des Beaux-Arts for a short period in 1918. He returned to Neuchâtel in 1920 and held his first exhibition there, then moved back to Paris in 1922, where he worked hard at painting and earned his living as a picture restorer. Exhibited at the Salon d'Automne in 1926, and from 1935 to 1939 at the Salon des Surindépendants. Having assimilated the joint influence of Cubism and Surrealism, he gradually departed from figurative painting and in 1944 exhibited a picture entitled **First Abstract Composition**. The Galerie Denise René organized a traveling exhibition of his work in Scandinavia (1946), while one-man shows were held in Paris (Galerie Lydia Conti, 1947, 1948, 1950; Galerie de Beaune, 1951; Galerie Galanis, 1954; Galerie du Musée de Poche, Gouaches, 1959); Brussels (1952; Palais des Beaux-Arts, 1953); Cologne (1952; Galerie Der Spiegel, 1953; 1957); Munich (1953); New York (Kootz Gallery, 1956, 1957, 1958); Milan (Galleria Apollinaire, 1958). His work has been included in many international exhibitions both in Paris and abroad: Salon de Mai, Paris (from 1949 to 1960); Venice Biennale (1948, 1954); Berlin and Innsbruck

(1950); Advancing French Art, New York, San Francisco, Chicago (1950, organized by Louis Carré); School of Paris 1900-1950, Royal Academy, London (1951); Pittori d'Oggi, Francia-Italia, Turin (1951, 1953); São Paulo Bienal (1951, 1953); Leverkusen (1954); Caracas Bienal (1955); Documenta I and II, Kassel (1955, 1959); Salon des Réalités Nouvelles, Paris (1956, 1958); Pittsburgh International (1958); Cinquante Ans d'Art Moderne, Brussels World's Fair (1958); School of Paris 1959: The Internationals, Walker Art Center, Minneapolis (1959). Awarded the Lissone Prize, Italy, 1957. Book illustrations (12 lithographs) for **Langage** by Ganzo, published by the Galerie Lydia Conti. Paris 1948.

Bibliography:

D. Chevalier, **Gérard Schneider**, in **Arts**, December 30, 1949. — R. V. Gindertael, **Schneider**, in **Art d'Aujourd'hui**, No. 6, June 1951. — R. Vrinat, **Portrait d'artiste: Schneider**, in **Actualité Artistique**, September 4, 1952. — Itsuji Yoshikawa, **Schneider**, in **Seijube Shincho**, 1952, and **Bokuki**, September 1954. — M. Ragon, **Schneider**, in **Cimaise**, April 1956. — M. Ragon, **Schneider**, in **Cimaise**, December 1958. — M. Brion, **Forme et Couleur de Schneider**, Preface to the Schneider Exhibition, Galleria Apollinaire, Milan 1958. — M. Pobé, **Gérard Schneider**, Paris 1959.

SINGIER, Gustave (1909)

Born at Warneton (West Flanders), Belgium. Moved to Paris with his family in 1919 and was already painting at the age of fourteen. For three years he attended art classes at the Ecole Boulle, drawing assiduously from life and copying the Old Masters. Until 1936 he worked as a designer for a firm of shop-fitters, devoting all his spare time to painting. Thereafter he exhibited regularly in Paris at the Salon des Indépendants (1936-1939), the Salon d'Automne (1937-1949), the Salon des Tuileries (1939-1942), and the Salon de Mai (1945-1960) of which he was a founder member. Professor of painting at the Académie Ranson, Paris, from 1951 to 1954. Took part in Vingt Peintres de Tradition Française, Galerie Braun, 1941, and Douze Peintres d'Aujourdhui, Galerie de France, 1943. Exhibited in 1946 with Le Moal and Manessier at the Galerie Drouin. One-man shows at the Galerie Billiet-Caputo, Paris (1949, paintings; 1950, watercolors); Blanche Gallery, Stockholm (1950); Galerie Apollo, Brussels (1951, watercolors); Galerie de France, Paris (1952, 1955, 1957, watercolors, 1959); Galleria Lattes, Turin (1953); Kestner Gesellschaft, Hanover, and museums of Lübeck, Duisburg, Elberfeld and Hamburg (1957). Has designed many tapestries, as well as stained-glass windows and sets for Monteverdi's **Orpheus** at the Aix Music Festival in 1955.

Bibliography:

C. Bourniquel, **Le Moal, Manessier, Singier**, Paris 1946. — G. Weelen, **Singier**, in **XX⁰ Siècle**, June 1956. — G. Charbonnier, **Singier**, Paris 1957. — G. Charbonnier, **Singier**, in **Prisme des Arts**, March 1957. — C. Bourniquel, **Singier**, in **Esprit**, March 1957. — Y. Taillandier, **Singier**, in **Connaissance des Arts**, January 1959. — Y. Taillandier, **Rencontre avec Singier**, in **XX⁰ Siècle**, February 1959.

SOULAGES, Pierre (1919)

Born at Rodez (Aveyron), France. While still attending the Lycée there, he showed a keen interest in prehistoric, Celt and Romanesque art, all well represented at the Musée Fenaille in Rodez. In 1939 he went to Paris where he had an opportunity of seeing Picasso and Cézanne exhibitions at the Galerie Paul Rosenberg; these made a lasting impression on him. Demobilized after the fall of France in 1940, he worked on a farm near Montpellier. In 1946 he settled in Paris for good and devoted himself entirely to painting. Exhibited in 1947 at the Salon des Surindépendants and then at the Salon de Mai, where he showed yearly thereafter. His work was represented in the Französische Abstrakte Malerei exhibition in Germany in 1948. Designed sets and costumes for **Héloïse et Abélard** by Roger Vailland in 1949. First one-man show the same year at the Galerie Lydia Conti, Paris. He took part in several group exhibitions in New York and London; in Do Figurativismo ao Abstraccionismo, São Paulo (organized by Léon Degand); the Festival of the Ruhr, Recklinghausen, 1950; Levende Farver, Copenhagen; Französische Malerei und Plastik, Düsseldorf and Berlin; and in the May Salon in Japan. In 1951 he designed sets and costumes for Graham Greene's **The Power and the Glory,** produced in Paris by Louis Jouvet. That same year he participated in the Pittori d'Oggi exhibition at Turin, in the traveling exhibition of Advancing French Art in the United States, and in several collective exhibitions in Paris (Galerie de France) and New York (Sidney Janis Gallery). One-man show at the Birch Gallery, Copenhagen in 1951, at the Otto Stangl Gallery, Munich, in 1952. That same year he took part in the Venice Biennale, Malerei in Paris Heute (Zurich), Rythmes et Couleurs (Lausanne) and other exhibitions in England, Chicago, New York, Paris and Tokyo. Awarded a prize at the São Paulo Bienal in 1953 and took part in the exhibition of Younger European Painters, Solomon R. Guggenheim Museum, New York. First one-man show in New York at the Kootz Gallery in 1954; the same year he exhibited in Chicago with Georges Mathieu. Participated in the exhibition Tendances Actuelles de l'Ecole de Paris at the Kunsthalle, Bern. One-man shows at the Kootz Gallery, New York (1955, 1956, 1957, 1959); Gimpel Gallery, London (1955, 1958); Galerie de France, Paris (1956, 1959); Galerie Berggruen, Paris (engravings, 1957); Galerie Gerd Rosen, Berlin (1958); Galerie Feigel, Basel (1958); Wise Gallery, Cleveland (1959). Took part in major exhibitions outside France: The New Decade, Museum of Modern Art, New York (1955); Mouvement dans l'Art Abstrait, Lausanne (1955); Tendencias recientes de la Pintura francesa, Spain (1955); Documenta I and II, Kassel (1955, 1959); Carnegie International, Pittsburgh (1955, 1958); International Art, Tokyo (1957); World's Fair, Brussels (1958).

Bibliography:

Catalogue, Mathieu-Soulages Exhibition, Arts Club, Chicago 1954. — J. Fitzsimmons, **Soulages,** in **Arts and Architecture,** Los Angeles, Vol. 71, June 1954. — J. Lassaigne, **Soulages,** in **XX⁰ Siècle,** N° 7, June 1956. — M. Ragon, **Soulages,** in **Cimaise,** February 1956. — H. Juin, **Soulages,** Paris 1958. — H. Juin, **Soulages,** in **Pour l'Art,** Lausanne, May 1960. — J. Leymarie, **Soulages,** in **Art International,** Zurich, May 1960. — R. V. Gindertael, **Soulages,** in **Quadrum,** N° 8, 1960.

SPAZZAPAN, Luigi (1889-1958)

Born at Gradisca, near Gorizia (Venetia), at that time a part of Austria. He grew up and went to school there, then studied at the Imperial Art Academy in Vienna, 1911-1913. He failed twice in competitive examinations and took private courses in painting and architecture.

As an Austrian citizen, he was called up and served in the Austro-Hungarian army during the First World War. Taken prisoner by the Russians, he escaped, was recaptured and escaped a second time. Sent to the Italian front, he was wounded and taken prisoner. After the war he became an Italian citizen and taught geometry and mathematics in his home town. He came into contact with the futurist movement at that time, but broke with it almost at once. Long trips throughout Europe, notably to Munich, Prague and London. Awarded a silver medal at the International Exhibition of Decorative Arts, Paris, 1925. After 1928 he made his home in Turin. Became one of the leading personalities along with the painter Moreni and the sculptor Mastroianni, in the art life of Turin after the Second World War. Took part in the following international exhibitions: Pittori d'Oggi, Francia-Italia, Turin (1952); the Venice Biennale (regularly); the São Paulo Bienal (1957); Documenta II, Kassel (1959). Died suddenly at Turin in 1958. Large-scale Spazzapan retrospective at the 1960 Venice Biennale.

Bibliography:

Antonio Morassi, **Spazzapan,** in **La Voce di Gorizia,** May 29, 1924. — Edoardo Persico, **Spazzapan,** in **Casabella,** September 1932. — Lionello Venturi, Preface, Spazzapan Exhibition, Galleria Codebò, Turin 1932. — Aldo Bertini, **Luigi Spazzapan,** in **Le Arti,** N° 1, October-November 1941. — Lionello Venturi, **16 Dessins de Luigi Spazzapan,** L'Orma, Turin 1946. — Michel Tapié, **Ricordo di Spazzapan,** in **Notizie,** April 1958. — G. Marchiori, **Spazzapan,** Turin 1960. — L. Carluccio, **Spazzapan,** Turin 1960. — Lionello Venturi, **Spazzapan,** De Luca, Rome 1960 (with a complete bibliography).

STAEL, Nicolas de (1914-1955)

Born in St Petersburg of a well-to-do family which, after the Revolution, emigrated to Poland and settled at Ostrow near Poznan. There his father died in 1921 and his mother in 1922; he and his two sisters were then entrusted to the care of a friend of the family, who sent them to Brussels where an engineer, M. Fricero, became their guardian. From 1922 to 1930 he studied at the Jesuit College of Saint-Michel in Brussels, and in 1930-1931 at the Collège Cardinal Mercier at Braine-l'Alleud. Entered the class of M. van Haelen at the Académie des Beaux-Arts, Brussels, in 1932. Made several trips to Holland, where he was deeply impressed by Rembrandt, Vermeer and Seghers, and did his first watercolors. Commissioned to do a decorative painting in the royal palace at Laeken. Went to Paris where he saw works by Cézanne, Matisse, Soutine and Braque. Spent nearly the whole of 1934 traveling in Spain, drawing and sketching daily. After a visit to Italy he returned to Belgium in 1935 and fitted up a studio at Uccle, near Brussels. Long trip to Morocco in 1936, where he worked hard (but later destroyed all the pictures produced during this period). After a brief trip to Algeria in 1937 he lived for a while at Naples, then returned to Paris and attended Fernand Léger's art school. Rented a studio in the Rue du Cherche-Midi in 1938 and drew at the Louvre, copying Chardin in particular. Enlisted in the French Foreign Legion in 1939 and was sent to Tunisia. Discharged in 1940 he settled at Nice, then moved back to Paris in 1943, where Jeanne Bucher encouraged him and helped him through a trying period of great material difficulties, buying drawings and pictures. Met Braque and Lanskoy in 1944 and became a close friend of both. Took part in the Peintures Abstraites exhibition with Domela, Kandinsky, and Magnelli, organized by the Galerie L'Esquisse, where he also had a one-man show the same year. Participated in the Salon de Mai in 1945 and exhibited at the Jeanne Bucher Gallery. Took a studio in Montparnasse, then moved to a studio in the Rue Gauguet in 1947. Met an American dealer, Theodor Schempp, who liked his work and introduced it in the United States. His mainstay among the Paris dealers at this time was Jacques Dubourg. Exhibited in 1948 with Lanskoy, Braque and Laurens at the Couvent du Saulchoir, Etiolles, and also at Montevideo. Trip to Holland and Belgium in 1949. De Staël exhibition in New York in 1950, organized by Theodor Schempp. His work was increasingly appreciated in Paris, by public and critics alike, and George Duthuit devoted a monograph to him in 1950. Even the State bought one of his pictures. One-man show at the Galerie Jacques Dubourg, Paris, 1950. Made a long stay in London in 1951 and published woodcuts illustrating poems by René Char. Exhibited at the Matthiesen Gallery, London, in 1952. Met the sculptor Vitullo, who initiated him into sculpture, but he executed only one work. Designed tapestries for the Aubusson manufactory. Dreamed of producing a ballet with Char and Lecuire, with music by Stravinsky, but the project was never realized. After a long trip to Italy in 1953 (Florence, Ravenna, Milan, Venice), he settled in the South of France. One-man shows at the Knoedler Gallery, New York (1953), and the Galerie Jacques Dubourg, Paris (1954). After a trip to Sicily he bought a château at Manerbes and made his home there. Did a series of etchings in 1954 for the Ballets-Minute of Lecuire. Traveled extensively along the French coast of the North Sea, lived for a time at Antibes on the Riviera, then made a trip to Spain. Jacques Dubourg organized one-man shows in 1955 in his Paris gallery and at the Musée d'Antibes. These two exhibitions called for an immense amount of work on the painter's part. Busy with drawings and book illustrations. Committed suicide at Antibes, March 16, 1955.

Bibliography:
G. Duthuit, **Nicolas de Staël**, Paris 1950. — R. V. Gindertael, **Nicolas de Staël**, Paris 1951. — P. Lecuire, **Voir Nicolas de Staël**, Paris 1953. — R. Cogniat, catalogue preface, **Pittori d'Oggi, Francia-Italia,** Turin 1955. — C. Zervos, **Nicolas de Staël,** in **Cahiers d'Art,** Paris 1955. — R. V. Gindertael, **Nicolas de Staël,** in **Cimaise,** June 1955. — H. Wescher, **De Staël,** in **Cimaise,** April 1956. — J. Cassou, Preface, De Staël Exhibition, Musée d'Art Moderne, Paris 1956. — D. Cooper, **Nicolas de Staël: In Memoriam,** in **The Burlington Magazine,** May 1956. — F. Meyer, Preface, De Staël Exhibition, Kunsthalle, Bern 1957. — D. Cooper, Preface to the Exhibition at the Musée Réattu, Arles 1958. — A. Tudal, **De Staël,** Editions du Musée de Poche, Paris 1958. — R. Guttuso, **Nicolas de Staël,** in **Il Contemporaneo,** October-November 1958. — D. Sutton, **Nicolas de Staël,** London-New York 1959. — W. Schmalenbach, Preface to the De Staël Exhibition at Documenta II, Kassel 1959. — F. Russoli, **Percorso di Nicolas de Staël,** and L. Landini, **Coscienza interiore e razionalità nell'opera di Nicolas de Staël,** Exhibition Catalogue, Museo Civico d'Arte Moderna, Turin 1960.

STILL, Clyfford (1904)

Born at Grandin, North Dakota. He grew up in southern Alberta, Canada, and Spokane, Washington. He visited New York in 1924, then studied at Spokane University (B. A. 1933) and received his M. A. from Washington State College, Pullman. From 1933 to 1944 he taught at Washington State, then moved to San Francisco and worked for a period in war industries. In 1943 the San Francisco Museum of Art exhibited twenty-two of his paintings. Visiting New York in 1946 he had another one-man show at Art of This Century. From 1946 to 1950 he taught at the California School of Fine Arts, San Francisco. In 1944 he taught at Richmond Professional Institute of the College of William and Mary, Virginia. In 1948 he organized a graduate painting course at the California School of Fine Arts. He was associated with the establishment of a student gallery in San Francisco, the Metart Gallery. Upon Still's departure from the School and from California in 1950, he was given a one-man show at this gallery. He came to New York in 1950 and taught at Hunter and Brooklyn Colleges, N. Y., 1952. His work was shown in: 15 Americans, Museum of Modern Art, New York, 1952; The New American Painting, organized by the Museum of Modern Art, shown in Basel, Milan, Madrid, Berlin, Amsterdam, Brussels, Paris, London, New York, 1958-1959; and Documenta II, Kassel, 1959. In 1959 the Albright Art Gallery, Buffalo, N. Y., presented a major retrospective exhibition of seventy-two paintings dating from 1936 to 1957; the catalogue contains an important preface by the painter himself. He lives in New York.

Bibliography:
Review of the Still Exhibition, Art of This Century, in **Art Digest,** Vol. 20, March 1, 1946. — Review, Still Exhibition, Metart Gallery, in **Art News,** Vol. 49, New York, October 1950. — Review, Still Exhibition, Betty Parsons Gallery, in **Art Digest,** Vol. 25, February 1, 1951. — **Five Americans at the Institute of Contemporary Arts,** in **Arts,** Vol. 32, May 1958. — R. Melville, **Spectacular Exhibitions of The New American Painting at the Tate Gallery,** in **Architectural Review,** Vol. 125, London, May 1959. — Paintings by Clyfford Still, exhibition catalogue, Albright Art Gallery, Buffalo, N. Y., 1959. — H. Crehan, **Clyfford Still: Black Angel in Buffalo,** in **Art News,** Vol. 58, December 1959. — E. C. Goossen, **Clyfford Still: Painting as Confrontation,** in **Art International,** Zurich, No. 1, 1960. — Herbert Read and H. H. Arnason, **Dialogue on Modern U. S Painting,** in **Art News,** Vol. 59, May 1960.

SUTHERLAND, Graham (1903)

Born in London, attended Epsom College from 1914 to 1918, and enrolled in 1921 in the Goldsmiths' College of Arts, London. Exhibited for the first time in 1925 at Gallery XXI, London (drawings and engravings). Taught etching and engraving at the Chelsea Schoo of Art from 1931. Discovered his vocation as a painter in Pembrokeshire, in South Wales, in 1935. Held his first one-man show of paintings in London in 1938, and a second in 1940 at the Leicester Gallery. Served as an Official War Artist from 1941 to 1945. Exhibited in New York at the Buchholz Gallery in 1945. Long stays in the South of France in 1947 and the following years. Exhibited tapestries at the Tate Gallery (1947) and paintings at the Hanover Gallery (1948), London. Sutherland Retrospective at the 1952 Venice Biennale and another large exhibition of his work at the Musée d'Art Moderne, Paris. Awarded a prize at the 1951 São Paulo Bienal. Exhibited at the Curt Valentin Gallery, New York, and the Stedelijk Museum, Amsterdam, in 1953; in 1954 at the Tate Gallery, London, and in Chicago, Boston, New York and the Venice Biennale. Took part in 1956 in the exhibition of Contemporary British Art, Silberman Galleries, New York, and in the traveling exhibition of Masters of British Art 1800-1950, organized by the Museum of Modern Art, New York. Exhibited with Henry Moore, John Chadwick and Armitage at the Galleria Blu, Milan, in 1958, and at Documenta II, Kassel, in 1959.

Bibliography:
E. Sackville-West, **Graham Sutherland,** Penguin Books, Harmondsworth 1943. — R. Melville, **Graham Sutherland,** London 1950. — A. Bowness, **Four English Artists,** Preface, Galleria Blu, Milan 1958 (with note by G. Marchiori).

TAL COAT, Pierre (1905)
Born at Clohars-Carnoët (Finistère), France. While still in his teens he decided to devote himself to drawing and sculpture. Employed as a painter in the pottery works at Quimper in 1924. The same year he settled in Paris and soon made a name for himself in the art world. In 1927 he moved back to Brittany. Several exhibitions of his work at the Galerie Bénézit, Paris, between 1929 and 1931. Settled in Paris again in 1932 and exhibited at the Galerie Billiet. Awarded the Prix Paul Guillaume for his portrait of Gertrude Stein (1934-1935). Traveled in the South of France in 1935. The Spanish Civil War inspired him to paint a series of violent and dramatic works: **Massacres.** Became friendly with Alberto Giacometti and Francis Gruber. One-man show at the Julien Levy Gallery, New York, in 1937. Long stays in 1939 in Brittany and at Ermenonville, where he painted landscapes; the same year he settled down near Aix-en-Provence, at the Château-Noir, where he continued to live until 1956. Exhibited at the Galerie de France, Paris, in 1945, 1949 (early works) and 1950 (recent works). Trips to Corsica (1953), the Cévennes (1954) and Brittany (1955). Exhibited at the Galerie Maeght, Paris, in 1954 and 1956. Long stay in the Dordogne in 1956 at the prehistoric site of Moustier. Then he made his home just outside Paris, first at Forges, then at Chevreuse. Exhibited with the sculptor Hajdu at the Kunsthalle, Bern (1957), and at the Galerie Maeght, Paris (1959).

Bibliography:
M. Florisoone, catalogue preface, Galerie de France, Paris 1945. — R. Cogniat, **Tal Coat,** in **Le Point,** N° XXXVI, 1947. — J. Lassaigne, catalogue preface, Galerie de France, Paris 1949. — H. Maldiney, catalogue preface, Galerie de France, Paris 1950. — H. Maldiney, **Tal Coat,** and A. Du Bouchet, **Ecart, non déchirement,** in **Derrière le Miroir,** N° 64, 1954. — A. Du Bouchet, **L'air, le rocher,** in **I Quattro Soli,** N° 3, 1955. — G. Duthuit, **Seul existe ce qui est paysage continuel,** in **Derrière le Miroir,** N° 82-83-84, 1956. — G. Limbour, **Autour de l'atelier de Tal Coat,** in **XXᵉ Siècle,** N° 7, 1956. — J. Lassaigne, **Unité de Tal Coat,** in **Quadrum,** N° 2, 1956. — F. Meyer, catalogue preface, Kunsthalle, Bern 1957. — P. Restany, **Tal Coat,** in **Cimaise,** June 1957. — H. Maldiney, **Tal Coat 1959,** in **Derrière le Miroir,** N° 114, 1959.

TÁPIES, Antonio (1923)
Born in Barcelona. Studied law, then gave it up in 1946 to devote himself to painting. Attended no art school but was entirely self-taught. With other young Spanish artists in Barcelona, he founded the Dau al Set group in 1948, which launched a magazine of the same name. He exhibited for the first time at the October Salon in Barcelona. In 1950 he obtained a grant from the French government, which enabled him to make a stay in Paris. First one-man show in Barcelona in 1950, followed by others at Santander and Madrid. Trips to Belgium and Holland in 1951, to New York in 1953. Exhibited in 1953 in Stockholm, Düsseldorf, Basel, Munich, Milan, Paris, Chicago. Won a prize at the third Spanish-American Biennial (1955), the Lissone Prize (1956) and the Carnegie International Prize at Pittsburgh (1958). At the 1958 Venice Biennale he won the prize awarded by the David E. Bright Foundation. Several one-man shows held in Paris, Düsseldorf and Rome.

Bibliography:
M. Tapié, **Antonio Tápies et l'œuvre complète,** Paris 1956. — P. Restany, **Tápies,** in **Cimaise,** November 1958. — J. Dupin, Preface, Tápies Exhibition, Galleria dell'Ariete, Milan 1958. — F. Choay, **L'Ecole espagnole,** in **L' Œil,** No. 51, 1959. — M. Tapié, **Antonio Tápies,** Barcelona 1959. — F. Meyer, Preface, Tápies Exhibition, Kunsthalle, Bern 1959. — G. C. Argan, **Tápies,** in **L'Europa Letteraria,** No. 3, Rome 1960.

TOBEY, Mark (1890)
Born at Centerville, Wisconsin, and grew up at Trempealeau, Wisconsin. He moved to Chicago, 1906, and in 1908 left school to begin work, attending Saturday classes at Chicago Art Institute. He visited New York, 1911, and supported himself by selling fashion sketches to magazines in Chicago and New York. First exhibition at Knoedler Gallery, New York, 1917. In 1918 he became interested in the Persian religion, Bahai; traveled in the western part of the United States. Settling in Seattle in 1922, he taught at the Cornish School until 1924. Through the Chinese painter, Teng Kwei, he learned the art of Chinese calligraphy. He went abroad in 1926, living for a time in France, and visiting other European countries and the Near East. He returned to Seattle in 1927; then went to England in 1930 to teach at Dartington Hall School, Devon. During the next seven years he traveled widely: to Mexico, 1931; to China and Japan, 1934, studying calligraphy. The Seattle Art Museum presented a one-man show in 1935. He returned in 1939 to Seattle, where he still lives. In 1944 the Willard Gallery New York, began exhibiting his work regularly. In 1951 the California Palace of the Legion of Honor, San Francisco, organized a retrospective exhibition, which circulated to western museums and was finally shown at the Whitney Museum of American Art, New York. During 1954 and 1955 he traveled in Europe and was given one-man shows at the London Institute of Contemporary Arts and the Galerie Jeanne Bucher, Paris. Major retrospectives have been held at the Chicago Art Institute, 1955, and the Pasadena Museum, 1960. In addition, he participated in the Venice Biennale, 1948, 1956, 1958 (Grand International Prize for Painting, awarded by the Municipality of Venice); São Paulo Bienal, 1951, 1955; Pittsburgh International, 1952, 1955, 1958; Guggenheim International Award, New York, 1958 (National Section Award), and Documenta II, Kassel, 1959.

Bibliography:
Review of the Tobey Exhibition, Willard Gallery, in **Art News,** New York, April 15, 1944, Vol. 43. — **Paintings by Mark Tobey,** exhibition catalogue, Portland Art Museum, San Francisco Museum of Art, Detroit Institute of Arts, 1945. — Julien Alvard, **Tobey,** in **Cimaise,** Paris, Série 2, No. 6, May 1955. — Janet Flanner, **Tobey, mystique errant,** in **L'Œil,** Paris, No. 6, June 15, 1955. — Léon Kochnitzky, **Mark Tobey,** in **Quadrum,** No. 4, Brussels 1957. — Frank O'Hara,

Presentation at the 29th Biennale, Venice 1958. — **Mark Tobey: A Retrospective Exhibition from Northwest Collections**, Seattle Museum, 1959. — Michel Courtois, **Mark Tobey, Des pictogrammes indiens à l'écriture blanche**, in **Cahiers du Musée de Poche**, No. 1, Paris, March 1959. — Dore Ashton, **Mark Tobey et la Rondeur parfaite**, in **XX⁰ Siècle**, No. 12, Paris May-June 1959. — C. von Wiegand, **The Vision of Mark Tobey**, in **Arts**, New York, May 1959, Vol. 33. — Colette Roberts, **Mark Tobey**, Grove Press, New York 1960.

TOMLIN, Bradley Walker (1899-1953)

Born at Syracuse, New York. He graduated from Syracuse University in 1921 with a Bachelor of Painting degree and was awarded the Hiram Gee Fellowship. He then moved to New York and in 1922 won a scholarship from the Louis Tiffany Foundation. Until 1929 he often designed covers for **Vogue** and **House and Garden.** His first one-man shows were exhibitions of watercolors in Skaneateles and Cazenovia, New York, 1922, and at the Anderson Galleries, New York, 1923. In 1923-1924 he visited England and France, where he worked at the Académie Colarossi and the Académie de la Grande-Chaumière in Paris. Back to New York, 1924; visited Woodstock, New York, summer 1925, and most summers thereafter. In 1926-1927, 1928 and 1934 he traveled in Europe again, visiting England, Italy and France. He taught at the Buckley School, New York, 1932-1933; Dalton Schools, New York, 1933-1934; Sarah Lawrence College, Bronxville, New York, 1932-1941. From 1941 he devoted himself entirely to painting. He died in New York, 1953. A memorial exhibition of his work was held at the Whitney Museum of American Art in 1957-1958. Paintings by Tomlin were exhibited at the São Paulo Bienal, 1951, 1953; the Pittsburgh International, 1952; and Documenta II, Kassel, 1959.

Bibliography:
Bradley Tomlin's Water Colors, in **Art News**, Vol. 21, March 10, 1923. — Margaret Breuning, **Tomlin's Paintings seen in Excellent Show,** in **Art Digest**, Vol. 18, January 15, 1944. — Thomas B. Hess, **Bradley Walker Tomlin,** in **Art News**, Vol. 49, May 1950. — Belle Krasne, **Of Time and Tomlin,** in **Art Digest**, Vol. 24, June 1, 1950. — Obituary Notice, **Art Digest**, Vol. 27, June 1953. — John I. H. Baur, **Bradley Walker Tomlin,** Macmillan, New York 1957. — M. Sawin, **Bradley Walker Tomlin,** Retrospective at the Whitney Museum, in **Arts**, Vol. 32, November 1957. — J. Ashbery, **The Pleasures of Color. Retrospective Now at the Whitney,** in **Art News**, Vol. 56, October 1957.

VASARELY, Victor (1908)

Born at Pecs, Hungary. He began medical studies in Budapest, then was tempted away from them by the offer of a scholarship at the Podolini-Volkmann School of Design. In 1928, at the age of twenty, he entered the "Mühely", the Budapest Bauhaus founded by Alexander Bortnyik. There he attended lectures given by Moholy-Nagy and discovered the work of Mondrian, Malevitch, Gropius and Kandinsky. That same year, 1928, he exhibited with Bortnyik at the Budapest Museum of Decorative Arts. First one-man show two years later at the Kovacs Akos Gallery, Budapest. In 1930 he left Hungary and went to Paris, where he has lived ever since. During the thirties, and up to 1944, Vasarely concentrated his energies on graphic work. After 1945 his chief interest swung back to painting, though he carried on his other activities at the same time, chiefly tapestry designing and lithography; in all these fields he has always been concerned with the problems of space whose premises he inherited from the Constructivists. His work has been represented in many group exhibitions: Galerie La Pléiade, Paris (1934); Salon des Surindépendants (1945, 1946, 1947); Salon des Réalités Nouvelles (from 1948 on); Quatre Surindépendants, Galerie Breteau, Paris (1947); Tendances de l'Art Abstrait, Galerie Denise René, Paris (1948); New York, Paris and São Paulo (1949); Zurich and Paris (1950); Galerie Denise René, Paris (1951, with Dewasne and Jacobsen); Italy, Yugoslavia and Scandinavia (1952); Rome, New York and Germany (1953); Milan Triennale (1954); Pittsburgh International and Documenta I, Kassel (1955); Germany, Japan and São Paulo (1956); Buenos Aires and Montevideo (1958). Awarded a gold medal at the Milan Triennale (1954), the Prix de la Critique, Brussels, and the International Prize, Valencia, Venezuela (1955). One-man shows at the Galerie Denise René, Paris (1944, 1946, 1949, 1952, 1959), Galerie Arne Bruun Rasmussen, Copenhagen (1950), Stockholm (1952, 1956), Palais des Beaux-Arts, Brussels (1954), Milan (1958), Paris (1959).

Bibliography:
J. Dewasne, **Vasarely,** Paris 1952. — L. Degand, **Vasarely,** in **Art d'Aujourd'hui**, June 1952. — **Témoignages pour l'art abstrait,** in **Art d'Aujourd'hui**, Paris 1952. — **Que pensent les peintres?,** in **Arts et Lettres**, No. 17, 1952. — R. V. Gindertael, **Le passage de la ligne,** in **Art d'Aujourd'hui**, March 1953. — R. Bordier, **L'art et la manière,** in **Art d'Aujourd'hui**, February 1954. — M. Seuphor, catalogue preface, Galerie Denise René, Paris, November-December 1955. — G. Habasque, **Vasarely et la plastique cinétique,** in **Quadrum**, No. 3, 1957.

VEDOVA, Emilio (1919)

Born in Venice. He had to go to work while still quite young and took odd jobs to earn a living, drawing and painting assiduously on his own, without attending an art school; even at this time his work began to attract attention. With his friend Hermann Pircher he went to Florence in 1938; there he studied at Silvio Pucci's Free School of Painting and moved in a circle of anti-Fascist writers and artists. Settling in Milan in 1942, he joined the Corrente art group, exhibited at the Galleria della Spiga, and took an active part in the Italian resistance movement. He at once joined the Fronte Nuovo delle Arti when it was formed in 1946, and participated in its group exhibitions at the Galleria della Spiga, Milan, 1947, and at the 1948 Venice Biennale. Awarded the Volpi Prize at the 1950 Venice Biennale. In 1951 he exhibited at the Viviano Gallery, New York, and the São Paulo Bienal, where he won a prize. Showed with the group of Eight Italian Painters at the 1952 Venice Biennale. In 1953 the Museum of Modern Art at Rio de Janeiro organized a large-scale exhibition of his work. Exhibited at Documenta I and II, Kassel (1955, 1959), the Tokyo Biennial (1955), London (1955), Vienna (1956), Munich (1956), Berlin (1957). Won a Guggenheim International Award in 1956 and participated in the Pittsburgh International in 1958. Large-scale Vedova exhibition organized at Warsaw and Poznan in 1958. Took part in Vitalità nell'Arte, Venice (1959), and European Art Today, Minneapolis (1959). He was awarded the Lissone Prize in 1959 and first prize for an Italian painter at the 1960 Venice Biennale.

Bibliography:

G. Guida, **Un artista di 16 anni: Emilio Vedova,** in **L'Illustrazione Vaticana,** August 16, 1937. — G. Marchiori, catalogue preface, Galleria del Pioppo, Mantua 1945. — U. Apollonio, **Vedova,** Venice 1950. — G. Marchiori, **Emilio Vedova,** Venice 1951. — U. Apollonio, **Peintres italiens d'aujourd'hui: Emilio Vedova,** in **Cahiers d'Art,** June 1953. — G. Marchiori, **Vedova,** in **Arti Visive,** 1954. — G. C. Argan, Presentation at the 28th Biennale, Venice 1956. — L. Venturi, **Emilio Vedova,** in **Commentari,** No, 1, 1956. — G. C. Argan, **Emilio Vedova, Premio Guggenheim Foundation,** in **I Quattro Soli,** No. 1, Turin 1956. — S. Branzi, **Vedova,** in **Scritti di Storia dell'Arte in onore di Lionello Venturi,** Rome 1956, pp. 239-246. — W. Haftmann, catalogue preface, Galerie Springer, Berlin 1957. — G. Mazzariol, **Emilio Vedova,** in **Quadrum,** No. 4, 1957. — E. Crispolti, **I manifesti universali di Vedova,** in **Civiltà delle Macchine,** No. 4, 1957. — N. Ponente, **Emilio Vedova,** in **Letteratura,** No. 29, 1957. — J. Starzynski, G. Marchiori and G. C. Argan, exhibition catalogue, Centralne Biuro Wystaw Artystycznych, Warsaw 1958. — G. C. Argan, Biennale Catalogue, Venice 1960. — G. C. Argan and J. Leymarie, **Emilio Vedova** (lithographs), Freiburg-im-Breisgau 1960.

VAN VELDE, Bram (1895)

Born at Zoeterwoude, near Leyden, Holland. At the age of twelve he was apprenticed to the Kramers firm of painters and decorators at The Hague. Began painting on his own while still in his teens, influenced by Breitner. Thanks to the generosity of the firm, he was able to live and work for a time at the artists' colony at Worpswede in North Germany. In 1925 he moved to Paris, and from 1926 on he exhibited regularly at the Salon des Indépendants, then at the Surindépendants. After a trip to Corsica, he went to Majorca and lived there permanently until 1936. Lost his wife during the Spanish Civil War and was compelled to leave Spain. Returning to Paris, he entered a long period of trying material difficulties which lasted throughout the war. E. Loeb took an interest in his work and organized an exhibition in 1946 at the Galerie Mai: a **succès d'estime** but a commercial failure. One-man shows at the Galerie Maeght, Paris (1948, 1952), Kootz Gallery, New York (1948), Galerie Michel Warren, Paris (1955, gouaches; 1957, gouaches and paintings), Kunsthalle. Bern (1958), and Albert Loeb Gallery, New York (1960).

Bibliography:

J. Greshoff, **Bram van Velde,** in **La Revue d'Art,** June 1929. — S. Beckett, **La peinture des Van Velde, ou le monde et le pantalon,** in **Cahiers d'Art,** 1945-1946. — S. Beckett, **Peintres de l'empêchement,** in **Derrière le Miroir,** No. 11-12, 1946. — G. Duthuit, **Bram van Velde, ou Aux colonnes d'Hercule,** in **Derrière le Miroir,** No. 42, 1952. — G. Duthuit, **Maille à partir avec Bram van Velde,** in **Cahiers d'Art,** No. 1, July 1952. — L. Degand, **Bram van Velde,** in **Aujourd'hui,** June 1957. — F. Meyer, Preface, Van Velde Exhibition, Kunsthalle, Bern 1958. — S. Beckett, G. Duthuit and J. Putnam, **Bram van Velde,** Paris 1958. — J. Putnam, **Bram van Velde,** in **Aujourd'hui,** No. 23, September 1959. — J. Putnam, **Bram van Velde,** in **L'Oeil,** No. 65, May 1960.

VAN VELDE, Geer (1898)

Born at Lisse, near Leyden (Holland), where he grew up and went to school. In 1925 he settled in Paris (where he still lives) and attended various art schools in Montparnasse, though holding aloof from any particular group. From 1926 to 1930 he exhibited regularly at the Salon des Indépendants, and in 1933 at The Hague with his brother Bram van Velde. Held his first important one-man show in London in 1938. From 1946 on he made yearly stays at Cagnes, on the French Riviera. One-man show at the Galerie Maeght in Paris in 1946, followed the same year, in the same gallery, by a joint exhibition with his brother Bram. Took part in the Salon des Tuileries and the Salon d'Automne in 1946, and showed at the Exhibition of French Art in Rio de Janeiro in 1949. Awarded first prize at the Menton Biennale in 1952 and exhibited at the Galerie Maeght, Paris, and at Recklinghausen (in the Ruhr). Though he lives in seclusion and shuns publicity, he takes part regularly in major exhibitions both in France and abroad. In 1959 he exhibited at Documenta II, Kassel.

Bibliography:

S. Beckett, **La peinture des Van Velde ou le monde et le pantalon,** in **Cahiers d'Art,** 1945-1946, pp. 349-353. — S. Beckett, **Peintres de l'empêchement,** in **Derrière le Miroir,** No. 11-12, 1946. — J. Kober, **Qualité de l'espace,** catalogue preface, Galerie Maeght, Paris 1946. — R. Chastel and F. Elgar, **Geer van Velde,** in **Derrière le Miroir,** No. 51, 1952.

VIEIRA DA SILVA, Maria-Elena (1908)

Born in Lisbon. At the age of twenty she went to Paris and studied sculpture with Despiau and Bourdelle and painting with Dufresne, Léger, Friesz and Hayter. In 1930 she married the Hungarian painter Arpad Szenes. She exhibited at the Salon d'Automne and the Salon des Surindépendants yearly from 1931 to 1933, and attended classes at the Académie Ranson in 1932. In 1933 the Galerie Jeanne Bucher, Paris, organized an exhibition of her illustrations for **Rô et Kô,** a children's book by P. Guéguen. She lived in Lisbon in 1935-1936 and worked hard at painting, helped and guided by her husband. In 1937 her work was exhibited at the Galerie Jeanne Bucher and she took part in group exhibitions in Paris. Designed several tapestries, woven by Madame Cuttoli. Took part in the Ecole de Paris exhibition at the Galerie Jeanne Bucher, Paris, 1938, and exhibited alone at the same gallery in 1939. She left France in 1940 and settled for the duration in Rio de Janeiro, where her work was exhibited at the Museum of Fine Arts in 1942. Took part in the Salon of Rio de Janeiro in 1943 and other exhibitions there in 1944. First one-man show in the United States at the Marian Willard Gallery, New York, 1946. That same year she participated in the Unesco exhibition at the Musée d'Art Moderne, Paris, and in the Salon des Réalités Nouvelles. She returned to Paris in 1947 and exhibited at the Salon d'Automne (1947, 1948, 1949) and La Hune (1950). Designed sets for **Parodie** by Adamov in 1952 and was awarded a prize at the 1953 São Paulo Bienal. Won prizes at the 1955 Caracas Bienal and the 1958 Pittsburgh International. Guggenheim Award in 1958. One-man shows at the Galerie Jeanne Bucher, Paris (1947, 1951, 1957), Galerie Pierre, Paris (1949, 1951, 1955), Blanche Gallery, Stockholm (1950), London (1952, 1953, 1957), Wuppertal (1957), Geneva (1957) and Hanover (1957). Besides exhibiting in Paris at the Salon de Mai (1951-1954, 1957, 1958) and the Salon des Réalités Nouvelles (1957), she has taken part in showings of French painting in Stockholm (1949), Berlin (1950), Düsseldorf (1950) and Zurich (1952), and such major international exhibitions as the Venice Biennale

(1950, 1954), Pittori d'Oggi, Francia-Italia, Turin (1951, 1959), the Pittsburgh International (1952, 1955, 1958), The New Decade, Museum of Modern Art, New York (1955), Documenta I and II, Kassel (1955, 1959), Contemporary Art, Tokyo (1956), Cinquante Ans d'Art Moderne, Brussels World's Fair (1958), School of Paris 1959: The Internationals, Walker Art Center, Minneapolis (1959).

Bibliography:

M. Seuphor, Catalogue Preface, Galerie Pierre, Paris 1949. — M. Seuphor, **Promenades autour de Vieira da Silva,** in **Cahiers d'Art,** 1949, pp. 331-335. — P. Descargues, **Vieira da Silva,** in **Peintres d'Aujourd'hui,** Paris 1949. — C. Estienne, Catalogue Preface, Galerie La Hune, Paris 1950. — J. Lassaigne, **Vieira da Silva,** in **Combat,** November 14, 1955. — Jean Grenier, **Vieira da Silva,** in **L'Express,** November 10, 1955. — C. H. Sibert, **V. da Silva,** in **Cimaise,** December 1955. — P. Guéguen, **Vieira da Silva,** in **XXᵉ Siècle,** No. 7, 1956. — J. Grenier, **Vieira da Silva,** in **L'Œil,** No. 14, February 1956. — R. de Solier, **Vieira da Silva,** Paris 1958. — W. Schmalenbach, Catalogue Preface, Hanover 1957-1958. — J. A. França, **V. da Silva,** Lisbon 1958.

WINTER, Fritz (1905)

Born at Altenbögge, Westphalia, Germany. First went to work as an electrician in the coal mines. From 1927 to 1930 he studied art at the Dessau Bauhaus, attending the classes of Schlemmer, Klee and Kandinsky. He worked for a while as Kandinsky's assistant. In 1929 he paid a visit to Davos (Grisons), Switzerland, where he met Ernst-Ludwig Kirchner, whose painting (and that of the Expressionists in general) he greatly admired. In 1930 he went to Berlin, where he met Gabo, and traveled in France and Switzerland. Appointed to a professorship in 1931 at Halle-an-der-Saale. He moved to Munich in 1933, but from that time on he was considered a "degenerate" artist by the Nazis and forbidden to paint. Called up at the outbreak of war, he served in the German army in Poland and on the Eastern Front. During a brief home leave in 1944 he painted **The Driving Forces of Nature.** Taken prisoner by the Russians in 1945, he was sent to Siberia. Set free in 1949, he returned to Germany and settled near Munich, where he lived until 1955. His first post-war exhibition was held in a Munich gallery in 1950. Appointed to a professorship in 1955 at the Art Academy, Kassel, where he now lives. One-man shows in Munich, Witten, Wuppertal, Stuttgart and Basel (1950), Munich retrospective exhibition, Günther Franke (1951), New York (1952), Venice (1952), Rome (1958, 1959), Milan (1960). He participated in the Venice Biennale in 1950 and again in 1956 (a whole room devoted to his work); the São Paulo Bienal (1955); The New Decade, Museum of Modern Art, New York (1955); German Art of the Twentieth Century, Museum of Modern Art, New York (1957); Arte Tedesca dal 1900 ad Oggi, Rome (1957); Documenta II, Kassel (1959). Awarded prizes at the 1950 Venice Biennale and the 1955 São Paulo Bienal, and a gold medal at the 1954 Milan Triennale.

Bibliography:

L. Grote, exhibition catalogues, Munich, Witten, Wuppertal, Stuttgart, Basel 1950. — W. Haftmann, **Fritz Winter,** Bern 1951. — D. Sutton, **Painting by Fritz Winter,** catalogue preface, Lefebvre Gallery, London, February-March 1953. — W. Grohmann, **Artistes allemands, Fritz Winter,** in **Cahiers d'Art,** No. 1, June 1953. — W. Grohmann, **Evoluzione di Fritz Winter,** in **I Quattro Soli,** No. 1, January 1957. — E. Crispolti, catalogue preface, Galleria Blu, Milan 1960.

WOLS (1913-1951)

Born in Berlin (his real name was Alfred Otto Wolfgang Schulze). Grew up at Dresden. After rather desultory studies, he attended the classes of Frobenius at the Institute of African Studies in Frankfort, then those of Walter Gropius at the Bauhaus, where he met Mies van der Rohe and Moholy-Nagy. In 1932 he settled in Paris, where he took up photography and came in contact with the Surrealists. Made a trip to Spain, visiting Barcelona and Ibiza. Back in Paris he met Miró, Calder, Tristan Tzara and Max Ernst. To earn a living he worked as a photographer and gave German lessons. Exhibited his photographs at the Librairie Les Pléiades in 1936 under the name of Wols. In 1937 he obtained exclusive photographic rights at the Pavillon de l'Elegance of the Paris World's Fair. When war was declared in 1939 he was interned as a German citizen; spent fourteen months in an internment camp, working hard at painting and drawing all the while. Set free late in 1940 he settled near Marseilles, at Dieulefit and Cassis where, with the help of H. P. Roché, he was able to go on working and sold a few gouaches and drawings. An exhibition of his gouaches was held in New York at the Betty Parsons Gallery in 1942. He returned to Paris in 1945 and the same year held a large one-man show at the Galerie Drouin; exhibited there again in 1947. Now began a long series of book illustrations: **Visages** and **Nourritures** (1948) by Sartre; **L'invité des morts** (1948) by Kafka; **Le Théâtre de Séraphin** (no date) by Artaud; **Poèmes chinois** translated by Jean Paulhan and **La Bergère d'Ecosse** (1948) by Jean Paulhan; **Baleine-ville** (1949) by Camille Bryen; **Naturelles** (1948) by René de Solier. Exhibited at the Galleria del Milione, Milan (1949), and in New York (1950). Died in Paris in 1951. Large-scale retrospective of his works at the 1958 Venice Biennale.

Bibliography:

Silveire, **Un petit homme de la lune,** and H. P. Roché, **Extraits de notes sur Wols,** exhibition catalogue, Galerie Drouin, Paris 1945. — U. Apollonio, **Wols, Forma e Natura,** in **Scritti di Storia dell'Arte in onore di Lionello Venturi,** Rome 1956. — N. Ponente, **Wols,** in **L'Esperienza Moderna,** No. 2, 1957. — G. Marchiori, **Nota su Wols,** exhibition catalogue, Galleria La Medusa, Notiziario della Galleria, No. 1, Rome, December 1957. — H. Rensing, Preface, Galerie Springer, Berlin 1957. — P. Restany, **Wols,** in **Cimaise,** November 1958. — U. Apollonio, Preface, Wols Retrospective, 29th Biennale, Venice 1958. — G. Dorfles, **Wols,** Milan 1958. — H. P. Roché, **Souvenirs sur Wols,** Catalogue of the Wols Exhibition (Gouaches), Galerie Claude Bernard, Paris 1958. — W. Grohmann, **Wols,** Catalogue, Wols Exhibition, Galerie Europe, Paris 1959. — Marcel Lecomte, **Souvenirs sur Wols,** in **Quadrum,** No. 7, 1959. — Catalogue, Wols Exhibition, Galleria Blu, Milan 1960.

Index

List of Colorplates

Contents

This volume of the collection "Painting ○ Color ○ History" was produced by the technical staff of Editions d'Art Albert Skira. Finished the fifteenth day of October nineteen hundred and sixty.

Text and colorplates by

SKIRA

Color Studios at Imprimeries Réunies S.A., Lausanne.

Plates engraved by
Guezelle & Renouard, Paris
except for those on pages 18, 19, 20, 41, 45, 50, 56, 102, 103, 105, 137 and 154, engraved by Schwitter AG., Basel.

Photographs

Hans Hinz, Basel (pages 14, 20, 26, 27, 30, 40, 41, 42, 50, 54, 56, 58, 62, 69, 72, 74, 98, 102, 105, 113, 123, 132, 137, 140, 141, 143, 154, 169), Claudio Emmer, Milan (pages 16, 17, 23, 43, 64, 65, 75, 78, 79, 80, 81, 86, 88, 89, 94, 117, 118, 120, 121, 148, 149, 152, 171), Louis Laniepce, Paris (pages 24, 32, 35, 36, 37, 38, 44, 46, 47, 52, 53, 55, 59, 70, 71, 92, 111, 115, 116, 122, 123, 124, 135, 158, 159, 160, 165, 166, 167, 172, 173), Henry B. Beville, Washington (pages 77, 93, 100, 103, 104, 126, 128-129, 130, 133, 150, 155), Zoltán Wegner, London (page 139), Eric Pollitzer, New York (page 19), Raymond, Cincinnati (page 18), Salchow, Cologne (page 157), Sidney Janis Gallery, New York (page 151) and Galerie de France, Paris (page 45).